The Economy
of Sweden

**PRAEGER SPECIAL STUDIES IN
INTERNATIONAL ECONOMICS AND DEVELOPMENT**

The Economy
of Sweden

A STUDY OF THE MODERN WELFARE STATE

Martin Schnitzer

PRAEGER PUBLISHERS
New York • Washington • London

The purpose of Praeger Special Studies is to make specialized research in U.S. and international economics and politics available to the academic, business, and government communities. For further information, write to the Special Projects Division, Praeger Publishers, Inc., 111 Fourth Avenue, New York, N.Y. 10003.

PRAEGER PUBLISHERS
111 Fourth Avenue, New York, N.Y. 10003, U.S.A.
5, Cromwell Place, London S.W.7, England

Published in the United States of America in 1970
by Praeger Publishers, Inc.

Library of Congress Catalog Card Number: 79-122086

Printed in the United States of America

Sweden, although a small country in terms of population, has an influence on contemporary Western society which is out of proportion to her size. Long known for its humanitarian activities during various catastrophies, Sweden has developed an economic system which is second to none in terms of providing a decent standard of living for everyone. An egalitarian society has been created in which extreme differences between rich and poor do not exist. Poverty, which is an expensive nuisance and a menace to the security of society, does not exist in Sweden. To a certain extent this may be attributable to a fortuitous set of circumstances which have existed in the country, but probably much more important has been the ability of the Swedes to develop measures which have placed an income floor under all types of persons.

There is no such thing as a perfect society. The United States is a wealthy industrial country with a high standard of living. For the most part, its economic system has functioned well in terms of productivity and the provision of opportunities for personal advancement. It can be faulted in that it has allowed poverty to coexist with wealth to an extent which should not be tolerated. Moreover, there is accorded to the holders of wealth privileges and requisites which simply fly in the face of a country founded on the Jeffersonian principle of equal rights for all, special privileges for none. There has also been a preoccupation with the quantity rather than the quality of life.

Despite Lenin's predictions to the contrary, there isn't a scintilla of evidence to indicate that any utopian system has been created in the Soviet Union. Although the means of production have been socialized, and thus owned by the state as the representative for all of the population, it cannot be

said that the state has acted as the compliant agent
of the people in the production of goods and services.
In fact, despite concessions from time to time, the
reverse is true. Not only has the Soviet Union failed
to overtake the advanced capitalistic countries in
terms of living standards, but grave deficiencies
continue to exist in several sectors of the Soviet
economy. The slow growth of agriculture presents a
serious problem. Perhaps the highest priority need
is the expansion of agricultural output. Another
major problem is an acute shortage of housing. There
has been a sharp deterioration in urban housing which
has been exacerbated by migration from rural areas
into the cities.

Through five trips to Sweden under the auspices
of the Joint Economic Committee of the U.S. Congress,
the author has been in a position to study first hand
the operation of the Swedish economy. On several
occasions, reports and monographs of the author on
various public policy approaches of the Swedish government have been published by the committee or by
journals. Considerable interest in Sweden resulted
from those publications. In fact, a study called
Unemployment Programs in Sweden which was published
in 1963 resulted in the distribution of more than
8,000 copies by the committee and the Government
Printing Office. Subsequent studies on Swedish tax
and social welfare policies also created interest
in the country.

The author is indebted to the numerous Swedes
with whom he made contact during his trips to Sweden,
and to the various members of the staff of the Swedish Embassy in Washington who read parts of the
manuscript. I am also indebted to William Bodde,
Political Officer at the American Embassy in Stockholm, who was responsible for the arrangements of
several of my visits to Stockholm, and to my wife,
Joan, who typed the manuscript.

CONTENTS

LIST OF TABLES, FIGURES, AND MAPS

xi

Table   Page

GLOSSARY

<u>Aftonbladet</u>	Swedish newspaper run by the trade unions
Kooperativa Förbundet (KF)	formed in 1899 by the uniting of consumer cooperatives
Konsum Stockholm	world's largest consumer cooperative
köpingar	boroughs
krona (pl. kronor)	Swedish currency unit (in this book, conversion of kronor into dollars will be done at the rate of 5 to 1 for the sake of computational simplicity; i.e., 1,000 kronor equals $200)
landskommuner	rural communes
Landsorganisationen Sverige (LO)	Confederation of Swedish Trade Unions
landsting	county council
länsstyrelsen	county administrative board
öre	1/100 of a krona
Statstjänstemännens Riksförbund (SR)	National Federation of Civil Servants
Sveriges Akademikers Centralorganisation (SACO)	Swedish Confederation of Professional Associations

Svenska Arbetsgiva- reföreningen (SAF)	Swedish Employers' Confeder- ation
städer	towns
Svetab	Swedish Industrial Establish- ment Company; founded in mid-1969 to create new employment opportunities
Tjänstemännens Centralorganisa- tion (TCO)	Central Organization of Salaried Employees

The Economy
of Sweden

CHAPTER **1** SWEDEN

INTRODUCTION

Most of the major industrial countries of the world do not fit within a rigid definitional framework of capitalism or socialism. It is more appropriate to use the term "mixed economic system" which means that these countries possess characteristics that are relevant to both capitalism and socialism. Although there is both public and private ownership of industry, it is important to realize the small degree to which countries like Sweden and the United Kingdom have used the weapon of formal nationalization of industry as demanded by the more doctrinaire socialists. In fact, in countries with mixed systems, most of what can be called the agents of production, that is, capital and land, are owned by private industries and individuals, and there is reliance upon the market system rather than upon central economic planning to allocate resources among scarce ends.

However, the role of the national government in these countries is of paramount economic and social importance for several reasons. First of all, the national budget is important because of its size relative to gross national product. It is the national budget which brings together most of the economic decisions a country makes. Budget decisions affect purchasing power, employment, inflation potential, and the rate of economic growth. Secondly, ownership of certain industries also gives the national government some leverage over the level of economic activity. Often these nationalized industries are very big capital users; although they may employ a small percentage of the labor force, they have at times approached the point of being responsible for nearly half of all investment in productive industry in such countries as France and the United Kingdom. Finally,

although monetary systems vary from country to country, it can be said that there is much greater government control over monetary and credit policies in
Sweden, France, and other countries with mixed economic systems than in the United States.

The modern welfare state is a recent manifestation of a powerful trend not only in Western society
but in the world as a whole. This trend involves an
effort to achieve more equality in the distribution
of real income. In a most vital sense, the distribution of income is a key problem in any society, and
failure to solve this problem can lead to costly
social upheavals. The welfare states of the West use
government power as an instrument for the redistribution of income in society, generally with the dual
objectives of greater equality in the distribution
of money income, and a guarantee of some minimum
standard of well-being for all citizens. These objectives may be carried out directly through a redistribution of money income, or indirectly through the
provision of services to some segments of the population on some basis other than the costs of these
services.

The most immediate consequence of the welfare
state is an expansion in the volume of transfer payments. The reason for this is clear because transfer
payments, as well as taxes, are the chief means by
which a government can provide for a greater degree
of equality in the distribution of income that is the
hallmark of the welfare state. The existence of a
tax-financed system of transfer payments will alter
a market-determined pattern of income distribution
in that most transfers of money income go to people.
Transfer payments, such as family allowances, old-
age retirement benefits, and unemployment compensation, have a direct effect on the money distribution
of income in a society. Taxes, of course, provide
the state with control over economic resources.

Unemployment, the bête noire of capitalism, has
ceased to be a major economic problem in the Western
countries despite Marxist predictions to the contrary.
For example, in the decade prior to the Second World
War, the average annual rate of unemployment in
Sweden and Great Britain was well over 10 percent.
Since the war, it has rarely exceeded 3 percent, and
for most of this period it has been less than 2 percent. But full-employment has brought with it one

problem to which Western countries have not found a
satisfactory solution. The problem is one of con-
tinually rising prices which have economic and social
costs. Since even relatively modest price increases
may quickly affect the balance of payments of many
of these countries, curbing inflation is an immediate
concomitant of economic growth. Balance-of-payments
considerations, therefore, would require more prompt
and vigorous action against inflation in Great
Britain and Sweden than in the United States.

SWEDEN

Although Sweden is a small country with a population of 8 million persons, its influence upon the
world is much larger than its size. It is a highly
developed industrial country which may well have the
highest overall living standard in the world. In
terms of per capita money income, it ranks second only
to the United States; in terms of a more equitable
distribution of real income, it can be rated superior
to the United States. However, a caveat is in order:
In making comparisons between the United States and
Sweden, it is necessary to remember that different
institutional arrangements govern each country.

Sweden is one of five countries which comprise
a cultural and geographical entity known as Scandinavia.* The five countries--Denmark, Finland, Iceland, Norway, and Sweden--have a population of
approximately 25 million persons, and possess higher
living standards than the great majority of nations.
Social welfare programs are comprehensive and are
designed to benefit all groups, regardless of income.
Attempts at income leveling have been expressed
through tax-financed social security and other welfare
measures as well as through the income tax structure
itself. The Scandinavian countries are bound together
by a common historical heritage. At one time, Sweden
was the dominant Baltic power, and maintained control
over Norway and Finland. Although these countries

---

*Technically Finland cannot be considered a
Scandinavian country, although it was once a part of
Sweden. Scandinavia includes Sweden, Norway, Denmark,
and Iceland.

attained their independence, Sweden still remains as
the most important of the Scandinavian countries
in terms of wealth, industrial development, and international prestige.

The economic system of Sweden has been called
the "middle way" by Marquis Childs.[1] This term, when
it was first used in the 1930s, referred to sort of
a middle-ground approach between the unfettered economic individualism of American capitalism and the
collectivism of Russian communism. The goal of
Swedish policy during the 1930s was to modify the excesses of capitalism while avoiding outright socialization of the agents of production. The system has
also been called "functional socialism," which means
that certain equity goals of socialism, such as a more
equitable distribution of income, have been realized
without recourse to formal nationalization of the
means of production.[2] Instead, there has been a selective socialization of some of the more important
functions within a totality of private ownership.
Although there is small, formal state ownership of
industry, the government exercises a considerable
degree of influence over the economy through public
consumption and public investment, and through income
transferred between different groups in society
through taxation.

The term mixed economic system seems to be as
appropriate as any in describing the Swedish economy.
In this system, some functions of ownership are
socialized, while others are not. However, mixed
economic systems do not constitute a special category
of economic system, held apart from capitalism and
communism, but instead constitute subgroups within
each system. In reality, it seems probable that
these subgroups are the only ones that actually exist.
If we compare the capitalistic and communistic countries along the lines of formal ownership of the
means of production, we would see that there is no
adherence to any norm. In Yugoslavia and Poland,
which are communist countries, most agricultural land
remains privately owned. In Yugoslavia, private enterprise is permitted to the extent that a private
employer can hire up to five workers. Apparently,
the Yugoslavs are also attempting to develop a market socialism in which market forces rather than central planning will determine what is to be produced.

Fiscal and monetary policies play an important
role in the mixed economy of Sweden. Fiscal measures--

government expenditures and taxes--change aggregate
demand directly by altering private income and expenditure streams, while monetary measures affect
aggregate demand indirectly by altering prices and
the absolute and relative supplies of different kinds
of financial assets. Fiscal policy controls the
provision of public goods and services through expenditures, and the redistribution of income through
taxes and transfer payments. Monetary policy produces a more indirect effect on the economy by influencing the aggregate amount and composition of
effective demand for goods and services and the interest rate charged in the financial markets. In
Sweden, the central bank (Sveriges Riksbank) is state
owned. Its functions have been, until recent years,
subverted to the economic policies of the Swedish
government. Full-employment and social welfare took
precedence over price stability, and an easy money
policy was pursued.

To understand a country, it is necessary to know
something about its institutional arrangements. The
Swedish foreign policy of nonalignment, which it followed during both the First and Second World Wars,
has been prompted to a major degree by the series of
conflicts in which it participated in the eighteenth
and nineteenth centuries, conflicts that gained little
in terms of territory and prestige, but which lost
much in terms of lives and property. The agricultural
revolution and the industrialization of Sweden in the
latter half of the nineteenth century resulted in
major population shifts. A flight from the country
began in which a large percentage of the population
moved from rural to urban areas; to some extent this
movement still continues. Moreover, between 1870
and 1914 nearly a million and a half Swedes went
overseas, largely to the United States. The outward
movement of population has ceased; indeed, since the
Second World War there has been a net inflow of mi-
grants from other countries.

Geography

Sweden is the third largest country in Western
Europe. Its area is 173,423 square miles, of which
158,486 are land and 14,937 are water. It occupies
the eastern part of the Scandinavian peninsula, and
is separated from Norway on the west by the Kjolen
mountain range. It is separated from Finland by the
Gulf of Bothnia in the east, but is joined by a common

land frontier 333 miles long. Sweden is an elongated
country, resembling California to a certain
extent. Its length from north to south is 1,000
miles, but its average width from east to west is
300 miles. Because of the great length from north
to south, the climate varies considerably, and this
has had an impact on the development of the country.
Not surprisingly, the major agricultural and industrial areas are found in the central and southern
parts of the country. However, the country's most
important natural resources are located in the
northern part.

     The three main territorial divisions of Sweden
are Gotaland, Svealand, and Norrland. Gotaland, comprising the southern quarter of the country, possesses
terrain, soil, and climate which are relatively
favorable to agriculture. The western part of Gotaland, which contains the industrial and shipping
center of Gothenberg, is the most rapidly growing
area of Sweden, chiefly because of an influx of population from the rural areas to the north. Svealand,
which comprises the central part of Sweden, contains
the capital city of Stockholm. Norrland occupies
roughly the northern half of Sweden. Although its
population is sparse, this region possess iron ore,
forests, and water power. Consequently, the nation's
largest pulp and paper mills are located there. In
addition, hydroelectric facilities supply electricity
to the more heavily populated areas in the south.
The intensive exploitation of these basic natural
resources, combined with a skilled labor force and
research, has transformed Sweden from a poor, rural
economy to a highly productive, industrialized economy in less than a hundred years. Basic industries
still account for a significant part of Sweden's
production; the country ranks third in the world in
the production of wood pulp and fifth in timber production.

     About 8 percent of Sweden's land area is arable
and agriculture accounts for about 4 percent of the
gross national product. Swedish agricultural prices
are fixed by the government as a means of maintaining
farm incomes at a level with the incomes of industrial workers. There is a reliance on high protection
in the form of import taxes. This protection has
resulted in a level of agricultural production that
has made the country nearly self-sufficient in caloric
terms. However, many Swedish agricultural products

are produced at high cost. The government has also encouraged the consolidation of small, unproductive farms into larger, more productive units. This policy has resulted in the closing down of numerous small farms, especially in the northern and central areas of the country.

Sweden possesses only poor coal deposits and largely uneconomical shale oil reserves, and is heavily dependent on imports of liquid and solid fuels. The rapid development of hydroelectric power capacity has made the country relatively less dependent on fuel imports than before the Second World War, but still only about one-third of its total energy requirements are produced internally. However, as mentioned above, a major reason for Sweden's high level of industrial development is its possession of other mineral resources, especially iron ore. High quality Swedish iron has been famous for centuries. More recently, Swedish steel has achieved a worldwide reputation.

History

Sweden is one of the world's oldest nations. Scandinavian tribes were settled in what is now Sweden by the end of the Ice Age, perhaps 12,000 or 15,000 years ago. Pliny in the first century A.D. mentioned Scandinavia, and Tacitus in 98 A.D. referred to the Svear, or Swedes, as "powerful by reason not only of their men and weapons, but also of their fleets." In the sixth and seventh centuries these inhabitants of central Sweden conquered and merged with the Götar, living in the southern section of the peninsula. By the end of the eighth century a kingdom of the Swedes emerged. In the great Viking outburst from 800 to 1060, the Swedes set up trading posts on the coasts of Europe and Russia. With the end of the Viking period, wars between the kingdoms of the Swedes, the Danes, and the Norwegians were common, but on occasion, as in the case of the Union of Kalmar in 1397, the Scandinavian people had a common monarch.

From early times, the office of King of Sweden was elective; he was chosen by provincial assemblies. From these assemblies, the Riksdag, a national legislature composed of four estates--nobles, clergy, burghers, and farmers--emerged. As early as 1350, there were two national codes of law; one for the

towns, the other for the rural districts. These
replaced earlier codes effective in the separate
counties and kingdoms which had preceded the national
government. Feudalism and serfdom never took hold,
and Sweden maintained a free peasantry throughout
the medieval period.

The history of modern Sweden begins with the
election of Gustavus Vasa as king in 1523. He broke
the economic power of the Hanseatic League, made the
dynasty hereditary, and made Lutheranism the national
religion. In 1611, Gustavus Adolphus became king.
Under him Sweden became the dominant Protestant power
of continental Europe in the great religious wars of
the seventeenth century. From the end of the Thirty
Years' War (1618-1648) to 1709, Sweden established
dominion over the entire Baltic area. The attempt of
the Swedish King Charles XII to gain control in Poland
culminated in the defeat of the Swedish army at Pol-
tava in 1709. This defeat marked the emergence of
Russian in place of Sweden as the dominant power in
Eastern Europe. After this period, Swedish influence
in Europe began to decline. A series of internecine
wars with Denmark and Russia throughout the eighteenth
century resulted in much loss of life and the dis-
sipation of national revenues, and eventually led to
a Swedish disengagement from costly European wars.

In 1809, the present constitution was adopted.
It remains in force today as Europe's oldest written
constitution. It sought to establish a balance of
power between the king and the Riksdag; the subsequent
passage of time has witnessed the atrophy of royal
power and the evolution of Sweden into a parliamentary
democracy. In the following year, 1810, one of Napo-
leon's marshals, Bernadotte (1763?-1844), was made
crown prince; he became king in 1810. The Bernadottes
continue as the royal dynasty of Sweden under the Act
of Succession.

The nineteenth century was marked by the rise of
the middle class, the modernization of agriculture,
and the industrialization of Sweden, a process which
accelerated after 1870. These factors culminated in
the development of a great modern democracy. A major
constitutional step in this process occurred in 1866
when the present Riksdag Act was adopted, replacing
the medieval four estates of nobles, clergy, burghers,
and farmers with a two-house parliament. Thereafter,
a modern party system and a parliamentary democracy
emerged.

The Political System

Sweden is a constitutional monarchy with a parliamentary government somewhat similar to that of Great Britain. The present monarch, Gustav Adolf VI, is descended from Jean Bernadotte who was elected heir to the Swedish throne in 1810. Since the Swedish order of succession to the throne is based on the priniciple of direct descent through the male line only, the future of the Bernadotte dynasty rests with Crown Prince Carl Gustaf, who will not attain the legal age of succession until April 30, 1971, when he becomes twenty-five. Although the monarchy possesses little power, there is some republican sentiment in Sweden. Moreover, its future is complicated by dynastic and constitutional factors. In view of a possible interregnum, should the present king die before 1971, a motion has been made by a group of Social Democrats to study the consequences of abolishing the monarchy in favor of a republic. It has passed the Riksdag and is now under consideration by a special commission of inquiry considering a revision of the Swedish Constitution of 1809.

The real political power rests in the Swedish Riksdag (Parliament), which consists of two chambers having virtually equal powers in budgetary and legislative matters. All legislation must be passed by both chambers separately except for fiscal bills which, if rejected by either chamber may subsequently be enacted by joint vote of the two combined chambers. An amendment to the constitution creating a unicameral parliament was passed in February, 1969, and will come into effect in 1971.

The Upper Chamber of the Riksdag consists of 151 members who are elected by indirect ballot by the provincial and municipal assemblies. Each member serves an eight-year term, and membership is renewed by one-eighth every year. The assemblies are elected by popular vote every four years. The Lower Chamber consists of 233 members who are elected by direct popular vote every four years. An electoral system based on a Swedish version of proportional representation is used. The number of seats a political party receives in the Riksdag reflects the percentage of the vote it polls in proportion to the total votes cast in each of the country's twenty-eight electoral districts. However, the parliamentary reform which

is to come into effect in January, 1971 will establish
a 350-member unicameral legislature elected every
three years. The first election to this single chamber will be held in September, 1970.

     There are five political parties in Sweden: the
Social Democrats, the Moderates, Liberals, Center,
and the Left-Communist Party. The Social Democrats
are the most important party, have dominated Swedish
politics for almost forty years. Although it was
originally a socialist party, over the years it has
modified considerably its doctrinaire support of
nationalization of industry. A nationalization program, adopted by the party at the end of the Second
World War, was never introduced into the Riksdag and
has been shelved until only recently when leftist
elements have advocated the nationalization of the
banking industry. However, Prime Minister Olof Palme
and other leaders of the Social Democratic Party have
been recorded as being opposed to this move. Instead
of nationalization, it can be said that over the years
the party's domestic policy has revolved around consistent attempts to strengthen and expand the welfare
of the lower-income groups. It actively supports a
continued redistribution of income and wealth through
high taxes on income, inheritance, and property. It
advocates increased government supervision of industry
and trade, and over the years it has introduced perhaps the most extensive and comprehensive social
security system in the world.

     There are three parties, which are called the
bourgeois parties, in Sweden. One party is the Mod-
erate-Union Party (formerly the Conservative Party),
which derives its support from the upper-middle
classes and career officers in the civil service and
armed forces. In terms of domestic policy, it advocates free enterprise and the tariff protection
of private industry. Another party is the Liberal
Party which is supported primarily by the urban middle class, small tradesmen, and intellectural elements. Domestically, it favors private enterprise,
free multilateral trade and low tariffs, and the
curbing of trusts and state monopolies. It is also
opposed to the nationalization of industry. The
third party is the Center Party which is supported
primarily by farmers and small tradesmen. Its domestic policies are similar to those of the Liberal
Party. The total vote received by the three burgeois
parties in national and provincial elections is almost

SWEDEN   13

equal to that received by the Social Democractic
Party. However, their inability form a viable coa-
lition has enabled the Social Democrats to maintain
political power.

There is also the Left-Communist Party, which
was formerly the Swedish Communist Party. It has
had minor success in Swedish national elections. The
invasion of Czechsolovakia by the Soviet Union and
internal factional disputes have reduced its effectiveness as a national party. Under a new election law,
which will be in effect in the 1970 election for a
unicameral legislature, a party must receive at least
4 percent of the total vote, or 12 percent in a single
election district, in order to be represented in the
Riksdag. In the 1968 national elections for the
Lower Chamber of the Riksdag, the Left-Communist
Party received 3 percent of the popular vote.

Table 1-1 presents the party composition of the
Lower and Upper Chambers of the Swedish Riksdag as of
1969.

TABLE 1-1

Party Composition of the
Swedish Riksdag

Political Party	Number of Seats	
	Upper Chamber	Lower Chamber
Moderates	25	32
Liberals	26	34
Center	20	39
Social Democrats	79	125
Communists	1	3
Total	151	233

Sweden has not been involved in a war for over
150 years. Its traditional foreign policy has been
one of nonalignment in times of peace with the objective of preserving its neutrality in times of war.
This policy was tested severely by the Germans during
the Second World War after they conquered both Norway
and Denmark. Sweden was isolated between the Germans
on one flank and the Russians on the other. The
Germans wanted the right to transport troops across
Swedish territory to the Finnish front to fight the

Russians. The Swedes allowed German troops to cross
the country from Norway to Finland and from Norway
down into Germany and back. This policy involved
primarily the transit of German soldiers on leave.
Although criticized for this policy, Sweden took the
rather pragmatic view that the Germans could either
invade their country or at least cut off all or most
of the coal essential to Swedish industry. Swedish
sentiment, however, was with the Allies, and covert
support was given to refugees from Denmark, Norway,
and other countries.

     In recent years Sweden has taken an active role
in international relations. Priority has been given
to the provision of technical assistance to underdeveloped countries. Family planning has played an
important role in the Swedish efforts, with extensive
projects of this nature in Ceylon and India. Sweden
also has a small peace corps, concentrated primarily
in East Africa. The principal beneficiaries of
Swedish foreign aid have been Ceylon, Ethiopia, India,
Kenya, the Sudan, and Tanzania. In cooperation with
Denmark and Norway, Sweden participates in joint
Nordic projects in Kenya, Korea, and Tanzania. In
1968, Swedish foreign aid amounted to .33 percent of
the gross national product. The governing Social
Democratic Party has announced its intention of increasing aid to underdeveloped countries to 1 percent
of the Swedish gross national product by 1974.

     In recent years, Swedish opposition to the policy
of the United States in Vietnam has become more outspoken. The Swedish government has sympathized with
North Vietnam and the program of the National Libera-
tion Front. The Social Democratic Party has been even
more outspoken in criticizing what it considers to be
United States aggression in Vietnam. This criticism
has been manifested in the granting of political
asylum to deserters from the United States armed
forces.

Local Government

     For administrative purposes Sweden is divided
into twenty-four counties and the city of Stockholm,
a total of twenty-five major political entities. Administration of each of these entities is in the hands
of an administrative board, the county board (läns-
styrelsen). The head of the board is the county
governor, who, like the county treasurer and the

county secretary, is appointed by the national government. In Stockholm, there is an appointed governor-
general and an elected city council; the latter appoints an executive committee, which has charge of
the municipal administration. In addition to the
county board, each county has an elected county council (landsting). One of its functions is the election of members to the Upper Chamber in the Swedish
Riksdag. It also has the power to make decisions
for the county on certain matters of general county
interest: education, medical care, and the like. A
portion of the local income tax goes to the county
for these purposes.

The larger cities may leave the jurisdiction of
the county council. Cities, thus separately governed
by their own municipal councils, are Stockholm, Göte-
borg, Malmö, Norrköping, Hälsingborg, and Gävle. The
primary unit of local government, however, is the
commune, or local district. This is an ancient local
unit which antedates the medieval parish, although
there was long a relationship. In the nineteenth
century civil matters were separated from church affairs and the communes became primarily civil districts. Communes may be divided into three classes:
rural communes (landskommuner), boroughs (köpingar),
and towns (städer). The distinctions between these
tended to disappear in recent years. Government of
the commune is in the hands of a local council. The
commune is primarily responsible for loval government
functions--education, welfare, and the like--and the
council has authority both to determine the rate of
the local income tax, and to appropriate money for
local needs. The communes also receive grants from
the national government, for education, housing, and
other purposes.

SUMMARY

In the United States, the United Kingdom, and
most Western countries, the end of the Second World
War found economic-policy debate focused upon the
likelihood of a fall in prices after the end of the
war and consequent danger of a depressive reaction
upon employment and output. Before the war, unemployment had been a serious problem in the Western
countries. There was a general fear that after the
war there would be a reversion to mass unemployment.

The main focus of economic policy, therefore, was
upon the problem of maintaining full-employment in
the face of difficulties in securing adequate supplies of raw materials and fuel, a hazard of a failure
of effective demand, and a tendency of prices to
fall. Principal responsibility for policy devices
to maintain a high level of employment, and to redistribute income was assumed by the national governments of the Western countries. The national
budgets of these countries became the catalyst
through which tax and expenditure policies were carried out. Mixed economic systems emerged, which combined some of the basic features of both capitalism
and socialism.

     The welfare state is a relatively recent de-
velopment in contemporary Western society. It is a
manifestation of a trend toward more equality in the
distribution of real income. In a most vital sense
the distribution of income represents a problem in
any society, and failure of society to solve this
problem in a satisfactory manner can lead to costly
social upheaval. In Sweden and other Western countries measures have been taken to effect a more
equitable distribution of income. The social security systems of these countries have been designed to
provide an array of benefits to cope with such uncertainties of industrial life as unemployment, disability, illness, and old age.

     Sweden, probably more than any Western country,
has been able to maintain a high level of employment
during the twenty-five years which have followed the
end of the Second World War. The general economic
policy of the Swedish government has been to achieve
a high level of employment, and fiscal and monetary
policies have been subordinated to this objective.
Sweden also has the most comprehensive set of welfare
measures of any country in the world. It has pioneered
the development of old-age pensions. Income redistribution has been effected through the use of taxation and government expenditures to a much greater
extent than in either the Soviet Union or the United
States; or for that matter, any other major industrial
country, with the possible exception of France. Sweden
has combined perhaps the highest standard of living
in the world with a highly developed social welfare
system to create what is perhaps the closest thing
to a utopian society in existence.

NOTES

1. Marquis Childs, <u>Sweden: The Middle Way</u> (New
Haven: Yale University Press, 1961).

2. Gunnar Adler, <u>Functional Socialism: A
Swedish Theory for Democratic Socialization</u> (Stockholm: Bokförlaget Prisma, 1969).

CHAPTER **2** GENERAL
CHARACTERISTICS
OF THE ECONOMY

INTRODUCTION

The Swedish economy contains some of the basic features of capitalism and socialism. It possesses certain characteristics which are also common to such other Western European countries as France, West Germany, and the United Kingdom. These characteristics are as follows:

1. There is a basic reliance on free enterprise and the market system. Most industry is privately owned. Production and distribution remain primarily in the hands of private enterprise. Nevertheless, the Swedish government plans an important role in the economy through the use of fiscal and monetary policies. Control over the national budget and credit gives the government leverage over the economic decisions of business firms.

2. There is a commitment to full-employment as a fundamental economic policy objective. Aggregate demand has been managed in such a way as to keep it at a high level. The government exerts its influence on total spending, production, employment, and prices through both sides of its budget. Its purchases of goods and services add directly to the demand for output and create money income for persons and business firms, while its expenditures for interest, social security benefits, and various other transfer payments also add to private incomes and spending power. Taken by themselves, therefore, government expenditures tend to expand money incomes and the market for business output. On the other side of the budget, tax collections extract from personal and business incomes large amounts of money that might have been spent for consumption purposes or for capital improvements.

3.   The term "welfare state" is certainly applicable to the Swedish economy. The main principles
of a welfare state are a commitment to an equitable
distribution of income and a minimum living standard
for all of its citizens, and to full-employment as
the most important social goal to be supported by
public policy. In Sweden, as well as in other countries with mixed economic systems, there has been an
objection to the concentration of income and wealth
in the hands of a few, which leads to considerable
income inequality. The rentier class, or coupon
clippers, is looked upon with disfavor. There has
been an attempt to correct this distribution of income through the use of progressive income taxation,
gift and inheritance taxes, and a vareity of transfer
payments which are designed to raise the incomes of
the lower-income groups.   -

4.   There is recognition that the objectives of
full-employment and social welfare can be accomplished
without recourse to the nationalization of industry.
Nationalization, at least for the present, is only a
shibboleth worshipped by die-hard socialists. In
Sweden, government ownership of industry has not followed the clear-cut pattern that developed in the
United Kingdom and France.* After the First World
War, the government became coowner of the iron mines
in Lapland by acquiring a participation in a subsidi-
ary of the Graensburg Corporation. Mixed enterprises
with government and private control have become a
charactertistic of Sweden's industrial structure.
Government control over private industry is substantial
as a result of fiscal, monetary, and regulatory measures of the kinds familiar in other highly developed
industrial countries.

----

*A wave of nationalization took place in the
United Kingdom and France in the period immediately
following the end of the Second World War. The main
reason for nationalization in the United Kingdom
was to use public investment as a compensatory device
for offsetting the investment vagaries of the private
sector and maintaining employment at a higher level
than during the prewar period. In France, the immediate postwar years were characterized by a policy
of economic "dirigisme," which included the nationalization of the gas and electric power industries
and the Bank of France.

5. In countries with mixed economic systems,
there is reliance on economic planning. However, the
extent of this reliance varies from the formal French
plans to no planning in West Germany. Economic planning in Sweden is not nearly so comprehensive as
French planning.* There is no formal plan which is
supposed to be operative over a specific time period.
Swedish planning takes the form of a forecast which
usually spans a five-year period. The purpose of
the forecast is to provide business firms with information about the prospects for the economy in
order to help them with their investment decisions.
The aim of Swedish planning is to outline a flexible
strategy for resolving the long-term difficulties
with which economic policy is faced, in order to ensure full-employment, rapid production increases,
and financial stability.

MARKET MECHANISMS

A fundamental dilemma of any economic system is
a scarcity of resources relative to wants. Decisions
are necessary to decide how a given volume of resources is allocated in production, and how the income derived from production is to be distributed to
the various agents (capital, labor, and land) that
are responsible for it. In a market system, the
forces which allocate resources in production and determine the rewards in distribution are supply and
demand. The relationship of supply and demand determines the relative values of individual resources and
commodities. Explained in terms of money, these
values are prices, and the pricing system is the un-
conscious planning mechanism which guides private individuals, in pursuit of maximum individual rewards,
to allocate fully the resources of the economic system.

----

*French economic planning is an example of in-
dicative planning. It is much less extreme or coercive than Russian planning, and it is essentially
viewed as a set of directives or guidelines which help
to guide the planning of private industry as well as
the public sector of the economy. However, there is
a certain amount of government intervention, which
has taken the form of indirect control over credit and
taxation to encourage desirable objectives.

Productive agents are, then, allocated or distributed on the basis of prices in a market system.

In countries operating with a market economy, consumer sovereignty is an important institution for the reason that consumer preferences in the market place determine what and how much will be produced. These preferences will be expressed through the price mechanism which operates on supply and demand in the markets for goods and services. If consumer demand for color television is great relative to the supply, prices will be bid higher than costs of production, and in response to demand, expansion will occur on the part of existing firms and new firms that may choose to enter the market. Eventually, the output of color television will be equal to the demand. However, if consumer demand is less than the supply of color television sets, prices will fall below costs, firms will stop producing sets, and eventually supply will adjust to demand.

An economy that relies upon market arrangements usually has two main types of economic units. One is the household, which consists of an individual or a family, and the other is the business firm. The household is a consumer and an owner of resources; the firm is a user of resources and a producer. This, however, does not preclude government ownership and operation of certain public services (post offices and communications), or natural monopolies. For example, in Germany, government ownership of certain industries predates Bismarck. In Prussia, state ownership of mines existed until 1865 when a mining law did away with state operations. With the formation of the German Empire, Bismarck realized the need for a co-ordinated railroad system under state control if Germany was to become strong militarily. Accordingly, he took steps to nationalize the railroad system, particularly in Prussia. By 1914, most of the rail-road system was under state control; by 1919, the entire system had been nationalized.

The commodity composition of the output of an economy which relies on market arrangements is deter-mined in the first instance by managers of business firms. These managers are directly responsible for converting resources into production. It is they who determine what products will be produced; guided, of course, by the actions of consumers in the market place. The profit motive is the lodestar that impels

managers to choose products which can be sold at
prices that are high relative to costs of production.

Owners of resources and consumers of products
exercise their influence on the composition of production through their influence on the costs of production and the prices of products. Resource owners
who prefer some utilization of their resources by
others will accept lower compensation for some uses
of the resources than for others. In this way they
encourage firms to produce the products resulting
from these uses. Consumers will pay high prices for
products which they want very much, and thus they
encourage firms to choose to produce these products.

There are a variety of names used to designate
an economy which relies extensively upon market arrangements. One is "free-enterprise economy," a name
suggesting economic decisions which are made by individuals free from direct orders from others, including those who operate collectively in the guise of
government. Freedom of enterprise would refer to the
right of an individual to select his own occupation,
to found and operate a business in any field, or invest his capital in whatever enterprise he chooses.
As a consumer, he is also free to buy the products of
his choice. There is a libertarian element in this
institution that is easy to reconcile with the development of political democracy in the United States
and in Western Europe. However, the element of self-
interest is probably a stronger rationale for freedom
of enterprise, for the reason that it is probably the
strongest motivating force in individual decisions.*
Tied to freedom of enterprise is economic motivation,
which involves the profit motive for the entrepreneur,
and the maximization of income for workers and their
families.

Another name for a market economy is capitalism,
a term emphasizing the importance of private or

---

*The idea is prevalent in a capitalistic or free-
enterprise system that acting in one's self-interest
benefits other members of society. Adam Smith, for
example, expressed the view that the wealth of nations
would increase most rapidly if every man was allowed
to follow whatever occupation seemed best in his own
eyes and be allowed to invest his capital in whatever
enterprise he thought would prove most profitable.

nongovernmental ownership of the agents of production,
and also indicating the existence of certain rights
of persons who own property. In addition to private
ownership of property, there are the institutional
arrangements which have been mentioned above--profit
as the motive which keeps men competing to organize
production and supply the market, and consumer sovereignty which when expressed in the market place affects what and how much will be produced.

However, consumers are unequal in their ability
to bid for goods and services for the reason that
incomes are not distributed equally. The question
of for whom goods are produced is resolved by the
price system operating in the market place. Some
consumers have more money than others and can bid
higher for certain goods. If this seems unfair, it
is necessary to point out that in a free market system, supply and demand largely determines the distribution of income to individuals. Labor, as an agent
of production, is rewarded according to its productivity. If it is scarce relative to the demand for
it, then its productivity is high and it can command
a large income; if it is abundant relative to demand,
then its productivity and income will be low.

Communism as an economic system represents a
significant departure from the arrangements of a market, or capitalistic, system. The communists contend
that there are several major flaws in a capitalistic
system: unemployment, income inequality, and social
waste. The communists would amend these flaws by
changing the institutions that presumably are responsible for them. There would be public ownership of
the agents of production. Income distribution would
also be a public function, and income disparities
based on the receipt of rental income or interest
would be eliminated. The institution of private property would be eliminated. Decisions concerning the
kinds and quantities of goods to be produced, the
allocation of available productive factors to various
industries and enterprises, and the distribution of
resources between consumption and capital formation
would be made by government planning.

In general terms capitalism can be defined as a
system in which the ownership of the means of production is vested with private individuals, and basic
production and distribution decisions are determined
in the market place. Contrariwise, communism can be

defined as a system in which the means of production
is vested with the state, and production and distribution decisions are made by central planning. However, there is an admixture of both capitalism and
communism even in the communist countries. For example, in Yugoslavia, more than 80 percent of the agricultural land is privately owned. Private enterprise
exists in industry and in the service areas subject
to certain employment limitations. Yugoslavia is
also attempting to develop a market socialism in which
the market mechanism rather than central planning
will determine production and distribution. In
Poland, most of the agricultural land continues to
remain in private hands. Even in the Soviet Union
there is some private ownership of the means of production, and the market system is allowed to function,
particularly in the agricultural sector.

The market economies of Western Europe and the
United States have succeeded to a considerable degree
in ameliorating unemployment and income inequality.
Despite Marxist predictions to the contrary, the
fundamental problem of unemployment, which plagued the
United States and other Western countries, appears
to be resolved. In countries like Sweden and the
United Kingdom, where the unemployment rate was in
excess of 10 percent during the 1930s, full-employment has been accomplished for most of the post-World
War II period. Communism, at least as far as it is
being practiced in the Soviet Union, China, and other
communist countries, is a far cry from the utopia that
its adherents claim for it. In fact, unemployment,
income inequality, and waste of economic resources
also exist in the communist countries. Central planning, too, has its defects.

It is the premise of this book that Sweden has
developed a system which appears to have resolved the
problems of unemployment, poverty, and income inequality that have affected Western civilization
during this century. Sweden is a showcase country--
a model which other countries can examine from the
standpoint of perhaps exploring the possibility of
utilizing various employment and social welfare approaches. It is necessary to remember, however, that
Sweden has been favored with certain developments
during this century, not the least of which was the
avoidance on involvement in the Second World War.
Its population is very homogeneous, whereas the reverse is true in the United States.

Primary attention will be placed on the role of the Swedish public sector and its concern with two functions which are also basic to the public sectors of other countries as well. These functions are economic stabilization and the redistribution of income. Economic stabilization can be considered from the standpoint of policies which are designed to maintain a high level of employment. Concern with employment involves the consideration of labor force utilization. Excessive unemployment of labor represents output lost, much of it for all time. However, economic stabilization also concerns the movement of price levels. The movement of prices is a matter for concern in a variety of ways. Price level changes affect the distribution of wealth and income and change the value of wages and other factor payments.

In the most vital sense the distribution of income is a key problem in any society, and the failure of the society to solve this problem in a satisfactory manner will inevitably lead to violent and costly social upheaval. In essence Marxism is nothing more than the most violent kind of challenge to the alleged failure of capitalism to achieve distributive justice. One has to only look at the United States to realize that much of the turmoil which has occurred during the 1960s can be attributed to inequities in the distribution of income. Poverty exists in the midst of plenty. In 1967, 12 percent of the total population of the United States was classified as living at poverty levels.[1] In particular, the incidence of poverty is highest in nonwhite households: about one household in three compared with about one in seven among white households. Compounding this inequity in the distribution of income is the fact that wealthy persons and special interest groups enjoy favorable treatment under the tax system and possess inordinate power in a democracy that is supposed to be based on the Jeffersonian principle of equal rights for all, special privileges for none.

Since the inception of capitalism, much of the social and economic history of the West has revolved around efforts to modify existing institutions and to create new arrangements to achieve more equality in the distribution of income. Sweden has created machinery for the redistribution of income as comprehensive as any now existing among Western nations. In particular, the nation's social security system has become an instrument for the redistribution of

income in the economy. In general, expenditures for
welfare purposes under the system transfer real and
monetary income from one group in the economy to
another. These expenditures, while they do not involve the use of real resources by the government,
do reflect, by and large, the use of government
power as an instrument for the redistribution of income. The social security system has had the effect
of boosting the share of labor income in the national
income total, but in an indirect fashion.

     Taxation is, of course, the chief instrumentality
through which resources, real and monetary, are diverted from private to public use; but the kind of
taxes resorted to have vastly different economic
effects. The taxation process diverts income to the
public sector either directly, by reducing the money
income of the consumer, as is the case with the taxation of incomes, or indirectly, by reducing his real
income through price changes, as is the case with
excise or consumption taxes. Sweden depends on direct
taxes for most of its governmental revenue, particularly at the local level. These taxes consist of
the personal income tax, corporate income tax, estate
and gift taxes, and social security taxes levied
against employees. The incidence of direct taxation
is simple because it is generally presumed that such
taxes cannot be shifted. This is certainly true for
the personal income tax and the social security tax
paid by the employee, although the ultimate incidence
of taxes on profits may be somewhat more complicated.
In a purely competitive world in which entrepreneurs
always operated at the point of profit maximization,
a tax on profits could not be shifted.

THE SWEDISH ECONOMIC SYSTEM

     The Swedish economy can be divided into three
sectors, each of which contributes to the total output
of goods and services. The private sector is the most
important in terms of consumption, production, and
employment. The government sector is also important,
not only from the standpoint that it contributes to
consumption and investment, but also because it plays
the paramount role in the maintenance of full-employment and the redistribution of income. For a variety
of reasons the government, national and local, has
entered into certain business activities which it

shares to a greater or lesser degree with private
enterprise. The consumer cooperative movement has
grown in Sweden to an extent probably unequaled elsewhere. Although cooperatives account for only a
small fraction of total industrial production, they
are especially important in the food business, accounting for about one-fourth of the nation's food
trade.

Sweden has the highest standard of living in
Western Europe, and in the world is second only to
the United States. In 1967, per capita gross national
product of Sweden was $3,241 compared to $3,966 for
the United States, $2,808 for Canada, and $1,709 for
the United Kingdom. In such outward manifestations
of living standards as numbers of automobiles, television sets, radios, and telephones per thousand
people, Sweden is second to the United States.

The Private Sector

Business and industry are primarily in the hands
of private industry. The nationalization or socialization of industry has not been a part of the program
of the Social Democratic Party, which has been in
power since the 1930s. Most of the gross national
product is contributed by the private sector of the
economy, and the basic institutions of capitalism,
freedom of enterprise, private ownership of property,
and consumer sovereignty prevail in Sweden subject
to certain modifications. Nevertheless, government
control is substantial as a result of fiscal, monetary, and regulatory measures of the kinds familiar
in other highly developed industrial countries, and
the Swedish government has large interests in various
sectors of the economy. In all branches of business,
ownership as measured by percentage of workers employed was divided in these proportions in 1967:
private, 82 percent; public, 15 percent; and cooperative enterprises, 3 percent.

A measure of the contribution of the private
sector to the Swedish economy can be obtained by comparing the amounts of private consumption and investment expenditures to gross national product. Using
this approach from the standpoint of the national
economy, aggregate demand is equal to the sum of consumption and investment expenditures. The familiar
Keynesian equation, $Y = C + I$, can be used where Y is

equal to total output, C represents consumption expenditures, and I represents investment expenditures.
C + I together represents aggregate demand. To this
another component can be added--government expenditures. However, it is possible to divide government
expenditures into the category of consumption or
investment expenditures.*

Table 2-1 presents the contribution of the private sector to the Swedish gross national product
for 1968. Private consumption and investment accounted for about 65 percent of total domestic consumption and investment. The foreign trade sector
of the economy is considered as a separate entity.

TABLE 2-1

The Swedish Gross National Product for 1968

	Millions of Kronor
Private consumption	73,009
Central government consumption	8,585
Local government consumption	15,441
Private domestic gross investment	23,762
Central government gross investment	9,445
Local government gross investment	11,802
Changes in stocks	366
Exports of goods and services	29,859
Less: Imports of goods and services	-30,809
Gross National Product	141,460
Less: Indirect taxes	-17,218
Plus: Subsidies	1,944
Gross National Product at Factor Cost	126,186

Source: Sekretariat for Economic Planning of the
Ministry of Finance and the National Institute of
Economic Research, "The Swedish Economy, 1969"
(Stockholm, 1969), Table 51, p. 56.

---

*Because of the special interest which centers
around government expenditures, these have in the
practice of national income accounting been treated
as a separate classification. Total domestic demand
is equal to C + I + G.

In the private sector of the Swedish economy, the problem of resource allocation is largely solved through the mechanism of the market. In a social sense, the market is a device for the organization of economic activity and it functions by transmitting consumer preferences, as revealed through the expenditure of income, to producers who, in the process of adjusting output to correspond with these preferences, direct economic resources into various and alternative uses. The result of this interplay between consumer preferences and the response of producers is a structure of prices and costs. This structure reflects the relative values that consumers place on the goods and services that the economy is capable of producing and, in so doing, indicates how resources ought to be allocated. As a mechanism for the allocation of economic resources, the market operates on the basis of individual choice, and the culmination of the whole process is the act of exchange whereby the consumer pays individually for any good or service he wishes to acquire.

Investment expenditures occupy a highly significant role in the Swedish economy. There are two reasons why this is so. First of all, the total demand, both private and public, for investment goods represents a large part of the gross national product. In 1968, for example, private and public investment represented almost one-third of the gross national product. Second, investment expenditures are significant because of their impact on the economy's productive capacity. Investment expenditures involve the acquisition of capitl goods, whose function is to produce other goods and services. This means that not only do investment expenditures affect the level of income and employment, but they are also a vital factor in economic growth, which depends to a great extent upon how rapidly productive capacity is being enlarged.

Table 2-2 presents the contribution of the private and public sectors to total gross investment for 1968. It is necessary to point out that public investment expenditures involve more than the acquisition of capital goods. Included as public investment are expenditures on roads, schools, and public utilities.

Savings play an important role in any industrial economy since they constitute the source of capital

TABLE 2-2

Private and Public Composition
of Gross Investment in 1968

	Millions of Kronor
Building and Construction	
Private	11,727
Central government	4,703
Local governments	10,560
Total	26,980
Machinery, Mining, and Agriculture	
Private	12,035
Central government	4,742
Local governments	1,242
Total	18,019
Total Investment by the Private and Public Sectors	
Private	23,762
Central government	9,445
Local governments	11,802
Grand Total	45,009

Source: Sekretariat for Economic Planning of the
Ministry of Finance and the National Institute of
Economic Research, "The Swedish Economy, 1969"
(Stockholm, 1969), p. 114.

formation. Savings in national income accounting are
obtained from three main sources: depreciation, retained earnings, and personal savings. Table 2-3
presents the volume of savings which originate in the
private and public sectors of the Swedish economy in
1965. It can be seen that the private sector provides the bulk of total savings in the economy.

The receipts from the sale of gross national
product, or its cost, consist of three items: national
income, capital depreciation, and indirect business
taxes. National income is income earned producing
goods and services during a given productive period.
National income can also be called "factor cost"

TABLE 2-3

Disposition of Saving in the
Swedish Economy for 1965

Millions of Kronor

Savings	
Private enterprises	4,953
National government	3,283
Local governments	61
Households	5,598
Total	13,895
Depreciation and Other Operating Provisions	
Private enterprises	11,537
National government	3,693
Local governments	3,878
Households	1,042
Total	20,150
Net Borrowing From Abroad	1,490
Miscellaneous	1,219
Total of Savings	36,754

Source: Statistiska Centralbyran, "National-
räkenskap, 1950-1965" (Stockholm, 1965), pp. 44-59.

because it is income going to the factors of production; land, labor, and capital. It consists of wages
and salaries, which are clearly labor income; income
of unincorporated enterprises, or proprietors income,
which is a mixture of both labor income and return to
capital; corporate profits, which is a return to capital; rental income, which is a mixture of property
income and labor income; and interest, which is a
return to financial capital.

Wages and salaries, or compensation of employees,
is the largest component of national income, and normally accounts for two-thirds of the total amount.
In Sweden most of wages and salaries emanate in the
private sector. In 1965, total wages and salaries

in Sweden amounted to 63.2 billion kronor. Of this
amount, 50.9 billion kronor was paid to workers employed in the private sector, 5.2 billion kronor was
paid to workers employed by the national government,
and the remainder was paid to workers employed by
local governments.[2] In 1965, corporate profits
amounted to 3.3 billion kronor, proprietors income
amounted to 7.3 billion kronor, rent, interest, and
other property income amounted to 3.7 billion kronor,
and government income from property and entrepreneur-
ship amounted to 3.5 billion kronor.[3] .The private
sector accounted for approximately 80 percent of
national income.

        Private consumption expenditures amounted to
73 billion kronor in 1968. This accounted for 51.6
percent of the gross national product. However, a
fundamental change has occurred in the last thirty
years which reflects an expansion in the role of the
public sector. A transformation of market forces has
accompanied the growth in government. It is pertinent
to note that in the period immediately prior to World
War II, private consumption expenditures were equivalent to about 66 percent of the national output. In
1950, private consumption still amounted to 62 percent of gross national product, but a shift to the
government in the use of output was accomplished
through a considerable increase in the rates of taxation. The ratio of disposable income to gross national product was thereby lowered; and, in turn,
there was a corresponding reduction in the ratio of
private consumption to gross national product. Conversely, public consumption, which amounted to 10
percent of the gross national product in 1950, increased to 17 percent in 1968.

        Another measure of the contribution of the pri-
vate sector to the Swedish economy is the income and
expenditures of manufacturing enterprises. In 1966,
gross operating income of private corporations, joint
stock companies, and cooperatives amounted to 60.2
billion kronor, and costs of manufacturing and other
expenditures amounted to 51 billion kronor.[4] In 1967,
total sales of seventy-five of the eighty companies
listed on the Stockholm Stock Exchange amounted to
46.7 billion kronor.[5] In the same year, public enterprises and companies in which the national government has a controlling interest had sales of 15.1
billion kronor. These figures, however, understate

the role that both private and public enterprises play in the economy.

Table 2-4 presents the contributions in terms of sales that the fifteen largest Swedish manufacturing companies make to the Swedish economy. Public ownership in the manufacturing and mining sector is limited primarily to companies which operate in northern Sweden, where climatic factors and other conditions have made this area unattractive to private enterprise. The largest government-owned business is Luossavaara-Kirunavaara (LKAB), which exploits the iron ore deposits in northern Sweden. There is much less government ownership of industry in Sweden than in France, where the Renault automoble company, the four largest deposit banks, most insurance companies, and the largest aircraft company are owned by the government.

The Public Sector

The public sector in Sweden is engaged in two major types of activities, both of which can be measured by the expenditures incurred in carrying them out. One activity involves the government in the provision of a broad array of goods and services to its citizens, including expenditures on roads, police protection, and education. These expenditures represent a transfer of resources from the private sector of the Swedish economy to the public sector, and also represent the contribution of the government sector to the total gross national product.

The other activity involves the use of transfer payments as an instrument for the redistribution of income, generally with the dual objectives of greater income equality, and the provision of some minimum standard of living for everyone. Transfer payments, as distinguished from government expenditures on goods and services, involve only the transfer of income from one group to another through taxation, and provide no equivalent value in terms of goods and services in exchange. There is no return flow to the government in goods and services. Transfer payments include family allowances, old-age pensions, maternity grants, and unemployment compensation. Some services, such as free medical care, are considered to be a direct expenditure on the part of the government for a service which absorbs resources the same way as other government expenditures for services.

TABLE 2-4

The Fifteen Largest Corporations in Sweden Based on Volume of
Sales in 1967

Corporations	Volume of Sales (millions of kronor)	Product
SKFa	3,514	Ball bearings
Volvo	3,410	Automobiles
ASEAb	2,765	Electric machinery
L.M. Ericsson	2,291	Telephones
Skanska Cementgjuteriet	2,120	Buildings
STABc	1,536	Matches, machinery
SAAB	1,451	Aircraft, automobiles
Alfa-Laval	1,335	Separators
BPA Byggproduktion	1,300	Buildings
Grangesberg	1,280	Iron ore, steel, shipping
Stora Kopparberg	1,264	Steel, pulp, paper
Scania-Vabis	1,154	Trucks
Svenska Metallverken	1,064	Nonferrous metals
Atlas Copco	1,058	Pneumatic equipment
Svenska Cellulosa	1,054	Pulp, paper

aAB Svenska Kullagerfabriken
bAllmanna Svenska Elektriska AB
cSvenska Tandsticks AB

Source: Stockholms Enskilda Bank, "Some Data About Sweden, 1969-1970" (Stockholm,
1969), p. 68.

34

Resource allocation from the private to the public sector is accomplished by the process of taxation. This means that the cost of public activity is borne in the final analysis by the Swedish taxpayers. Taxes represent a withdrawal of funds from the private sector of the economy to the public sector. The burden of taxation in Sweden can be explained to a considerable degree by the existence of a very extensive social security program. Expenditures on social welfare measures are financed either out of general revenues, or by special fees and charges which are levied on individuals and companies.

In any discussion of the economic significance of public activity, it is not the absolute level of public expenditures that is important, but their level relative to other major expenditure components, such as consumption and investment. The economic significance of the public sector as a supplier of social goods can be determined by computing government expenditures for goods and services as a percentage of gross national product. This will show what proportion of total output is being absorbed by public bodies and presumably being utilized for the satisfaction of social rather than private wants. Taxes provide a government with control over economic resources, and their relationship to gross national product indicates the extent to which resources are diverted from the private to the public sector. The degree to which the government has become an instrument for the redistribution of income can be measured by computing transfer expenditures as a percent of national income. When transfer payments are computed as a percent of this total, it will show the proportion of earned income that has been redistributed by action of the public sector.

The Swedish public sector, that is, the national and local governments, absorbs a substantial proportion of the resources of the gross national product in the form of goods and services for investment and consumption. A considerable proportion of expenditures in the public sector, particularly by the national government, consists of income transfers to other sectors of the economy. While these outlays do not in themselves make any demands on real resources, the direct transfers from the national government to household and to local governments in particular do result in an immediate demand for goods and services.

A significant economic dimension of total governmental activity is its total outlay not only for the purchase of goods and services, but interest on its debt, subsidies, and transfer payments for welfare and similar purposes. The combined expenditures of national and local governments eliminating duplication that arises in such a total from grants-in-aid from the national government to local governments amounted to 44.4 billion kronor in 1967 out of a total gross national product of 123.8 billion kronor. The breakdown of government outlays compared to gross national product is presented in Table. 2-5.

TABLE 2-5

Total Outlays of the Swedish Public Sector
Relative to Gross National Product

Governmental Outlays	Billions of Kronor
Purchases of goods and services	26,065
Transfer payments	14,563
Subsidies	1,818
Interest on the public debt	1,925
Total Governmental Outlays	44,371
Gross National Product	123,770
Government Outlays as a % of GNP	35.9

Source: Organization for Economic Cooperation and Development, "National Accounts of OECD Countries, 1958-1967" (Paris, 1969), p. 256.

A measure of the contribution of the public sector to the Swedish economy is the share of public consumption and investment expenditures relative to gross national product. Public consumption expenditures involve needs of a collective nature which are supplied by the national and local governments, and would include police protection, the judicial system, and public administration. It would also include services received through education and medical care, which are enjoyed individually by private persons, but which are financed and operated by national and local government authorities. Transfer payments, such as family allowances, old-age benefits, and unemployment compensation, are excluded for the reason that their recipients are free to use them for private consumption or savings. Public consumption involves goods and services which are supplied by the government. The purchase of educational materials and teachers' salaries would count as public consumption. Educational grants would count as income transfers.

Public investment would involve expenditures on physical facilities and would include several categories of investment: investment in public utilities, railways, and other government-owned enterprises; public investment which involves highway construction, water supply and drainage systems; and investments which are needed for educational facilities and hospitals. The development of an urban society in Sweden has been followed by an increase in the need for public housing, water and sewage systems, and streets and communications. The high birth rate of the late 1940s and educational advancements have necessitated the building of new schools. Pressure for increased public investment has been particularly acute at the local government level, and public investments by local authorities have grown more rapidly over the past two decades than public investment by the national government.

In 1968, public consumption and investment expenditures amounted to 45.2 billion kronor out of a gross national product of 141.5 billion kronor, or 32 percent of the gross national product. The share of the public sector has increased during the period since the end of World War II. In 1946, 17 percent of gross national product was utilized by the public sector compared to 32 percent in 1968. Most of the increase occurred during the time periods 1947 to 1953 and 1962 to 1963. Part of this increase can be attributable to problems caused by the rapid urbanization of Swedish society which has taken place over the last twenty years, and part can be attributable to the increased participation of the government in certain sectors of the economy.

Total governmental outlays on consumption and investment has increased from 17 percent of gross national product in 1946 to 32 percent in 1968. Most of this increase was recorded during the period 1947-1953 and the period 1963-1968. Local governments have shown the most rapid expansion so that since 1955 their share of the public sector has been greater than that of the national government. Actually, more than half of national government revenues go to local governments and private individuals in the form of transfer payments, loans, and subsidies.

Transfer payments in national income accounting by convention, are excluded from gross national product for the reason that they involve transfers of income by the government from one group of persons to other groups, rather than the acquisition of resources necessary to the production of government output. Transfer expenditures, in other words, provide income, real or monetary, to the recipients of such expenditures, but the government unit does not receive either goods and services in return. Transfer payments to households constitute an important part of total governmental transactions. In 1967, transfer payments to households amounted to 14.1 billion kronor, which represented 12.9 percent of personal income.[6]

Another measure of the participation of the public sector in the Swedish economy is the extent to which income flows are affected by taxation. No other Western country diverts a greater percentage of its gross national product from the private to the public sector than does Sweden. In 1967, total taxes including social security contributions amounted to 41 percent of the gross national product. In France, the ratio was 38 percent, and in the United States the ratio was 26 percent.[7] In 1967, direct taxes amounted to 33 percent of national income in Sweden compared to 27 percent in France, 22 percent in the United States, and 15 percent in Japan.*

---

*In national income accounting, indirect business taxes and depreciation allowances are subtracted from gross national product to arrive at national income. National income represents the cost of producing gross national product. Comparing direct taxes to national income is one measure of the extent to which income from the private sector is diverted to the public sector.

The French figure of 27 percent is misleading. The major direct tax is social security contributions,

Despite the dominance of the private sector of the economy, government, both national and local, has entered into business in many areas. It has done so in varying degrees, in different forms, for various reasons, and without any preconceived plan. Mixed enterprises with government and private control have been established as a characteristic type of Sweden's industrial structure. These can be found in the wood and wood pulp industries, in the generation of electric power, and in the railways. In housing, national and local government units play a large part, with the national government's share represented by loans, subsidies, and the like, rather than direct ownership.

Certain activities of economic importance are legal monopolies, in some cases operated by a government agency or corporation and in others by a "mixed corporation" in which government and industry share ownership. Some of the activities involved are in the nature of public utilities which are typically operated by the national government, including the postal and telephone services, and the government monopoly of the manufacture, importation, and sale (other than at retail) of tobacco. This is exercised by Svenska Tobaksmonopolet, a corporation in which all of the shares are owned by the government. The radio and television industry has a special position; it is a monopoly which has exclusive rights of radio and television broadcasting. It is controlled by the government, which appoints a majority of the directors, but is owned by private interests. A mixed corporation is the ASEA-ATOM nuclear power corporation which was founded in 1968: Half of the shares are owned by the national government.

The national government also owns 95.7 percent of Luossavaara-Kirunavaara (LKAB), owner of the great

---

which are paid primarily by employers. Although OECD statistics count this as a direct tax, it can be reasoned that this tax constitutes an indirect levy against the employer which can be shifted. From the employer's point of view, social security taxes are simply a part of labor costs, and like other costs of production, they will be borne by the consumer. This is particularly true where such taxes constitute a significant part of total labor costs, as is the case in France.

Kiruna iron ore mine. The government's interest,
dating back to 1907 and increased to the present figure by the exercise of stock options, was acquired
in order to oust foreign interests from the field.
In the 1890s, the center of iron ore exploitation
shifted from central Sweden to the area of Lapland
in the extreme north, where mining towns like Kiruna
rapidly grew. Most of the iron ore was exported
from Sweden by an international cartel which controlled iron ore mines, steel mills, and railroads
in Sweden and northern Africa. The national government also owns 100 percent of Norrbottens Järnverk,
a pig iron producer set up in the north of Sweden
during World War II to maintain supplies and employment; as a result of renewed unemployment in the
area in the recession of 1957-1958, the national
government expanded its operations of the plant.

The government, national and local, has entered
into other business activities which it shares to
a greater or lesser degree with private enterprise.
For example, in 1967, in the field of electricity
production, 45 percent of total output was produced
by the national government, 13 percent was produced
by local government units, and 42 percent was produced by private enterprise.[8] In the banking and
financial sector of the Swedish economy, there is
both public and private ownership of the financial
institutions. The central bank is a state bank, formally subordinated to the Swedish Parliament. Commercial banks are, for the most part, privately owned.
The exception is the Sveriges Kreditbank, which is
the third largest of the five major commercial banks.
This bank represented a merger of two smaller banks
originally taken over by the national government when
faced with financial difficulty.

Swedish public enterprises, such as the state
railways and the post office, are expected to cover
operating costs from their current receipts, and show
some return on the capital invested in them. Their
assets and liabilities are included in the national
government's capital budget. All long-term capital
is supplied by the national government, but depreciation funds and any reported surplus has to be paid
to the government. Government-owned business corporations, such as LKAB and the tobacco company, Svenska
Tobaksmonopolet, transfer their profits to the
national government. Dividends are paid to shareholders. Government-owned business corporations

are shown in the capital budget only when they are
set up, or have their share capital increased.

Table 2-6 indicates the extent of government
ownership in various sectors of the Swedish economy
as measured by sales, operating profits, and fixed
investments for 1967. Excluded from the table are
government credit institutions, including a government investment bank which was created in 1967. The
purpose of this bank is to give financial support
to business firms that comply with the objectives of
location and labor market policies.

A new state-owned company, Svenska Industrie-
tableringsaktiebolaget (Swedish Industrial Establishment Company), Svetab, was formed in the middle of
1969. The main reason for the formation of the
company was to create new employment opportunities
through the creation of companies, wholly or partly
owned by the government. Primary attention is to be
paid to developing new enterprises or taking over
already-existing companies in areas with employment
problems, such as in the forest and rural regions
in northern Sweden. The share capital of the company
is 8 million kronor. The Swedish government has subscribed to the entire stock. Svetab's operations
will be financed by borrowing.

In late 1969, the government and the Pharamceut-
ical Society of Sweden concluded an agreement on the
formation of a pharmacy company in which the government will have the controlling interest. Providing
that the agreement is approved by Parliament, which
is likely, the new company will take over the privately owned pharmacies in January, 1971. The pharmacy company will also take over the pharmaceuticals
manufacturing company owned by the Pharmaceutical
Society. This company will be merged with the state-
controlled pharmacy company. The reason that is
given for the nationalization of the pharmacies is
that the government wishes to exert a greater influence on the price of medicines. Nearly two-thirds
of the retail turnover of pharmacies--over 1 billion
kronor a year--is paid by national health insurance
and by hospitals.

Governments can significantly condition or alter market response through the use of subsidies to
supply goods and services at less than cost. The in-
tent of subsidies is to achieve a desired social or

TABLE 2-6

Public Enterprises and Companies in Which the National
Government Has a Controlling Interest

Public Enterprises	Sales (millions of kronor)	Operating Profit (millions of kronor)	Fixed Assets (millions of kronor)
Board of Telecommunications	2,439	682.1	672.2
State Railways	2,303	170.0	415.0
Post Office	1,200	16.0	16.1
Airport Administration	122	32.6	16.2
State Power Board	867	588.3	400.9
State Forest Service	413	47.8	25.1
National Defense Industries	336	31.0	35.5
	7,680	1,567.8	1,581.0
Government-Owned Business Companies			
LKAB	856	327.0	160.0
Karlskrona Shipyard	73	4.9	1.4
Uddevalla Shipyard	273	31.7	2.9
Svenska Tobaksmonopolet	323	64.1	13.8
Retail Alcohol Monopoly	2,492	120.1	25.3
The Swedish Lottery	357	151.1	-----
The Swedish Soccer Pools	328	91.5	3.5
Sweden's share of SAS	1,308	174.4	254.4
Other companies	2,445	162.3	194.8
	8,455	1,127.1	656.1

Source: Ministry of Finance, "The Swedish Budget, 1969-1970" (Stockholm, 1969),
pp. 64-65.

42

economic objective by providing a product or service
that would otherwise be offered at a market-determined
price. For example, a government can offer capital
to governmental or private enterprises at less than
the prevailing interest rates in financial markets.
A government through the remission of taxes or other
charges can influence plant location. Still another
form of subsidy is the provision of government insurance or medical care at rates less than those which
would normally prevail in the market.

In 1967, approximately 4 percent of total government expenditures in Sweden took the form of subsidies. Regional development policy is one area in
which subsidies are used. To promote the location of
industry in northern Sweden, subsidies which cannot
be in excess of 35 percent of investment costs are
granted to business firms. The subsidies do not have
to be repaid. Subsidies are also of some importance
in agriculture, with price supports being used to keep
farm incomes in some degree of parity with incomes in
the rest of the economy. Other subsidies have been
directed toward housing and hospital construction,
medical care, and health research facilities. Certain
public enterprises, such as the air transportation
industry, are also favored with subsidies.

Cooperatives

The cooperative movement developed in Europe as
a reaction against the excesses of the industrial
revolution. Between 1840 and 1860, the major forms of
cooperatives had developed and also those concepts
which became characteristic of the cooperative system.
In general, cooperatives developed as representatives
of producers and consumers. The basic idea in back
of the cooperative movement involved the association
of individuals collectively for solving problems of
mutual interest. They may associate as producers for
the collective purchase of goods used in production, or
as consumers for purchasing in common consumer goods
or services. Normally, a considerable part of the
capital involved in the operation of a cooperative is
contributed by its members, who have certain voting
privileges and who are entitled to receive dividends,
if any, from the earnings.

The Swedish cooperative movement dates back to
1850 and was patterned after the Rochdale Pioneer

Cooperative Society in England.* Consumer cooperatives were formed, but most were unsuccessful. Their
failure was attributable primarily to a lack of man-
agerial expertise and to a lack of capital. These
cooperatives united in 1899 to form the Kooperativa
Förbundet, known throughout Sweden as KF. Its development was rapid. After World War I, Kooperativa
Förbundent took up a systematic fight designed to
bring down consumer prices by eliminating or restricting the oppressive practices of certain powerful
national and international monopolies. Major examples were the fights against monopolies in flour,
fertilizers, electric lamps, and margarine. In the
case of flour, a strong private cartel of flour mills
had been established after 1920. There was a wide
disproportion between grain and flour prices. In
1922, Kooperativa Förbundet entered the industry by
buying up one of the largest flour mills in Sweden,
with the result that prices to consumers were reduced at once.

The Swedish cooperatives play an important role
in certain areas of the Swedish economy. In 1965,
the cooperatives were responsible for 20 percent of
all retail sales, 30 percent of the total retail
trade in food, 15 percent of all of the petroleum
products sold, 80 percent of the output in agriculture and fishing, and 10 percent of the value of life
insurance policies issued. Although cooperatives
were responsible for only 2 percent of total industrial production, they produced 45 percent of the
nation's pottery, china, and earthenware, 35 percent
of the flour, 30 percent of the light bulbs, 25 percent of margarine, and 10 percent of bakery products.

Consumer Cooperatives

Kooperativa Förbundet is the central and most
important consumer cooperative. A number of retail

---

*The Rochdale Pioneer Cooperative was formed in
1844 by twenty-eight artisans, who were mostly
weavers. It proposed to sell products at market
prices and to capitalize profits, establishing reserves destined to be plowed back and a fund for educational and promotional purposes. The principles
of the Rochdale Cooperative are still the principles
of consumer cooperatives all over the world.

cooperatives are affiliated with this organization
and each is required to invest in share capital a
sum equivalent to 1 percent of its purchases from
KF during the year before the current accounting
period. The shares in KF are, in principle, not
withdrawable. However, in connection with liquidation, a retail cooperative may, with the consent of
the board of directors, be refunded its shares. In
addition to the purchase of share capital, each cooperative is required to pay an annual subscription
fee of 25 öre for each member. These subscriptions
are used for educational and promotional work on the
part of KF. These subscriptions, however, cover only
a very small part of the costs for this type of work
carried out by KF.

At the end of 1967, the number of cooperatives
affiliated with KF was 275. Total membership amounted
to 1,404,000 persons. Both with regard to membership
and geographical size, the consumer cooperatives vary
greatly. The world's largest consumer cooperative,
Konsum Stockholm, has some 230,000 members in the
city of Stockholm. Konsum operates the second largest
department store, PUB, in Stockholm, which has an annual volume of sales of around 150 million kronor.
In addition, Konsum owns department stores in the
suburbs surrounding Stockholm, restaurants, bakeries,
a meat processing factory, and breweries. The total
value of Konsum's sales in 1967 was 960 million
kronor.*

KF itself is more than just an amalgam of cooperatives. In terms of sales, it (and its subsidiaries)
is the largest concern in Sweden. Sales to its
affiliated cooperative socities in 1967 amounted to
3.3 billion kronor, and sales to other buyers and
exports amounted to another 1.3 billion kronor. KF's
industrial activity is diverse; it ranges from the
production of foodstuffs to the manufacture of such
special products as paper, porcelain, and bathtubs.
Several of KF's industries are among the largest in

---

*In Konsum the surplus from the trading activity
is returned to the members in proportion to their
purchases. To obtain this dividend the amounts of the
receipts that are received when making purchases are
added together and handed into Konsum at the end of
the year.

the country. This is the case with regard to the
flour mills, Tre Kronor (Three Crowns) in Stockholm
and Tre Lejon (Three Lions) in Gothenburg, and the
electric light bulb factory, Luma, in Stockholm. In
addition KF has factories which supply heavy industry--
rubber products, foam plastics, paper and forestry
products, and oils. There is also the mutual insurance enterprise, Folksam, which is the second largest
insurance company in the country. It is organized
along parliamentary lines, with supreme decision-
making authority vested in its general assembly. Of
the forty-five general assembly members, thirty are
appointed at KF's district congresses, and fifteen
by LO, the Confederation of Swedish Trade Unions.

Producers Cooperatives

     Producers cooperatives are of particular impor-
tance in agriculture. Outside of this area, producers
cooperatives exist in such fields as bakeries and
meat packing. Most are affiliated with KF. Apart
from KF and the consumer cooperative movement, there
is a farm cooperative movement of great importance.
The Agricultural Federation, Sveriges Lantbruksförbund,
consists of thirteen separate cooperative organizations; practically every Swedish farmer belongs to
at least one of these. As a consequence a farmer
has to acquire shares in all of the different cooperatives in which he is a member. The share obligations
are different for most of the cooperatives, but in
general share payments are due within fifteen years.
The share capital may be fixed on a per capita basis
and represent the same sum for all members, or based
in proportion to the number of cattle or produce
delivered. The system which is preferred in the
Swedish agricultural cooperatives is the fixing of
the share capital in proportion to the quanities of
products delivered to the cooperatives.

     Agricultural cooperatives are responsible for
the great majority of farm produce sold in the country. In 1966, cooperative dairy associations were
responsible for 98 percent of the dairy products sold;
their sales amounted to 1.8 billion kronor. Cooperative slaughterhouses sold 83 percent of all meat
animals, and similarly had sales exceeding 2 billion
kronor. Other important cooperative groups covered
sugar beets, eggs, cows and pigs, vegetables, and
lumber. In 1966, the total volume of sales for all
agricultural cooperatives amounted to 7.7 billion

kronor.[9] In addition, a large share of farm machines,
fertilizers, building materials, and other items is
purchased by farmers through purchasing cooperatives.
There are also cooperative farm mortgage banks. In
1966, there were 525 cooperative farm banks, with
assets of 3.1 billion kronor and loans outstanding
of 2.5 billion kronor.[10]

SUMMARY

In countries operating with a market system,
the market is a device for the organization of economic activity, and it functions by transmitting consumer preferences, as revealed through the expenditure of income, to producers who, in the process of
adjusting output to correspond with these preferences,
direct resources into various and alternative uses.
As a mechanism for the allocation of economic resources, the market operates on the basis of individual choice, and the culmination of the whole process
is the act of exchange whereby the consumer pays
directly and individually for any good or service
he wishes to acquire. The presumption is that the
price he is willing to pay in the market for a good
or a service reflects the value or benefit he expects
to derive from its use.

The mixed economy typifies the economic system
that is prevalent in Western noncommunist countries
today. There is both public and private ownership
of the agents of production. Although the market is
the primary allocator of resources, the indivisible
character of most social goods makes it manifestly
impossible to utilize this mechanism which is firmly
rooted in the act of individual exchange. As a consequence, economic resources are allocated to public
use through the medium of taxation.

In terms of economic well-being and an equitable
distribution of resources for its citizens, Sweden
must be considered a model country. Its performance
can be rated as far superior to the authoritarian-
planned economy of the Soviet Union. Although it
ranks second behind the United States from the standpoint of per capita income, it has accomplished a
more equitable distribution of both real and monetary
incomes. There is not the extreme disparity between
the incomes of the rich and poor that exists in the

United States, and physical or overt poverty does
not exist.

The Swedish economy can be divided into private,
public, and cooperative sectors. Actually, the cooperative sector can be considered a part of the
private sector. Although the private sector is dominant in terms of consumption and output, the influence
of the public sector upon the economy is considerable.
The point has been made that governmental influence
in the market place has become particularly pronounced
in Sweden and other Western market economies. One
measure of the economic dimension of total governmental activity is its total outlay not only for the
purchase of goods and services, but also for interest,
subsidies, and transfer payments. In 1967, total
governmental outlays in Sweden amounted to almost
36 percent of the gross national product. The diversion of income from the private to the public sector
through the medium of taxation is a second measure.
In 1967, taxes in Sweden amounted to 41 percent of
the gross national product. The government also enters the market as a producer and seller of goods and
services.

In Chapters 3, 4, and 5 the influence of the
governmental sector upon the Swedish economy will be
analyzed. Chapter 3 is concerned with taxation and
expenditures of the national government; Chapter 4
is concerned with economic stabilization policies; and
Chapter 5 pertains to income redistribution through
taxation, transfer payments, and full-employment
policies.

NOTES

1. Economic Report of the President, 91st
Cong., 1st Sess., House Doc. 28 (Washington, D.C.:
Government Printing Office, 1969), p. 153.

2. Statistiska Centralbyran, "Statistiska
Meddelander, 1966" (Stockholm, 1966), p. 54.

3. These figures are approximately correct.
See Sekretariat for Economic Planning of the Ministry
of Finance and the National Institute of Economic

Research, "Riksrevisionsverkets Inkomstberäkning,"
(Stockholm, 1965), p. 7; Organization for Economic Co-
operation and Development, "National Accounts of
OECD Countries, 1958-1967" (Paris, 1969), p. 261.

    4.   Statistiska Centralbyran, "Statistisk
Årsbok, 1968" (Stockholm, 1968), p. 360. The data
exclude enterprises with less than 50 employees.

    5.   Tiido Uutma and Jaak Järv, "Company Reports
for 1968--A Comparison with Earlier Years,"
Skandinaviska Banken Quarterly Review (Third Quarter,
1969), p. 73.

    6.   Organization for Economic Cooperation and
Development, op. cit., p. 256.

    7.   Ibid., Tables 1 and 7.

    8.   Stockholms Enskilda Bank, "Some Data About
Sweden, 1969-1970" (Stockholm, 1969), p. 89.

    9.   "Statistisk Årsbok, 1968," op. cit., p. 102.

    10. Ibid., p. 200.

CHAPTER **3** THE FISCAL SYSTEM

INTRODUCTION

The level of taxation in Sweden in relation to
gross national product is the highest of any Western
industrial country. Receipts from Swedish taxation
and social security contributions amounted to 41.1
percent of the Swedish gross national product in 1966.
There is no country in the world that relies more
heavily on the income tax as the prime source of both
national and local government revenues. In the field
of local revenue, it is especially noteworthy that
the local governments rely almost exclusively on the
local income tax; there is no other local tax of any
consequence. Not only is the local income tax uniform (except as to rate) throughout Sweden, as a
matter of both law and administration, but it is
integrated almost completely with the national income tax. The same legislative rules govern both
national and local income taxes, almost without
exception.

Government expenditures on goods and services--
national and local--and transfer payments comprise a
considerable part of gross national product. In
particular, government expenditure through transfer
payments has had a great impact on income redistribution in Sweden. This transfer of income is accomplished by an extensive system of allowances and
subsidies. Although the national income tax introduces an element of progression into the tax system,
it only accounts for about 1 percent of all income
redistributed by taxation and transfers. Government
expenditures on goods and services comprises the
activities of the national and local governments.
In addition to the standard expenditures on national
defense, education, and housing, other expenditures

50

are made through the public enterprises and the
government-owned business companies.

THE SWEDISH BUDGETARY SYSTEM

A feature of Swedish practice is the "divided
budget"; divided between a current operating budget
and a capital budget. In effect the former deals
with the national government as a going concern,
while the latter deals with the government's capital
investments. On the revenue side, the operating
budget shows tax receipts and the profits of the
government's capital funds and economic enterprises--
receipts from the tobacco, alcohol, and telephone
monopolies, the post office, and the like. The expenditures side of the current operating budget shows
the customary government expenditures for national
defense, education, social welfare, roads, and the
like. It also includes payments to the capital funds
covered by the capital budget, as well as capital
losses. The capital funds include a national debt
fund and a fund for the depreciation of new capital
investments.

All current expenditures of the national government, including interest on the debt, are entered in
the current budget, and are financed out of tax revenues and earnings from government enterprises. Capital expenditures are reserved for the capital budget.
In fact, the Swedish capital budget only shows the
new borrowing requirements for capital expenditures,
while the total capital expenditure, with some exceptions, is shown in a special budget of capital
expenditures.* Obviously, depreciation and obsoles-
cence must be covered by current taxes or, if the
project is self-liquidating, by the proceeds of the
sale of the state-produced commodity. Just as in
the case of private investment, the original capital

------

*The special budget of capital expenditures
includes total expenditures financed out of depreciation allowances within the capital funds, liquidation of assets, depreciation allowances set in the
current budget, and new borrowing requirements. The
total amount of the special budget is approximately
5.4 billion kronor for 1969-1970.

sum financed by borrowing never has to be paid back
so long as additional savings continue to seek investment outlets.

The Swedish capital budget for the fiscal year
1969-1970 is presented in Table 3-1.

TABLE 3-1

The Swedish Capital Budget for 1969-1970
(Millions of Kronor)

Revenue		Expenditures	
New borrowing	2,825,249	Public enter- prise funds	497,097
		Real estate fund	144,291
		Defense real estate fund	42,006
		State loan funds	1,571,454
		State loan aid fund	257,074
		Fund for state owned shares	300,000
		Fund for advances to the government	14,600
		Miscellaneous capital funds	67,466
			2,864,788
		Deduction for cap- ital repayment	39,539
	2,825,249		2,825,249

Source: Ministry of Finance, "The Swedish
Budget, 1969-1970" (Stockholm, 1969), p. 72.

The current and capital budgets formally comprise
the state budget, which is submitted to the Riksdag
in January of every year. In addition, a national
budget, or economic survey, is also submitted.[1] Its
contents can be described as a discussion of the
general economic development of the coming year, so
far as this can be estimated on the basis of the
preliminary national economic accounts for the calendar year just ended. It can also be said to show
the expected results of the economic policy that is

presented simultaneously in the state budget. The
quantitative part of the national budget takes the
form of a balance of resources for the coming year:
a table showing the expected total supply of goods
and services within the country, and the use of these
for different purposes. The estimated balance of
resources is based on the national income accounts
for the previous year, and statistical material from
a number of government agencies concerning both the
preceding and the coming year, the latter frequently
in the form of statistics on plans.

    The main part of social welfare expenditures are
not carried in the state budget. Of the five basic
components of the social security system, only the
basic pension scheme is carried in the current operating budget. The other four components--the supplementary pension, health insurance, industrial injuries,
and unemployment benefit schemes--are financed from
autonomous budgets which are not presented to the
Riksdag. However, the health insurance and unemployment benefit schemes receive grants from the current
operating budget. The bulk of Swedish social welfare
expenditures are financed not by general national
revenues, but by special taxes or levies on employees
and, to a lesser extent, on employers. These taxes
and contributions go to special funds rather than to
the national treasury, and are handled in separate
budgets.

                        TAXATION

    The Swedish tax system is relatively easy to
describe. The income tax is the most important
national and local tax and is levied against both
individuals and companies. In 1968, the income tax
accounted for 30 billion kronor out of total tax
collections of 48 billion kronor. Another tax, which
is of increasing importance as a source of revenue,
is the value-added tax. This tax is of recent origin,
and is patterned after the French value-added tax,
which has caught the fiscal fancy of many European
countries. Sumptuary taxes, particularly those on
alcohol and tobacco, are also of importance. In
recent years indirect taxes have increased in importance relative to direct taxes as sources of government
revenue. For example, the general sales tax, which
was recently replaced by the value-added tax, accounted

for 19.7 percent of total national government revenue
in the fiscal year 1968-1969, compared to 9.1 percent
in 1960-1961.

Table 3-2 presents tax revenues for both the
national and local governments for the fiscal year
1968-1969. Excluded from the table are revenues from
the public enterprise funds and other sources of non-
tax revenues, such as receipts from annual depreciation allowances and the liquidation of assets. For
the fiscal year 1969-1970, total tax receipts including the value-added tax (which went into effect in
January, 1969) are estimated at around 53 billion
kronor, an increase of 10 percent over the fiscal
year 1968-1969. The value-added tax is expected to
produce around 7 billion kronor in revenue to the
national government.

Income Taxes

Sweden has a national and local income tax. The
national income tax is progressive, but all local income taxes are proportional. The rates, however,
vary from commune to commune. The average rate of
all local income taxes in 1968 was 19.34 percent of
taxable income. Local income taxes are levied at
the same rate for individuals, partnerships, corporations, and trusts. The national and local income
taxes are collected together by one administrative
organization, usually by means of withholding from
wages and salaries. The county governor's office
pays to each commune local income taxes collected on
its behalf.

Income in Sweden is defined as the total of net
income from all sources: wages and salaries, interest, dividends, business activity, rent, and capital
gains. Capital gains, unlike in the United States,
are treated as regular income, and are subject to
both the national and local income taxes. There are
variations in the treatment of capital gains. For
example, capital gains derived from stocks and bonds
are taxed on the full gain if the securities are held
for two years or less, and at a decreasing rate if
held longer than two years. After a five-year period,
10 percent of the capital gain is taxed as ordinary
income. Capital gains from the sale of real estate
are also taxed as ordinary income. If the property
has been held for less than two years, the tax is on

the full amount of the gain; after two years, the tax
is on 75 percent of the gain. Acquisition and improvement costs of up to 3,000 kronor a year can be
deducted from the sales price of the property.

TABLE 3-2

National and Local Tax Revenues for
the Fiscal Year 1968-1969

National Taxes	Millions of Kronor
Income & capital tax, including	
old-age pension fees	14,200[a]
Death duty and gift tax	200
Other direct taxes	233
Sales tax	6,800
General employer contribution	300
Liquor tax	2,230
Tobacco tax	1,500
Gasoline tax	2,023
Customs	880
Energy tax	900
Annual car tax	1,000
Miscellaneous taxes	1,619
	31,885

Local Taxes	
Local income tax	16,100
	47,985

[a]This sum can be divided approximately as follows: income tax from individuals, 10.3 billion
kronor; income tax from companies, 1.2 billion kronor; capital taxes, 400 million kronor; and old-age
pension fees, 2.3 billion kronor.

Source: Skattebetalarnas Förening, "Fakta för
Skattebetalare" (Stockholm, 1968).

Deductions and allowances may be credited against
total net income. While the local income tax is deductible from income for purposes of the national
income tax, the latter is not deductible for any purpose. Nor is either tax available as a credit against
the other. As an alternative to the deduction of the
local income tax, a standard deduction of 2,250 kronor

for single persons, and 4,500 kronor for married couples is permitted. Otherwise, deductions are standard
for both the local and national income taxes. Included are pension premiums, compulsory health insurance fees, and certain contributions. Life insurance
and voluntary health insurance premiums are also deductible, with a limit of 250 kronor for a single person and 500 kronor for a married couple. A married
woman who is employed may deduct 300 kronor from her
earned income. If her children are under sixteen,
she may deduct an additional 25 percent of her income, up to a maximum of 2,700 kronor. Swedish taxpayers are allowed to deduct 400 or 800 kronor, depending on their marital status, in interest. Losses
are in general deductible from income; however, capital losses can only be offset against capital gains
derived during the same tax year.

After deductions have been made, there are standard exemptions or allowances for married and single
people. There are no allowances for children, these
were replaced in 1948 by cash grants which currently
amount to 900 kronor for each child.

The National Income Tax

The national income tax rates range at present
from 10 percent to 65 percent. These rates are only
base rates; annually the Riksdag must determine what
percentage of the base rates is to be applied for
the year in question. This results in a "mobile tax"
which gives the tax system a degree of flexibility to
meet changing revenue or economic needs. By a simple
rate statute, the Riksdag can raise or lower rates
without reopening the entire statute or even the rate
structure itself.

The rates of the national income tax are presented in Table 3-3.

The Swedish national income tax is computed the
same way as the federal personal income tax in the
United States. Progression is accomplished by the
"bracket" method, whereby each successive higher rate
applies only to income in excess of the previous
bracket maximum. Furthermore, continuing exemptions
reduce somewhat the overall burden of the scheduled
rates. Actually, therefore, the overall effective
rates on total incomes are less than the maximum
bracket rates applied to these incomes. For example,

TABLE 3-3

National Income Tax Rates for Married and Single Taxpayers

Taxable Income	Rate for Married Couple[a]	Taxable Income	Rate for Single Person
0-12,000 kronor	10%	0-6,000 kronor	10%
12,000-16,000	15	6,000-8,000	15
16,000-20,000	22	8,000-10,000	22
20,000-24,000	27	10,000-15,000	27
24,000-30,000	34	15,000-20,000	31
30,000-40,000	42	20,000-25,000	36
40,000-60,000	48	25,000-30,000	40
60,000-100,000	54	30,000-40,000	44
100,000-150,000	59	40,000-60,000	49
150,000 & Over	65	60,000-100,000	54
		100,000-150,000	59
		150,000 & Over	65

[a]Married couples can have their income taxed as one unit or separately. If their income is taxed separately, it is subject to the tax rates for single persons.

Source: Skattebetalarnas Förening, "Fakta för Skattebetalare" (Stockholm, 1968).

the marginal tax on taxable incomes between 30,000
and 40,000 kronor is 42 percent. However, the effective tax rate is much less. The total national
tax on a net taxable income of 39,000 kronor would
be 9,580 kronor. The effective tax rate is 24.6 percent compared to a marginal tax rate of 42 percent.

Although the rates of the national income tax
are high, it is necessary to remember that they are
levied on net taxable income which has allowed for
deductions and exemptions mentioned previously.
Moreover, as the rates of progression begin to become
effective only in the higher income brackets, the
local income tax actually places a heavier burden on
gross incomes of up to 36,000 kronor for single taxpayers and 55,000 kronor for married taxpayers. On
a net taxable income of 15,000 kronor, a married couple would pay approximately 2,700 kronor. Of this
amount, approximately 2,100 kronor would be paid in
local income taxes and the remainder would be the
national income tax.

The Local Income Tax

The communal system of local government in Sweden
underlies the structure of the local income tax rate.
While only one local income tax is levied, the rate
is made up of several separate components. For example, the local income tax rate for the County of
Kalmar was 20.66 percent in 1968, but was divided
into a communal portion of 12.35 percent,* a portion
for the support of the state church of 0.98 percent,
and the remaining portion of 7.33 percent goes to
the county council. These amounts are set by the
commune and county councils. The rate for the state
church is determined when the local church council
submits its budget to the commune council, which then
includes in the rate of the local tax an amount sufficient to meet any deficit. The combined average
rate of all local taxes for the whole of Sweden for
1968 was 19.34 percent of taxable income, (i.e.,
assessable income after deductions and exemptions).
Of this, 13.24 percent went to the communes, 0.79 percent went to the support of the state church, and the
remainder to the counties.

---

*As previously noted, communes may be divided in-
to three main classes: landskommuner, köpinger, and
städer.

The national and local income taxes are computed together and are generally withheld by the employer. However, every person earning an annual income of at least 2,400 kronor or owning capital assets valued at 100,000 kronor or more is required to fill out and submit an annual tax return in February of each year which states his income during the previous year and the amount of his capital assets at the end of that year.

The following example of the computation of the national and local income taxes can be used to illustrate some of the fundamentals of income taxation in Sweden: The taxpayer is a married person whose wife has no earned income. Net income after general deductions is assumed to be 15,000 kronor, and the local tax is assumed to be 20 percent. The local income tax, as mentioned previously, can be taken as a deduction from income or, as an alternative, a standard deduction of 4,500 kronor can be taken.

Local Income Tax

Net income	15,000 kronor
Allowance (standard allowance of 2,250 kronor per person)	4,500
Taxable income	10,500
Local tax (20 percent of 10,500)	2,100

National Income Tax

Net income	15,000
Deduction for the local income tax	4,500
Allowance	4,500
Taxable income	6,000
National tax (10 percent of 6,000)	600

In addition to national and local income taxes on personal incomes, there is a basic old-age pension which is financed by a tax on the employee of 5 percent of income, with a maximum payment of 1,500 kronor a year. The three taxes are withheld as a single deduction from an employee's income by the employer. Since the deduction covers both national and local income taxes, and since the rate of the latter tax varies from commune to commune, it is necessary to publish a series of withholding tables, which are designed to take this factor into account.

Table 3-4 presents the total amount of national and local income taxes and old-age pension payments that selected types of taxpayers would have to pay at different income levels.* The local income tax is assumed to be 18 percent. Health insurance premiums are also withheld and constitute a part of total tax payments.

TABLE 3-4

Tax Payments for Selected Types of Taxpayers

Monthly Income (Kronor)	Unmarried Person	Married Person Whose Wife Does Not Work[a]	Married Couple, Both Work	Unmarried Person With Children Under 15 Years
2,000	735	548	643	435
3,000	1,251	1,002	1,111	862
4,500	2,077	1,780	1,907	1,631
5,800	2,834	2,526	2,643	2,368
8,300	4,371	4,050	4,175	3,879

[a]Or wife earns less than 3,000 kronor a year.

Source: Ministry of Finance, Skattetabel för Beräkning av Preliminär A-Skatt för Ar 1969 (Stockholm, 1969).

State and local income taxes and the basic old-age pension take a much higher percentage of taxable income of wage and salary earners in Sweden than in either the United States or the Soviet Union. For example, a Swedish family with one wage earner would pay a tax of 548 kronor ($109) on a monthly income of 2,000 kronor ($400). This income would be around

---

*Health insurance premiums are also a part of tax payments. The premium is based on income, with the maximum payment for a single wage earner set at 500 kronor a year. The payment of the premium does not distort U.S. and Swedish tax comparisons, as the amount would rarely exceed 40 kronor a month.

the average for Sweden. The effective tax rate of
27.4 percent is much higher than the rate on a comparable income in the United States.

Assume, for example, that an American family
with one wage earner makes $400 a month and resides
in Virginia, which has a state income tax; for the
sake of simplicity, there are no children to claim
as dependents.* There are three basic deductions--
the federal income taxes, state income taxes, and
social security contributions--so that similar comparisons can be made with Swedish tax payments. The
family would pay total taxes of $71.10. The effec-
tive tax rate is 17.8 percent, which can be compared
to the effective tax rate of 27.4 percent for the
Swedish family with a comparable income. The same
family making $900 a month would pay $202.36 in
federal and state income taxes and social security
contributions. The effective tax rate is 22.5 percent, which can be compared to an effective tax rate
of 39.7 percent for a Swedish family making $900 a
month. On an income of $1,650 a month, the American
family would pay a combined tax of $412.67, for an
effective tax rate of 25 percent. The comparable
effective Swedish tax rate is 48.8 percent.

For most Swedes, the local income tax takes a
greater amount of personal income than the national
income tax. For example, Table 3-5 presents average
state and local income taxes for single and married
taxpayers for different income levels.

Provisions designed to limit the total impact of
national and local taxation on individual incomes have
been in effect for some years. Since the national
income tax rate may reach a maximum of 65 percent,
and local income taxes range from 18 to 21 percent,
there are cases in which the total burden of these
taxes could be quite large. There is also a progressive tax on capital assets in excess of 100,000
kronor. Combined income and capital taxes could
exceed 100 percent of total income. To avoid such a
possibility, Swedish tax laws contain a special

---

*As previously noted, there are no exemptions
for children under the Swedish tax system. Instead,
a family allowance of 900 kronor a year is paid for
each child.

limitation clause which states that the national and
local income taxes and the capital tax cannot exceed
80 percent of a taxpayer's income for a given year.

TABLE 3-5

A Comparison of National and Local Income
Taxes at Different Income Levels

Yearly Income (Kronor)	Single Taxpayer		Married Taxpayer[a]	
	State Income Tax	Local Income Tax	State Income Tax	Local Income Tax
6,000	119	688	--	210
10,000	506	1,462	55	1,010
15,000	1,296	2,452	529	1,958
20,000	2,358	3,444	1,025	2,950
30,000	4,859	5,428	2,623	4,934
50,000	11,415	9,418	8,190	8,924
100,000	31,782	19,418	28,073	18,924

[a]No children, one wage earner.

Source: Ministry of Finance, "The Swedish
Budget, 1969-1970" (Stockholm, 1969), p. 108.

Direct taxes on the population are unimportant
in the Soviet revenue system. The personal income
tax accounted for only 7 percent of total state budget
revenues in 1966. It is progressive in nature, and
in 1960 ranged from a minimum of 0.15 percent to a
maximum of 13 percent of monthly earnings withheld
by the Soviet enterprises and paid to the Ministry
of Finance. The income tax is differentiated between
economic groups, with certain groups such as workers
and salaried employees paying a lower tax than other
groups such as doctors, lawyers, and artisans with
incomes from private practice. The personal income
tax was supposed to have been abolished in the Soviet
Union by 1965, but this has not come about, although
some liberalization in the amount of income which is
exempted from the tax has occurred. As of 1967, the
amount of income exempted from the tax was 60 rubles
($66.66) a month.[2]

There are two reasons for the lack of reliance on the personal income tax in the Soviet Union. First of all, virtually all wage and salary earners are employed by state enterprises, or enterprises which are closely controlled by the state. Therefore, a personal income tax would only be an administrative device for doing what could be done with less trouble by adjustment of the wages and salaries originally paid. Second, the Soviet Union relies on wage differentials to allocate labor. Material incentives play a very important role in stimulating worker productivity. A direct tax, such as the personal income tax, it is felt, would have a more negative impact on work incentives than indirect taxes. An indirect tax, such as a sales tax, is more invisible than the income tax and would not have the effect of reducing the take-home pay of the worker. In the Soviet Union, staged reductions in the rate of the personal income tax have been carried out.

The significance of personal income taxation in Sweden can be illustrated by comparing it to personal income. In 1966, it amounted to 20.7 percent of Swedish personal income--a percentage which is quite high in comparison to the relationships in other countries. For example, in 1966 in the United States personal income taxes amounted to 12 percent of personal income. In the United Kingdom, which also relies extensively on income taxation, the ratio was 11.7 percent. In France and Japan, the percentage relationships were 4.9 and 5.6, respectively. In Norway, the ratio between personal income taxes and personal income was 16.3 percent.[3]

The Corporate Income Tax

As mentioned previously, the national and local income taxes are levied on the incomes of individuals and corporations. The national income tax is levied on corporations at a flat rate of 40 percent, and the local income tax rate is levied at the same rates as for individuals. Since the latter tax is deductible for national income tax purposes, the combined rates amount to about 49 percent of taxable income. Both the national and local income taxes are assessed against corporations in the assessment year on incomes earned in the previous year. This year may be either a calendar or a fiscal year. Corporations are exempt from the national capital tax.

Economic associations, such as cooperatives, savings banks, and mortgage banks, pay the national income tax at a lower rate. The net taxable income of cooperatives and banks are subject to a tax rate of 32 percent. Life insurance companies pay an income tax of 10 percent on net profits. Local income taxes are levied at the same rate as those applied to individuals and corporations. However, while economic associations are of some importance, most large-scale enterprises in Sweden are carried on in the corporate form; what is perhaps the oldest corporation, Stora Kopparbergs Bergslags AB, has been active in Sweden since before the discovery of America.

The corporate income tax is levied on net taxable income. To determine net income, a corporation may deduct from its gross receipts all normal operating expenses. It can deduct interest on borrowed capital, certain taxes including the local income tax, pensions, maintenance and repairs, wages and salaries, and rent. In addition, there are special rules governing the taxation of corporate income which are designed to increase the efficiency of Swedish industry as a competitor in world markets. These rules govern depreciation, inventory valuation, and the use of investment reserves for economic stabilization. Through these rules, and in the changes that it has made in them from time to time, the Swedish government has been motivated not only by tax considerations, but also by a desire to influence the investment decisions of business firms.[4]

Wealth and Inheritance Taxes

Sweden levies a national tax on net wealth, inheritances, and gifts. In terms of their yield to national tax revenues, they contribute little. In the fiscal year 1968-1969, total revenue of the wealth, inheritance, and gift taxes amounted to 570 million kronor from national government tax revenues of 31.9 billion kronor. It can be said, however, that the main purpose of these taxes is to accomplish a more equal distribution of income. When they are combined with personal income taxes, it is apparent that income differentials have been narrowed considerably.

The Capital Tax

A taxpayer who owns capital assets in excess of 100,000 kronor has to pay, in addition to taxes on income from these assets, a special capital tax. With few exceptions, virtually every kind of property--real or movable, tangible or intangible--is subject to the tax; in general, only such items as household goods and certain kinds of personal insurance are exempt. For purposes of the tax, the assets of husbands and wives are lumped together. Debts are deductible from the value of all assets, so the tax is levied on net wealth. Since there is double taxation, a special reduction clause provides relief to taxpayers with large amounts of capital assets, but small incomes. The amount of taxable wealth can in no case exceed a sum which is thirty times the taxpayer's combined net income from all sources as computed for purposes of the national income tax. This taxable amount, however, cannot be reduced to less than one-half of his total assets.

The tax is levied at progressive rates which range from 0.8 percent on net wealth between 100,000 and 150,000 kronor to 1.8 percent on net wealth in excess of 1,000,000 kronor. The tax on 1,000,000 kronor would amount to 13,100 kronor. National and local income taxes would also be levied on income which is derived from the ownership of the capital assets. If this income is 50,000 kronor a year, then the capital tax of 13,100 kronor would be added to the national and local income taxes which would amount to approximately 17,000 kronor (assuming that the only source of income comes from the ownership of the capital asset, and that a family is paying the tax). This means that actual disposable income would amount to less than 40 percent of the 50,000 kronor.

The Inheritance Tax

The Swedish inheritance tax has special rates which are based on the consanguinity of the inheritors to the person who is deceased. There are four rates which are levied upon inheritances. The lowest rate is paid by those inheritors who were closest to the deceased. Half of joint property left to a surviving spouse is not subject to the inheritance tax. Surviving children are also entitled to a tax-free deduction of 2,000 kronor for each year by which their ages are

less than twenty-one. Debts and expenses are deductible in computing the tax. The rate is progressive
and ranges from 3 percent on inheritances from 6,000
to 12,000 kronor to 60 percent on inheritances in
excess of 5 million kronor.

Higher rates are levied on other beneficiaries.
Parents, brothers, and sisters of a deceased person
pay rates which range from 6 percent on taxable inheritances of 2,000 to 5,000 kronor to 65 percent
on inheritances in excess of 1 million kronor. Lega-
cies to beneficiaries, such as churches and charities,
are taxed at a rate of 10 percent on amounts of 1,000
to 5,000 kronor. The rate increases to 30 percent on
inheritances of 60,000 kronor or more. Other benefi-
ciaries--servants, cousins, friends--would pay the
highest inheritance tax rates which range from 20
percent on inheritances of 1,000 to 5,000 kronor to
65 percent on inheritances of 50,000 kronor or more.

Gift Tax

The gift tax is designed to prevent an evasion
of inheritance taxes. In its basic features, it
closely parallels the inheritance tax. In both instances liability is imposed upon the recipient. The
gift tax is progressive in rate and cumulative in its
application; within certain limitations, prior gifts
from the same donor are added to current gifts to
determine the rate applicable to the latter. The
gift tax is paid by any person who receives a gift.
The rates of the tax are the same as those for the
inheritance tax, with the rate increasing as the
degree of consanguinity of the beneficiary to the
donor decreases.

Gifts which do not exceed 2,000 kronor a year
are not subject to the gift tax. Also, certain types
of recipients (e.g., churches, foundations, and char-
itable organizations) are exempt from the tax. Inter
vivos gifts of furniture and interior chattels intended for the personal use of a recipient or his
family are also exempt from the tax, although such a
transfer on death is taxable.

The Value-Added Tax

The value-added tax was introduced in Sweden in
January, 1969, replacing a general retail sales tax

which had been in existence for a number of years.
This tax is also used in West Germany, France, Denmark, and Holland, and is scheduled to go into effect
in Luxembourg in 1970. Simply stated, the value-added
tax is a tax on what a firm adds in value to the goods
it handles. The tax base, in general, is the difference between a firm's total receipts from sales and
its payments for materials. The tax base, in other
words, is the growth in value attributable to each
firm's activities. In essence, it is a tax on wages,
profit, and other payments for the factors of production. It is usually imposed at each stage of the
production process, not at just the retail stage or
the wholesale level.

The value-added tax is normally associated with
the fiscal system of France. The French were the
first to utilize it as a major source of tax revenue.
It accounts for around one-third of the tax receipts
of the national government. The French value-added
tax is levied only on the value added by a given
enterprise. Value-added is the difference between
the sales price of the product and the cost of the
various inputs used by the enterprise in the course
of the manufacturing and distribution process. Because the tax is only levied on the value added by
the enterprise, it is not a cumulative levy like the
general turnover tax which has been used by several
other European countries, and thus does not pyramid.*
The French value-added tax is calculated by applying
the tax rate to gross sales and then crediting against
the tax due, all taxes paid on purchases; thus each
taxpayer pays a tax only on the difference--the value
he has added. Rates vary, with lower rates applied
to goods regarded as necessities, and higher rates
applied to goods regarded as luxuries.

The Swedish value-added tax is a rather comprehensive levy on general consumption items--goods and

---

*Unlike the turnover tax, the tax on value added
gives credit for levies paid at earlier stages in the
distribution chain. The turnover tax, once the favored revenue tool in Europe, had the effect of building up--getting fatter on itself--as goods moved from
raw material suppliers to ultimate consumers. A 10
percent levy on a ton of steel, for instance, is added
to the selling price of a steel desk, on which another
10 percent tax is imposed.

services and imports of taxable goods to Sweden. Exports are excluded from the tax. With few exemptions, all goods and services are subject to the tax. The tax is levied on heating fuels, growing crops, hunting and fishing rights, consumer and capital goods, stocks and bonds, and lottery tickets. Services are also taxable. For example, cleaning and repair work, catering and leasing, transportation with the exception of passenger service, hotel rooms, and alteration and maintenance work are all subject to the tax. Buildings that are constructed for sale are also liable for the value-added tax.*

The value-added tax is an ad valorem tax payable on the price that the consumer pays, and can be considered a broad form of consumption tax. The rate of the tax is 10 percent of the taxable value, which is the price paid by the consumer with the amount of the tax included. The rate corresponds to 11.1 percent of the price before the tax. For certain transactions, the tax rate is based on reduced taxable values according to special reduction rules. For example, there is a reduction rule of 60 percent which is applicable to the purchase of machinery. The effective rate of the tax is reduced to 6 percent of the total price including the tax, or 6.38 percent when it is excluded.

Swedish exports are exempt from the value-added tax. The exemption is comprehensive and takes a variety of forms. First, if delivery is made outside of Sweden, the territorial principle, restricting the value-added tax to transactions carried out in Sweden, results in tax exemption. Second, even if delivery is made in Sweden, a sale of a product for export is exempt. Finally, a Swedish exporter not only is exempt from the tax on his export sales, but may recover the tax borne on his purchases of materials and components incorporated in the product exported. A Swedish automobile manufacturer selling a car to a United States buyer, for example, is exempt from the

---

*There are certain exemptions from the tax. For example, prescribed medicines are exempt. Electric power and other fuels subject to a special energy tax are exempt. Items upon which no value has been added are generally exempt, such as the sale of a second-hand passenger car.

tax on that sale and may recover from the government
the tax paid by him and by his suppliers on the steel,
paint, wheels, and other products incorporated into
the export.*

Although the value-added tax adds a certain
amount of regression into the Swedish fiscal system,
Sweden has few of the many indirect taxes that may
be found in the fiscal systems of other European
countries. There are the levies on alcohol and cigarettes which are common in most countries, but Sweden is one of the few countries in Europe in which
direct taxes on income account for more government
revenue than indirect taxes. Direct taxes on income
in Sweden also account for more revenue relative to
indirect taxation than is the case in the United
States and in Japan.

Sumptuary Taxes

Sumptuary taxes are designed to penalize the
consumption of certain products which are generally
considered to be harmful. The taxation of tobacco
and liquor represents a specific example. These
taxes have often been rationalized on the grounds
that the use of these products is socially undesirable. In fact, however, the very high rates of these
taxes reflect a desire to take an advantage of in-
elastic demand for tobacco and liquor to increase
revenues. Rates must be high before demand is notice-
ably affected, and short of this point a burden is
placed upon the lower income groups, who in the
aggregate pay the bulk of the tax.

Liquor and tobacco taxes are an important source
of revenue to the Swedish national government. In
1968, they accounted for approximately 13 percent of

------

*Advocates of the value-added tax see it as a
handy device for countries that want to boost exports
by exempting foreign sales from domestic levies. Because the tax is always assessed separately, the government can easily rebate the levy to exporters at
any stage in the production process. The government,
by the same token, can easily assess the tax on imports, subjecting foreign-made goods to the same
taxes to goods that are made at home.

national tax revenues. Sales of liquor are limited
to the two government-owned monopolies, one the im-
porter and wholesaler and the other the retailer. A
sales tax is added to the price of liquor when sales
are made from the wholesaler to the retailer. For
example, on wines the standard rate is 3.8 kronor per
litre for wines with an alcoholic content of more
than 14 percent. Then an ad valorem surcharge is
added to the retail price of liquor. On wine this
amounts to 36 percent. The value-added tax is then
imposed on the sales price of the liquor. On wine
this amounts to 36 percent. The value-added tax is
then imposed on the sales price of the liquor to the
consumer. In general, taxes account for about 80
percent of the retail price of a bottle of whisky
and about 52 percent of the price of an ordinary
light wine.

The government also has a monopoly on the manufacture, importation, and sale, other than at retail,
of tobacco. The tax on tobacco is composed of two
elements; a flat rate calculated per piece or per
package in the case of cigars and cigarettes, and the
value-added tax which is imposed on the sales price
to the consumer. The combined rates are very high.
For example, the total tax on a package of Philip
Morris cigarettes amounts to 92 percent of the sales
price.

The Burden of Taxation in Sweden

When direct and indirect taxes and social security contributions are compared to gross national
product, it is evident that a considerable percentage
of the gross national product is diverted from the
private to the public sector of the Swedish economy.
A recent article by Erik Lundberg revealed that taxes
and social security contributions represent around
44 percent of the Swedish gross national product.[5]
The comparable statistic which he developed for the
United States is 27.3 percent. He also estimated
that a 100 million kronor increase in gross national
product would be accompanied by an increase in taxes
of close to 50 million kronor.

Table 3-6 presents the average burden of direct
and indirect taxes for various classes of income
earners in Sweden. Included under the category of
direct taxes are the national and local income taxes,

the old-age pension, and the national health insurance premium; all of which are withheld by employers
from the wages and salaries of employees. Indirect
taxes would include sales and excise taxes. Transfer
payments, which would redound to the advantage of
those in the lower-income groups, are not included
in the table.

TABLE 3-6

Burden of Swedish Taxation for
Various Income Classes[a]

Income Classes (kronor)	Direct Taxes (kronor)	Indirect[b] Taxes (kronor)	Total Taxes (kronor)	Percentage of Income
8,000	1,020	1,675	2,695	34
10,000	1,480	2,045	3,525	35
15,000	3,250	2,820	6,070	40
20,000	5,000	3,600	8,600	43
30,000	9,160	5,000	14,160	47
40,000	14,020	6,235	20,255	51
50,000	19,285	7,370	26,655	53
100,000	49,090	12,220	61,310	61
200,000	115,270	20,335	135,605	68

[a]Taxes are for a family with one wage earner.

[b]Indirect taxes are estimates.

Source: Skattebetalarnas Förening, "Fakta för
Skattebetalare" (Stockholm, 1968), p. 6.

GOVERNMENT EXPENDITURES

National and local government expenditures consist of government purchases of goods and services,
public investment, transfer payments, and subsidies.
In 1968, total governmental expenditures of all types
amounted to approximately 62 billion kronor. National
government expenditures include those activities which
are financed directly out of the current, or operating, and capital budgets and those activities which
are financed from separate sources--the social security system, public enterprises, and government-owned

business enterprises. Local government expenditures
can be divided into two categories; those made on
consumption and those made on investment. Consumption expenditures include expenditures on education,
health, and social services; and investment expenditures include expenditures on roads and the operation
of electric, gas, and water utilities. In 1968, total
local government expenditures amounted to approximately 26 billion kronor.

Central Government Expenditures

National government expenditures are contained
in both the current and capital budget and are scheduled to amount to around 42 billion kronor for the
fiscal year 1969-1970. The three most important
categories of expenditures are national defense,
education, and social welfare. The main part of
social welfare expenditures, however, is carried in
separate budgets.* Social welfare expenditures financed directly out of the current operating budget
include the basic old-age pension, family allowances,
and housing subsidies. Grants are paid from the
operating budget for health insurance and unemployment benefits.

Table 3-7 presents a breakdown of the major national government expenditures as contained in the draft
budget for the fiscal year 1969-1970. (The draft budget
contains both current and capital budget expenditures.)

Social welfare expenditures account for the
largest percentage of national government expenditures. Transfer payments to households defrayed out
of the current operating budget and autonomous budgets
amounted to 12.6 billion kronor in 1968.** The most

---

*This arrangement is similar to the French budg-
etary system. The French Social Budget is a separate
entity which includes all social welfare expenditures.
This budget includes most of the transfer expenditures
as opposed to government purchases of goods and services which are contained in the regular budget.
**These transfers are mainly concerned with the
redistributive function of government. They do not
absorb resources; rather their chief effect is that
of redistributing income between individuals and
social and economic groups. Excluded from the amount
of 12.6 billion kronor is medical care and other ser-

important social welfare payments are as follows:
family allowances, old-age pensions, unemployment
compensation, and health insurance benefits.

TABLE 3-7

National Government Expenditures
for the Fiscal Year 1969-1970

Expenditures	Millions of Kronor
Education and research	8,110
Social security	7,100
Labor market and regional development	2,110
Communications and power	4,230
Judiciary and police	1,660
Family and housing allowances	2,260
Defense	6,030
Housing	1,470
Miscellaneous	8,990
Total	41,960

Source: Ministry of Finance, "The Swedish
Budget, 1969-1970" (Stockholm, 1969), p. 28.

In few countries do transfer payments from the
social security system account for a greater proportion of national income than in Sweden.* In 1966,
for example, transfer payments amounted to 12.5 percent of national income, against 6.3 percent in the

---

vices which are provided by the public sector. These
activities can be treated as social goods which orig-
iate in the public sector.
     *The degree to which a government has become an
instrument for the redistribution of income can be
measured by computing transfer payments as a percentage of national income. National income is a measure
of income earned by resource owners for supplying the
services of economic resources to the production process. If transfers are computed as a percent of this
total, it will show the proportion of earned income
that has been redistributed by the action of the
public sector.

United States and 9.8 percent in the United Kingdom.6
Moreover, in 1966, social security payments amounted
to 12.4 percent of household incomes and equaled 19.6
percent of the sum spent on private consumption. In
1964, the gross national product of Sweden was 91.1
billion kronor. Taxes amounted to 33 billion kronor,
and transfer payments amounted to 8.9 billion kronor.
The two basic income transfers--old-age pensions and
family allowances--amounted to 6.7 billion kronor,
which represented 8 percent of personal income and
12 percent of disposable income in Sweden.7 Transfer
payments expressed as a percentage of gross national
product amounted to 9.8 percent in Sweden compared
to 5.1 percent in the United States.

National defense also constitutes an important
part of budgetary expenditures. Although Sweden has
pursued a policy of nonalignment in its relations
with other countries, defense expenditures amount to
approximately 15 percent of total expenditures of the
current operating budget and 4 percent of the gross
national product. The Swedish defense system is
based upon the maintenance of a general conscription
system which is common in the continental European
armies. Swedish males between the ages of eighteen
and forty-seven are eligible for conscription. The
length of service is normally ten months of basic
training with additional training required at inter-
vals of from two to four years.

Labor market policy, which aims at the maintenance of a high level of employment, constitutes
another important area of national government expenditures. The purpose of labor market policy is
to promote adjustments between the supply of and the
demand for labor. It includes job training, relocation assistance to help unemployed workers move to
existing job opportunities, public works to employ
workers who suffer seasonal unemployment, special
measures to help handicapped workers, and other
measures which are generally designed to create employment. Labor market policy is an integral part
of a national economic policy which is designed to
maintain a high level of economic activity.

Expenditures on education accounted for 16 percent of national government expenditures for the
fiscal year 1968-1969. Included in this percentage
were grants to local governments for educational
purposes, support of technical research, and the

construction of new educational facilities. A new
university was recently constructed at Umea in the
northern part of the country, and a technical institute and a center for medical training and research
is in the process of being established at Linköping.
Study grants are also made available to students.
For example, for students at the university level,
general study grants of 1,750 kronor a year are available, and additional interest-free loans with an
amortization period of up to twenty years are also
available. In Sweden, public education at all levels
is free.

National government grants to local governments
are also an important expenditure. It is estimated
that total grants to local governments will amount
to around 8.1 billion kronor for the fiscal year 1969-
1970.[8] These grants are for both general and specific
purposes. Tax equalization grants are an example of
general grants. Their purpose is to enable local governments to provide standard social services. In
Sweden, particularly in the sparsely populated northern
part of the country, poorer localities have to levy
higher taxes to compensate for a lower tax base than
the more prosperous localities. The tax equalization
grants are supposed to guarantee localities revenues
based on a certain minimum tax basis and to assist
those with a high tax rate. The tax-basis guarantee
varies between 90 and 125 percent of the average local
income tax rate for the country as a whole. Grants
to assist localities with an above average tax rate
increases progressively with this rate. Grants for
specific purposes pertain to the support of schools
and housing.

Public enterprises have autonomous budgets of
current expenditures, though their investments are
included in the capital budget. In addition, the
capital budget contains loan funds for housing,
education, and regional development. Regional development loans are made available to business firms
that locate in northern Sweden. They carry an interest rate of 7½ percent a year, which can be waived
in certain cases for a maximum of three years. Housing loans serve as a means for controlling the volume
of residential construction in the country.

Local Government Expenditures

Revenue for local government expenditures comes from three primary sources: the local income tax, grants from the central government, and income from public utilities and other enterprises owned by local governments. The local income tax raises approximately 98 percent of the tax revenues of the local government units; the balance comes from a local dog tax and from the share enjoyed by the local communes in a national tax on admissions.

Table 3-8 presents a breakdown of local government revenues and expenditures for 1969. It is significant to note that local government expenditures are almost as large as those made by the national government.

TABLE 3-8

Local Government Revenue and
Expenditures for 1969

Revenue	Millions of Kronor
Taxes	16,900
Central government grants	8,430
Other income	3,580
Total Revenue	28,910

Expenditures	
Gross investments	6,880
Consumption	17,220
Transfers	4,640
Net inflow to government enterprises	1,130
Other financial transactions	640
Total Expenditures	30,510

Source: Secretariat for Economic Planning of the Ministry of Finance and the National Institute of Economic Research, "The Swedish Economy, 1969" (Stockholm, 1969), p. 118.

Local government expenditures are particularly important in the social service areas. One of the

most important functions of the county councils has
been to manage hospitals and other types of medical
care. Each county council is responsible for the
operation of at least one county hospital and one or
more general hospitals. Under the medical care activities of the county councils comes the district
nurse organization and the family welfare programs.
The county councils have also taken over the responsibility for operating mental institutions from the
national government, as well as the public medical
services administered by the provincial medical officers. The county councils are also in charge of
the public dental care programs which are carried
out at central and district dental clinics.

Education expenditures account for approximately
one-fourth of total local government expenditures.
Responsibility for the provision of education is held
jointly by the communes and county councils. The
communes are responsible for the operation of primary
schools within their territorial jurisdiction, and
the county councils are responsible for the operation
of the folk high school and the agricultural and
industrial trade schools.

Communes also provide a variety of other services.
These services are normally activities that, though
not legally stipulated, are deemed as necessary for
the well-being of the residents of the communes.
Many of these activities are often operated as public
corporations. Among the activities most often carried out by the municipally-owned corporations are
public transportation and power plants. Housing construction has, in recent years, turned out to be an
activity which to an increasing degree has been
handled by localities, and has been proven to be
especially suited for municipally-owned corporations.
The number of housing corporations is in excess of
500 and in number dominate the municipally-owned
corporations.

A measure of the extent of local governmental
participation in the Swedish economy is presented in
Table 3-9. Local government consumption of goods
and services amounted to 9 percent of the gross national product for 1967. The major part of public
consumption expenditures comes under local government
auspices. But as already mentioned, the local authorities are dependent upon grants from the national government for the financing of local activities.

TABLE 3-9

Local Government Consumption for 1967

General Services	Millions of Kronor
Administration	1,294
Defense	4
Social and Cultural Services	
Education	4,615
Health	4,596
Social security	1,437
Religion	537
Community Services	
Roads and waterways	478
Fire protection and sanitation	339
Miscellaneous	146
Total Local Government Consumption	13,446

Source: Sekretariat for Economic Planning of
the Ministry of Finance and the National Institute
of Economic Research, "The Swedish Economy, 1969"
(Stockholm, 1969), Table 53, appendix, p. 60.

SUMMARY

Individuals in Sweden are subject to national
and local income taxes, both of which are collected
by the central government. Local income tax payments
are then allocated to the province, municipality, and
parish in which the taxpayer lives. Every person
earning an income of 2,400 kronor or owning capital
assets valued at 100,000 kronor has to pay income
taxes. Income taxes are collected at the source.
These are preliminary taxes which must ordinarily be
paid during the year in which the income is received.
A final assessment is made during the year following
the income year and this is used as the basis for
computing the final tax.

Income for local income tax purposes is defined
as income from all income sources. Income from

employment includes deferred income payments such as
pensions and annuities, while capital income is classified as interest, dividends, income from business
activities, and income from land and houses. Taxpayers are permitted certain general deductions from
net income from all sources. Among these deductions
are periodic contributions to dependents, premiums
paid for annuities, pensions, and life insurance, and
losses as defined in the tax code. A wife who is
gainfully employed is entitled to a special work deduction of up to 3,000 kronor. In addition, after
these general deductions have been made, taxpayers are
given a personal or family exemption which is deductible from net income. The local income tax is not
progressive. In 1968, the average rate was 19.34
percent.

Income for national income tax purposes is determined prior to deductions and personal exemptions in
the same manner as for the local income tax. A Swedish taxpayer is permitted to make the same general
deductions in preparing his national income tax return as for the local income tax return. However,
in addition, the taxpayer preparing a national income
tax return may also deduct from income the amount of
the local income and real estate taxes paid in the
preceding year. The rate of the national income tax
is progressive and ranges from 10 percent on taxable
income of 6,000 kronor or less to 65 percent on incomes of 150,000 kronor or more.

Corporations are subject to the same local income
taxes as are individuals, but are not granted the personal or family exemptions. The local tax rates are
also the same, and the national income tax rate is
fixed at 40 percent of annual net profits after deductions for local income tax payments. This means,
however, that profits are subject to double taxation.
Companies must, first of all, pay the local income
tax on their taxable profits. After deducting this
tax from taxable profits, they pay the national income tax on the remaining profits.

Among the other taxes collected by Sweden are
the value-added tax, which is the most important indirect tax; inheritance and gift taxes; excise taxes
on alcohol and tobacco; and a consumption tax on
gasoline. Then, too, fees and charges of different
kinds are levied for specific purposes. Contributions
for old-age pensions and health insurance are examples.

The Swedish tax system possesses two characteristics which are as follows: (1) There is more reliance on income taxation than in any other Western
industrial country, and (2) the burden of taxes relative to gross national product is the highest of any
Western country. Income taxation accounts for around
65 percent of total national and local tax revenues.
At the local level it accounts for 98 percent of tax
revenues. Total taxes and social security contributions from all sources amount to around 41 percent
of the gross national product. It can be added that
Sweden's extreme position in this respect would probably be more striking if calculated at the margin.*

Government expenditures are a major component
of aggregate demand. Most expenditures of the national government are reflected in the current and
capital budgets. A certain amount, about 4.3 billion
kronor in 1968, bypasses the current budget and goes
to the social insurance system through autonomous
budgets. From here it is paid out in the form of
various transfer payments. The exception to this
rule is contributions to the supplementary pension
scheme which are saved in the National Pension Fund.
Income transfers to individuals, private organizations, and local governments account for at least
one-half of total national government expenditures.
About one-third of local government income in 1969
was composed of grants from the national government.
The national government, thereby, has a great deal
of control over certain aspects of local government
activity, particularly education.

----

*It is estimated that a 100 million kronor in-
crease in Sweden's gross national income would be
accompanied by a total rise in taxes and social
security contributions of close to 50 million kronor.

NOTES

1. Gosta Rehn, "The National Budget and Economic Policy," Skandinaviska Banken Quarterly Review (Second Quarter, 1968).

2. Bureau of the Census, The Soviet Financial System: Structure, Operations, and Statistics, International Population Statistics Reports, series P-90, no. 23 (Washington, D.C.: Government Printing Office, 1969).

3. See Organization for Economic Cooperation and Development, National Accounts of OECD Countries, 1957-1966 (Brussels, 1968), pp. 50, 64, 126, 210, 246, and 282.

4. For an analysis of depreciation and inventory valuation rules, see Martin Schnitzer, "The Swedish Investment Reserve: A Device For Economic Stabilization" (Washington, D.C.: American Enterprise Institute, 1967), pp. 57-63.

5. Erik Lundberg, "Sweden's Economy in an International Perspective," Skandinaviska Banken Quarterly Review (First Quarter, 1968), pp. 1-5.

6. National Accounts of OECD Countries, 1957-1966, op. cit., p. 246.

7. Statistiska Centralbyran, "Socialvarden 1964" (Stockholm, 1966), p. 104.

8. Ministry of Finance, "The Swedish Budget, 1969-1970" (Stockholm, 1969), p. 57.

CHAPTER **4** STABILIZATION
POLICIES

INTRODUCTION

There are no clear boundaries between stabilization policies and other types of government activities.
In general, it can be said that stabilization policies
involve the use of a government's fiscal and monetary
powers to influence employment, output, and growth in
productive capacity, as well as the level of prices.
Certain parameter changes are made in the operation
of these policies, which include changes in the level
of money and credit, and changes in tax rates and
government expenditures. In addition, there is manpower policy which attempts to create jobs for specific individuals, groups, and locations, and controls
policy, which can involve the control of capital movements. There are also what can be called built-in
stabilizing mechanisms which can be significant. An
execellent example is the progressive income tax which
can absorb a substantial proportion of increases in
income.

The central objective of economic policy in Sweden since the end of the Second World War has been
the maintenance of a high level of employment. This
objective stems from circumstances which prevailed
in Sweden between the two world wars. The average
unemployment rate in the period 1923-1930 was 11 percent; in the period 1930-1933, the unemployment rate
was 19 percent; and in the period 1933-1937, the
average rate was 16 percent.[1] After the Second World
War, Sweden made use of a national income budget as a
means of providing the general framework for the coordination of economic policy, both public and private. Economic policy coordination between public
and private groups was extensive and thorough, and
fiscal and monetary policies were utilized to maintain

high levels of aggregate demand. As a result, unemployment has averaged less than 2 percent since the war, and the supply of labor in some areas is so short that many workers have been brought in from other countries.

It can be said that the public sector has been the most significant factor behind the high level of employment. The Swedish national budget exerts a strong impact on the economy in terms of the level of expenditures and taxes, and whether or not the budget is balanced; and the composition of expenditures and taxes. Government expenditures are a part of the economy's total outlays on goods and services, and exercise their influence by generating demand and, therefore, employment and income. It has been pointed out that national government expenditures account for around 28 percent of the Swedish gross national product. The contribution of the public sector to investment is also large. Sweden was the first Western country to use its budget to move the economy from underutilization of its human and physical capacities to a position of high employment of these resources. In addition, budget policy has also been used to increase the growth rate. For example, the Swedish government has experimented rather freely with various depreciation methods for the purpose of stimulating investment.

Although national unemployment rates have been low during the postwar period, certain problems exist in the Swedish economy. Seasonal unemployment, which often ranges several percentage points above the average annual unemployment rate, is prevalent. Long-term structural changes have been taking place in several industries--textiles, forestry, clothing, and shoes and leather--which have caused areas of unemployment to exist throughout the country. Northern Sweden in particular is an area in which unemployment rates have been several percentage points above the national average. The upgrading of job skills in response to improved technology has resulted in some unemployment among semiskilled and unskilled workers. Finally, the export-oriented nature of the economy has made Sweden vulnerable to a decline in exports.

Moreover, the full and overfull employment which has existed in most of the country has put pressure on the price level. In fact, the problem during much of the postwar period has been to control inflation.

The consumer price index has shown an average increase
of approximately 5 percent since 1960. Since even
relatively modest price increases may quickly affect
the Swedish balance of payments, curbing inflation
has been a necessary concomitant of economic growth.
Balance-of-payments considerations require more prompt
and vigorous action against inflation in Sweden than
in the United States. On the other hand, political
stability in Sweden depends to an appreciable extent
on maintaining high rates of employment, and the
anti-inflationary action required to prevent balance-
of-payment difficulties may involve greater political
strain than in the United States.

Sweden has been a forerunner in the development
and use of fiscal devices aimed at attaining employment and economic growth.* In addition to liberal
depreciation allowances, which are applied to equipment and machinery, reliance has been placed on a
rather unique fiscal device called investment reserve as a means of influencing the timing of business
investment. This device is designed to use tax credits
and tax reductions to enable firms to build up reserves of investment funds which can be used for investment during a recession. An essential feature of the
reserve is the degree of control it gives business
taxpayers over the amount of profit to be reported
for tax purposes. It can also be considered as a
valuable complement to general fiscal and monetary
policy measures in that it has both a fiscal and
monetary effect on the level of aggregate demand.

In addition to the use of tax incentives to stabilize the level of investment, there are policies
which involve the use of public works and other devices to alleviate seasonal and cyclical unemployment.
There are also policies which are designed to stimulate

-----

*The World Tax Series volume, Taxation in Sweden,
makes this statement: "No country has sought more
vigorously to use taxation, together with other fiscal, monetary, and regulatory measures, as a tool to
affect the business cycle. Sweden has employed
pioneering income tax devices designed at least in
part to make the economy more resistant to depression
and to influence the propensity of business to invest;
in this way, it has sought to enlist private capital
in the task of leveling the business cycle."

the occupational and geographical mobility of labor,
including a reliance on relocation assistance to move
unemployed workers which is unmatched by any country
in the world. All policies, including the investment
reserve, are considered as a part of Swedish labor
market policy, and are administered by the Labor Market Board.

THE INVESTMENT RESERVE

The investment reserve is a device, incorporated
in the Swedish tax structure, designed to help iron
out economic fluctuations by encouraging private
corporate savings in periods of high profits and private capital expenditures in periods of unemployment.
Companies are encouraged to set aside part of their
pretax profits in a reserve, and if these funds are
disbursed for investments in buildings, machinery,
and inventories during a period when investment is
desirable for employment purposes, substantial tax
privileges are obtainable.

The investment reserve law was enacted in 1938.
The basic intent of the legislation creating the
reserve was the provision of a tax device which, by
permitting postponement of taxation, would enable
companies to build up reserves for use in the event
of a future depression as a source of investment and
hence employment. However, it has been put to practical use as an instrument of fiscal policy only in
the past twelve years.

The investment reserve possesses flexibility in
that it can be used without the approval of Parliament. This reduces considerably the lapse of time
that accompanies legislative enactment of fiscal
policy measures. Decisions to utilize the reserve
are made jointly by the Labor Market Board and the
Ministry of Finance. Implementation of the investment reserve is the responsibility of the Labor Market Board.

The Labor Market Board also is responsible for
the implementation of employment policy in Sweden.
The board has the responsibility for putting into
operation various employment-creating measures, such
as supervision of the investment reserve funds. It
is also responsible for the operation of the public

employment service, planning of projects suitable to
be carried out as emergency public works, direction
of the start and discontinuance of such works, licensing of starting permits for buildings, and stimulating occupational and geographical mobility of
workers.

The Labor Market Board is also responsible for
economic forecasting. Forecasts are based on county
labor board surveys of business and employment conditions which are made twice a year. These surveys
include data on the amount of incoming orders, volume
of production, inventories, planned investment in
buildings and machinery, unfilled vacancies, and expected layoffs or increases in personnel.

The Use of the Investment Reserve

Companies are permitted to set aside, at their
own discretion, up to 40 percent of pretax income as
an investment reserve for economic stabilization.*
This amount is deductible from income for the purpose
of both the national and local income taxes.** Forty-
six percent of the amount must be deposited in a
non-interest-bearing account in the Central Bank of
Sweden (Riksbank), and the remaining 54 percent remains a part of a company's working capital. No
government permission is needed to set aside this
reserve. However, control over the use of the reserve is exercised by the Labor Market Board.

------

*Actually, there are two types of investment re-
serves--investment reserves for forestry and investment reserves for business. This book is concerned
with the latter only.
**Swedish corporations are subject to both na-
tional and local taxes on income. The national income tax is levied on corporations at a flat rate of
40 percent. The local income tax, averaging 15 percent, is levied at a flat rate on all corporations.
The amount of the local income tax assessed during
the year against a corporation is a deduction which
is subtracted from net income to give the assessable
income for national income tax purposes. The effec-
ive tax rate, national and local, is approximately 49
percent: $\frac{15,100}{100} + \frac{40.85}{100} = 49$ percent.

For example, assume a pretax income of 2,500,000 kronor ($480,000). A company may set aside 1 million kronor as an investment reserve. Forty-six percent of this amount (460,000 kronor) must be set aside in the Riksbank and is, in effect, neutralized until needed during a downturn in economic activity. The remaining 54 percent (540,000 kronor) belongs to the company as a part of ordinary working capital. The company may use this amount for any purpose at any time it so desires.

The purposes for which an investment reserve can be used are as follows:

1. To write off the cost of erecting, enlarging, or reconstructing a building. However, the amount that can be written off in a tax return must not exceed the expenditure actually in the fiscal year, a condition which applies also to the other types of investment.

2. To contribute toward the erection, enlargement, or reconstruction of dwellings of present or former employees of the corporation.

3. To defray the cost of repair and maintenance of buildings which are used in their regular activities by corporations engaged in mining or manufacturing.

4. To write off the cost of machinery and other equipment intended for permanent use which have been purchased or of vessels which have been purchased or rebuilt during the fiscal year.

5. To cover the cost of the repair of vessels.

6. To depreciate stocks of raw materials and of semifinished and finished products up to an amount equal to the expenditures for the production or procurement of stocks during the fiscal year.

7. To cover the costs of prospecting the other preproduction work during the year in mines, quarries, and similar deposits under exploitation.

8. To promote the sale abroad of commodities which the corporation produces in Sweden. This use of investment reserves, however, is subject to special authorization.*

---

*The investment reserve regulations for industry were amended on July 1, 1963, to make provisions for

The 46 percent of the reserve in the Riksbank
and the remaining 54 percent, which is a part of
working capital, may be released for any of the above
purposes when the Ministry of Finance considers economic conditions to be worsening.* The reserves are
to be released during a recession when they are needed
to stimulate investment. The significance of the
reserves lies in the fact that up to 100 percent of
an investment can be written off immediately. When
the investment reserve is used for the permissible
purposes, the amount used is not restored to taxable
income, but the asset charged to the reserve is not
subject to depreciation allowance.

Several examples of how the investment reserves
may be utilized are as follows:

1. Assume, as in the previous example, that a
company has set aside 1 million kronor (approximately
$190,000) as an investment reserve. Forty-six percent
has been deposited in the Riksbank in a special non-
interest-bearing account. The remaining 54 percent
has been charged to working capital. The company has
used the 54 percent in the operation of the business.**

---

an inventory investment account. Under this provision,
firms may be allowed to transfer in their investment
accounts their investment reserve or a part of it to
an inventory investment account for a period of four
years. During this period, a firm may be allowed to
dispose of the corresponding amount of the reserve
deposited in the Riksbank, thereby improving its
liquidity position. The firm is entitled to a special
investment deduction of 10 percent, computed on the
amount by which the value of all inventories has increased during the period in question. The deduction,
however, cannot exceed 10 percent of the amount transferred to the inventory investment account. After the
prescribed period, the transferred amount must be
brought back to taxation, but a firm can neutralize
this by making new allocations to investment reserves.
   *A corporation establishes an investment reserve
by debiting its profit and loss account and crediting
the investment reserve account.
   **It is left to the company to manage its liquid-
ity position with a view to the needs of a possible
release. Thus, when reserves are released, the
company must have on hand, or be able to raise, more
than half of the amount it is required to invest.

A downturn in business activity occurs. The
Ministry of Finance decides that the time is propitious for the release of the investment reserves
and notifies the Labor Market Board to this effect.
The Ministry of Finance, on the basis of forecasts
and consultation with the Labor Market Board, makes
the decision to release the investment funds. The
Labor Market Board is responsible for the implementation of the release of the funds. It notifies firms
with investment reserve funds that the funds can be
utilized for investment. When the permission to use
the funds has been granted by the Labor Market Board,
the blocked funds are released to the firms by the
Riksbank (Bank of Sweden).

The time lag between recognition of the problem
and implementation of stabilization policy, although
reduced by the elimination of the cumbersome legislative process, still is subject to human errors in
forecasting and decision making. However, the
recognition lag itself is reduced considerably by a
system for advanced information on impending employment changes which is based on agreements between
the Labor Market Board and different employer associations. The Labor Market Board then gives permission to individual companies to use their investment reserves for any of the purposes previously
mentioned. Permission can be given in several ways.
One alternative is to grant general permission to
all firms that have set up investment reserves.
Permission, however, can be restricted to certain
industries or local areas, where the rate of employment is expected to be low. Another alternative is
to grant permits by approving individual applications,
specifying the projects for which the applicants wish
to use the investment reserve. This method was used
during the recessions of 1958-1959 and 1962-1963.

The company decides to use the entire 1 million
kronor for the purchase of new equipment. It may
withdraw the entire 460,000 kronor which it has on
deposit with the Riksbank. As for the remaining
540,000 kronor which has been kept in the business
and used, the company must reproduce this amount,
because it is a part of the investment reserve.

2.   Assume, however, that the company decides
to use only a part of the total reserve; for example,
100,000 kronor. The company was to take 46 percent
of this amount (46,000 kronor) from its deposit in
the Riksbank. The amount of its deposit is reduced

by 46,000 kronor, and the remainder is 414,000 kronor
(460,000 minus 46,000). As for the remaining 54 percent of the amount (54,000 kronor), the company must
produce this amount. It is deducted from that part
of the investment reserve (540,000 kronor) which
has been retained by the company and which has been
charged to working capital. When this deduction has
been made, the original amount has been reduced to
486,000 kronor (540,000 minus 54,000).

Not only is the investment reserve not restorable
to taxable income, but in order to stimulate the use
of this program even more, an extra investment deduction, 10 percent of the reserve used, is permitted
in the tax assessment in its next income tax return.
In other words, a company which uses its investment
reserves in 1962 is permitted to deduct 10 percent
of the amount from taxable profits in its income
returns for 1963.

3. For example, assume that a company sets
aside 1 million kronor in an investment reserve fund
in 1960. In 1962, a recession occurred, the reserve
funds were released, and the company used its entire
amount for new equipment. Ten percent of this amount
(100,000 kronor) was deductible from pretax income in
1963. Assume a pretax income of 3 million kronor.
The 100,000 is deductible from this amount, and the
income for tax purposes is now 2,900,000 kronor.

If an investment reserve is used without the
authorization of the Labor Market Board, the amount
involved plus a penalty of 10 percent of the reserve
is added to taxable income during the next assessment
period.

4. For example, assume the company in the afore-
mentioned example decides to use its entire investment
reserve (1 million kronor) without the authorization
of the Labor Market Board. This amount plus a penalty
of 10 percent (100,000 kronor) is restored to taxable
income. (Needless to say, this does not happen frequently.)

There is general permission after five years
have elapsed, irrespective of business conditions,
to withdraw up to 30 percent of the reserves provided
they are used for the allowable purposes. However,
in this case a company will not receive the extra
10 percent investment deduction.

5. For example, assume a company set aside 1 million kronor as an investment reserve in 1958. In 1963--a good year for the Swedish economy--the company decided to utilize part of its reserve to purchase machinery. It may use up to 30 percent of its reserve (300,000 kronor) for the acquisition; it decides to use this amount. Thirty percent of the amount on deposit in the Riksbank (460,000 kronor) can be withdrawn. This amounts to 138,000 kronor. Thirty percent of the reserve kept by the company (540,000 kronor) may also be withdrawn. This amounts to 162,000 kronor.

Through the system of investment reserves, the government has been able to influence a counter-cyclical movement of private investment. An increase in the investment reserve serves the purpose of damp-ening boom conditions for the reason that investment spending will be postponed.* This postponement of investment spending reduces the level of aggregate demand. The release of the investment reserve dur-ing a recession has the effect of stimulating invest-ment. Companies utilize their investment reserves, on various investment projects, thus raising the level of aggregate demand.

The 46 percent sterilization reserve in the Riksbank has an important advantage from the stand-point of business-cycle policy in that the reserve cannot be invested before permission to do so has been obtained from the Labor Market Board. This, however, assumes that the Labor Market Board possesses an unusual degree of omniscience from the standpoint of the appropriate timing of the release of the funds.

During the boom of 1960 a further inducement was added to the investment reserve program. If a firm wished, it could pay into the Riksbank an amount equal to 100 percent of the reserve. A tax rebate was granted, which was as follows:

1. If a company placed its reserve with the Riksbank before August 1, 1960, it could deduct

_____

*There will be a loss of tax revenue to the gov-ernment. If this results in deficit financing by the government to finance the various social welfare programs, the effect would be to circumvent the in-tent of the investment reserve.

from its taxable income during this year an amount
equal to 12 percent of its reserve.

2.   If the reserve was placed in the Riksbank
between August 1 and November 1, 1960, the corresponding deduction was 8 percent.

The amount of the reserve in excess of the required 46 percent was repayable at the end of 1961.
However, in 1961 boom conditions again prevailed
and companies which had deposited the full amount
of their reserves to the Riksbank in 1960 were granted
a further inducement to leave them in for another
year or until the end of 1962.*   The deduction permitted from taxable income in 1961 was 10.5 percent
of the full reserve.

Tax deductions similar to those of 1960 were
given to companies in 1961 if they agreed to deposit
the full 100 percent of the reserve in the Riksbank.
A tax deduction of 12 percent was given if a deposit
was made before July 1, 1961, and 8 percent if a
deposit was made before October 1, 1961, with 54 percent of the deposit repayable at the end of 1962.
This tax deduction could still be claimed if the
reserves were released for authorized purposes.

Tax Advantages of the Investment Reserve

There are several tax advantages which accrue
to firms that use the investment reserve. They can
be briefly summarized as follows:

1.   An advantage is gained when a company sets
aside the 46 percent for deposit in the Riksbank.
In the original example, the company set aside in
the total investment reserve fund an amount of 1
million kronor out of a pretax income of 2,500,000
kronor.   Forty-six percent was deposited in the
Riksbank, and the remaining 54 percent was kept by
the company. The company initially retains the difference between the income tax (49 percent of the
income) and the amount deposited in the Riksbank
(46 percent of the investment reserve), or, in the
example, 490,000 kronor (49 percent of 1 million

---

*In fact, a recession did occur and the reserves
were released.

kronor) less 460,000 kronor (46 percent of 1 million kronor). The difference of 30,000 kronor represents an initial gain to the company.

2. When the reserve is used (assume the full amount of 1 million kronor), the company is entitled to an extra investment deduction of 100,000 kronor from taxable income in the next tax year. Since the tax rate is 49 percent, the company saves 49,000 kronor.

3. In certain cases, the investment may be written off at once by the amount withdrawn from the reserve.*

However, these advantages to the corporation must be compared to the gains which would have accrued from the normal liberal depreciation allowances that could have been used. The net advantage is the difference between the advantages obtained with an investment reserve and those obtainable through the use of normal depreciation allowances.

Allocations to Investment Reserves

Although investment-reserve provisions have been in effect since 1938, the original law was regarded as experimental in nature and funds allocated to reserve accounts were negligible in magnitude. However, important changes in the law were made in 1947.

_____

*It should also be mentioned that for major projects requiring up to two years for completion, the government can authorize not only the use of existing reserves, but also future allocations to the investment reserve. In either case, a ceiling of 75 percent of the project is set. The total amount a company can be authorized to draw on existing reserves and future allocations must not exceed 75 percent of the total cost of the project. This means that a company can write off up to 75 percent of the cost of the project as soon as the expenditure is made, instead of the far smaller depreciation allowances permitted. However, government authorization is required. The project must be justified from the standpoint of public policy, unemployment, and the public welfare.

Companies were allowed to set aside up to 20 percent of net income as a reserve for future investment, deductible from income for both the national and local income tax. All a company had to do was to allocate the reserve to its accounts; no physical segregation in an account in the Bank of Sweden was required.

However, there was criticism of the 1947 legislation for the reason that the tax-free retention of the reserve increased corporate liquidity during periods when the economy was operating at full capacity. Temporary legislation during the early 1950s suspended the right to make allocations to investment reserves, except in special situations.

In 1955, new legislation again permitted the use of deductible investment reserves. The amount of net income that could be allocated to an investment reserve was increased to 40 percent. However, 40 percent of the amount allocated had to be deposited in a special non-interest-bearing blocked account in the Riksbank. The remaining 60 percent could be retained by the company. In 1957, the amount that had to be deposited in the blocked account was changed to 46 percent to bring it in line with the effective national and local income tax rates.

Prior to 1947, allocations to investment reserves were negligible. The liberalized provisions of the 1947 legislation caused an increase in allocations to the investment reserves, and by the end of 1955, Swedish corporations had set aside approximately 247 million kronor in reserves under the provisions of the 1947 law. However, a marked increase in allocations to investment reserves occurred during the 1955-1961 period. Although a large percentage of the reserve had to be deposited in the Riksbank, increased tax benefits well compensated companies for this inconvenience.

Allocations to investment reserves have increased considerably over the pre-1955 period. The largest allocation occurred in 1960, when the full amount of the reserve had to be deposited in the form of blocked accounts in the Riksbank. The average annual allocations for recent years has been around 600 million kronor. (See Table 4-1.)

TABLE 4-1

Allocation of Investment Reserves
to the Riksbank

Year	Millions of Kronor
1959	530
1960	1,063
1961	520
1962	439
1963	521
1964	684
1965	662
1966	530
1967	779

Source: Data provided by the Labor Market
Board.

Application of the Investment Reserve

To encourage Swedish firms to take measures calculated to even out business fluctuations, Swedish
law provides that they may set aside a certain portion
of their profits free of the income tax. These reserves must be deposited either in a fund for industry
or a fund for forestry, but 46 percent of the amount
deposited must be placed in a special account in the
national bank. These deposits are under the supervision of the Labor Market Board, and can be used
only under certain conditions and for purposes prescribed by law. Special tax concessions are granted
to business firms that utilize the investment reserve
fund.

The first time the investment reserve was released for the purpose of economic stabilization was
during the 1958-1959 recession. In 1960-1961, the
entire reserve (100 percent) was sterilized in the
Riksbank as an anti-inflationary measure and during
the 1962-1963 recession, the investment reserve was
released for the second time. In 1967, it was released again.

When the investment reserve funds were released
during the 1958-1959 recession, general permission

was given for the release of forestry reserves. However, more circumscribed permission was given for the
release of the investment reserve for business. A
basic criterion for permission to use the reserves
was that projects should be started at times which
corresponded with the highest level of unemployment.
This criterion was particularly applicable to investments in buildings, with the basic objective to start
the construction during the winter months when unemployment was the highest. Projects also had to
conform to a time schedule approved by the county
labor boards. The money involved could only be used
during a certain period. The length of the period
depended on the size and nature of the project, the
obvious concern here being the timing and duration
of projects. There was the danger that the duration
of many projects would be longer than the duration
of the recession. A total of 1 billion kronor was
used for housing construction, roads, forestry,
machinery, and equipment.

From the standpoint of creating employment, at
least in the construction industry, the release of
the funds had a propitious effect. The construction
industry is affected to a major degree by adverse
climatic factors in the winter months, which cause
seasonal unemployment, particularly in Stockholm and
the larger cities. Investment funds that were released
to cover the cost of constructing buildings usually
carried the stipulation that the work done should be
started at such a time that would as sufficiently as
possible contribute to the maintenance of employment
during the winter months.

Employment derived from the use of the investment-
reserve funds during the 1958-1959 period was as follows:[2]

1. In November, 1958, 2,000 workers were employed
on building projects financed with investment-reserve
funds. Total unemployment in Sweden during that month
was approximately 100,000. The 2,000 workers represented about 8 percent of the total number of workers
employed in building construction.

2. In February, 1959, the number of workers employed on building projects financed with investment-
reserve funds had increased to 4,000. This amounted
to 17 percent of the total number of workers employed
in building construction.

3. In August, 1959, the number of employed workers had increased to 6,400. The maximum employment-creating effect from the use of the investment reserves was derived during this period which lasted through the fall and winter of 1959-1960. However, this maximum effect was not achieved until a considerable time period had elapsed after the original permission had been given to use the investment reserves.*

4. In February, 1960, 6,300 workers were employed on projects financed with investment reserves, 21 percent of the total employed in building construction.**

To restrict liquidity, the basic investment-reserve provisions were changed in 1960 and 1961 to allow Swedish enterprises to obtain an additional deduction from taxable income provided that they deposited the full amount of the reserve (100 percent as opposed to 46 percent) in blocked accounts in the Riksbank during the tax year. As stated previously, in 1960 the tax deduction was an amount equal to 12 percent of the reserve payment if accomplished before August 1. If the deposit was made between August 1 and November 1, the tax deduction was 8 percent. In 1961, the same percentage applied to deposits before July 1 and October 1, respectively.

The sterilization of the entire reserve, or 100 percent reserve, had some effect on liquidity. There was a marked increase in the amount of new investment reserves registered over preceding years. Total new reserves registered in 1958 amounted to 419 million kronor; in 1959, 530 million kronor; and in 1960, 1,063 million kronor. The total amount of 100 percent reserves registered in 1960 amounted to 770 million kronor, and in 1961, 285 million kronor.***

---

*Permission to use the investment-reserve funds was terminated in September, 1959. The economic upturn began in the summer of 1959. By 1960, special tax incentives were being offered to increase the amounts deposited in the Riksbank.

**The data exclude projects for which special government permits were needed, and forestry projects.

***The 770 million kronor were sterilized during the period from July to the end of 1960, and the 285 million kronor were sterilized from January to July of 1961.

The direct effect was to sterilize 770 million kronor of the liquid funds of Swedish industrial firms for the latter part of 1960 and 285 million kronor out of liquid funds for the first half-year of 1961. This, in turn, served to reduce commercial bank liquidity, and also put a brake on the tendencies of the more liquid companies to lend to customers or to subcontractors.* The overall effect of the sterilization was also to put pressure on the level of interest rates upward.

One measure of the effect of 100 percent sterilization of the investment reserve is the liquidity ratio of Swedish commercial banks.** The liquidity ratio showed a decrease during the time that sterilization was in effect. Table 4-2 indicates changes in the liquidity ratio of the commercial banks.

However, these changes in the liquidity ratio may be attributable only in part to the sterilization of the investment reserve. The Riksbank instituted stringent monetary policy measures, including a penalty rate over and above the official discount rate, to discourage borrowing on the part of the commercial banks.

As an anti-inflationary measure, sterilization of the investment reserve had some effect on the price level through a reduction in the lending potential of the Swedish commercial banks. Also a considerable volume of funds which might have been invested were neutralized. However, the specific effect is very difficult to measure. As mentioned previously, Swedish monetary policy was switched to a restrictive direction. During 1960, the Swedish government introduced a turnover tax which, in itself, was bound to exert some effect on the economy.

Gross private domestic investment increased at an accelerated rate over previous years. In 1960,

---

*To a certain extent, the effect is similar to Federal Reserve open-market operations.
**The liquidity ratio for Swedish commercial banks is obtained by dividing net claims on the Riksbank's, claims on the National Debt Office and on other commerical banks, and housing bonds, by demand deposits (all deposits).

gross private domestic investment amounted to 12.5
billion kronor, an increase of 17 percent over the
preceding year. In 1961, gross private domestic
investment amounted to 14.2 billion kronor. Direct
investment in manufacturing amounted to 4.5 billion
kronor in 1960--a 20 percent increase over the preceding year, and 5.5 billion in 1961.

TABLE 4-2

Liquidity Ratios for Swedish Commercial
Banks by Months 1960-1961

Months	1960	1961
January	48.7%	40.4%
February	49.8	41.3
March	45.7	37.6
April	44.4	37.7
May	42.3	34.3
June	41.2	35.9
July	38.7	37.1
August	39.2	38.7
September	37.6	34.6
October	40.9	38.6
November	38.1	37.7
December	41.1	41.2

Source: Sveriges Riksbank, Affarsbankernas
Genomsnittliga Likviditet, Statistikkontoret (Stockholm, 1965).

Sterilization of over 1 billion kronor in investment reserve funds undoubtedly reduced the level of
investment in 1960 and 1961. No one knows to what
extent, and it is significant to note that in 1963
when the investment reserve system was changed by
Parliament to include release of the funds for the
purpose of encouraging the location of industry in
northern Sweden,* it was recommended by a study
commission that 100 percent sterilization of the

*This change created problems and was dropped in
1965.

investment reserves not be made a permanent part of
the system.*

Unemployment in the pulp and paper and building
construction industries led to the second release of
the investment reserves. Permission to use the investment reserves was first given to the pulp and
paper industry in December, 1961. In May, 1962, the
Labor Market Board, concerned about an expected substantial increase in unemployment in building construction for the fall and winter months, authorized
a general release of investment reserves for building
projects. These projects had to begin before November, 1962, and the reserves were available for projects carried out during the time period July, 1962
to April, 1963. In this way the maximum effect on
employment was produced during the winter months
when unemployment in building construction is at its
highest.

By the latter part of 1962, the recession had
spread to the metal and machine tool industry. Orders
were falling off and unemployment occurred. The Labor
Market Board and the Ministry of Finance decided in
November of 1962 to authorize the use of investment
reserves for machinery investments.** Permission was
given to use the reserves for this purpose. Orders
had to be placed before May, 1963. Through March,
1963, permits to use investment reserves for machinery investments amounted to 280 million kronor
($54,000,000).*** Coupled with this release of

---

*When questioned by the author why the investment
reserves had not been sterilized in 1965, when the
price level rose by 9 percent, or in 1966, when it
also rose, officials of the Riksbank and Labor Market
Board were of the opinion that: (1) no clear-cut
evidence was available to show that sterilization in
1960 and 1961 had an anti-inflationary effect, and
(2) general monetary measures instituted by the Riksbank would accomplish as much without having to pay
the price of the inducements for sterilization.
**The Ministry of Finance is responsible for
general economic policy; the Labor Market Board is
responsible for its implementation.
***The great majority of this amount went for
purchases of machinery and equipment from the shipbuilding, metal, and machine tool industries.

investment reserves was a speedup of state and local
government orders to the metal and machine tool
industry.

Industrial plant construction, however, was the
sector of investment on which the release of investment reserves had the greatest employment-creating
effect. For example, in August of 1962, the total
number of workers employed in plant construction
amounted to 28,560; of this number, 1,600 workers, or
6 percent, were employed on projects using investment
reserves. In November, 1962, the total work force had
increased to 34,860; however, of this total, 8,500
workers or 24.5 percent were employed on projects
using investment reserves. In February of 1963,
10,100 workers or 31 percent of all workers were
employed on investment reserve projects.

The investment reserve was released for the third
time in 1967. A decision was made by the Labor Market
Board to permit the use of the reserves for forestry
to stimulate the forest industry. Permission was also
granted by the board to release the regular business
investment-reserve funds. Their use, however, was
restricted to construction and machinery investments.
Construction projects had to be completed during the
time period May, 1967 to March, 1968, and orders for
machinery had to be filled by June, 1968. In October,
1967, further permission was given to use the investment reserve for the purpose of inventory accumulation.
Permission to use the reserves was then extended into
1968, and their use was expanded to cover mining and
quarrying. During the 1967-1968 period more than 1
billion kronor in investment-reserve funds were released to stimulate investment in various industries.

An Evaluation of the Investment Reserve

The effectiveness of any stabilization measure--
fiscal or monetary--depends to a major degree on timing. All too often, stabilization measures, if taken
at all, are taken only after the need for them is
apparent. One has only to look at stabilization policy
in the United States. Fiscal policy, to be effective,
must work two ways: as a stabilizing device during
both periods of unemployment and declining output,
and during periods of full-employment and rising
prices. The rather inept efforts to eliminate the
investment credit and to maintain the surtax in 1969

reflected not only inappropriate timing, but a basic
weakness of fiscal policy--the unwillingness of politicians to raise taxes or cut government--even
though these measures may be absolutely necessary.

Fiscal policy involves five time lags. The first
lag involves the time lost between the recognition of
the need for action and the initiating of it; the
second is in the process of legislative action, the
third involves changes in the flow of expenditures;
the fourth involves the change in consumer and investment demand for output brought about by the fiscal
change; and the fifth involves the change in output
which is brought about in response to a change in
consumer and investment demand. A time period of a
year or more can elapse before the fiscal change
actually makes its effect on the economy. A basic
desideratum of fiscal policy is to find the appropriate devices that can reduce the time lags in
operation.

In a parliamentary system, such as Sweden's,
fiscal policy measures can be effected within a
shorter period than is possible in the United States.
In Sweden, for example, the Ministry of Finance and
the Labor Market Board can carry out appropriate
fiscal policy measures independent of control by the
Swedish Parliament. This may be contrasted to the
American legislative system where fiscal policy
changes usually face a time-consuming process. Administrative fiscal proposals must face the legislative machinery. Hearings usually are held and changes
in the proposals are made to make them more acceptable
to Congress and to interested pressure groups.

Timing in the release of the investment reserve
has shown some improvement since its original release
in the 1958-1959 recession. The major criticism of
its operational effectiveness during this recession
related to timing. There is a fundamental dilemma
of economic stabilization policy--the reconciliation
of the long period of time which elapses between the
decision to adopt a stabilization measure and its
effect, and the short period of time in which changes
in employment can be forecast with any degree of
certainty. As it turned out, the maximum employment
effect of the reserve was not felt until fifteen
months after the permission for the release was
granted by the Labor Market Board in May, 1958. By
that time, the recession was over and the upturn was

well under way. There was also some delay and inde-
cisiveness on the part of the Labor Market Board to
release the reserve, attributable in part to a defi-
ciency in forecasting.[3]

    The timing of the release of the investment re-
serve during the 1962-1963 recession was far superior
to the timing in the 1958-1959 recession. The county
offices of the Labor Market Board had noted an increase in anticipated layoffs by industrial firms
late in 1961 and early in 1962. Investment surveys
taken in October, 1961 and March, 1962 by the Labor
Market Board also indicated a decline in planned
industrial investment. In the first part of 1962,
the county offices of the Labor Market Board con-
tacted business firms possessing investment-reserve
funds and indicated that a release of the funds was
imminent. In May, 1962, the release of the reserve
funds for construction was announced. It was stipulated that projects be started before November 1,
for the reason that a substantial increase in construction activity was needed during the winter
months when unemployment in the construction industry
is normally quite high.

    It was also evident that as far as a release of
investment-reserve funds was concerned, a powerful
impact of short duration could be secured at short
notice. The time lag between the announcement of
the release of the funds and their initial impact on
investment was small. The announcement took place
in early May of 1962, and by September a substantial
net increase in industrial construction had taken
place. The maximum impact of the release of the
funds took place in February of 1963, less than a
year after the announcement of the release. By May
of 1963, the impact had tapered off considerably.
The bulk of the investment effect took place in the
winter months of 1962-1963, during which a decline
in investment activity in the construction sector had
been forecast. For the whole period of release--July
1, 1962 to April 30, 1963--investment-reserve funds
amounted to 39 percent of total industrial investment
in Sweden.

    The employment effect of the investment-reserve
funds is summarized in Table 4-3. Although the effect
was favorable, rural areas in northern Sweden where
unemployment has been well above the national average
for the last decade were affected only moderately by
the release.

TABLE 4-3

Total Employment Effect of Investment-Reserve
Financed Projects

Years and Months	Total Employment Effect[a]
1962	
August	1,300
November	8,200
1963	
February	10,200
May	8,200
August	5,700

[a]This refers to employment on construction projects only.

Source: Martin Schnitzer, "The Swedish Investment Reserve: A Device for Economic Stabilization"
(Washington, D.C.:   American Enterprise Institute
for Public Policy Research, 1967), p. 37.

During the 1967-1968 recession, the release of
the investment reserve was well-timed, primarily
because the authorization was given at an early stage
of the downward trend and was limited to a relatively
short time period.   In terms of the employment effect,
the release of the reserve provided employment for
14,100 workers during the period February through
March, 1968--a period when seasonal unemployment is
at its highest point in Sweden.[4]   The release of the
investment reserve, coupled with government expenditures on public relief works projects, had a multi-
plier affect on aggregate demand which provided
employment for an additional 20,000 workers.

However, extenuating circumstances make it
impossible to assign the investment reserve a high
rating as a countercyclical fiscal instrument.   First
of all, it is uncertain how effective it would be in
the absence of a number of other programs which are
used by the Swedish government--public works, government orders to industry, increases in housing construction, and relocation of unemployed workers.
General fiscal and monetary policy measures are also

used. It is difficult to isolate the effects of the
investment reserve from the overall effects of stabilization policies in general.

Secondly, the operational effectiveness of the
program has been tried during a period of relatively
high levels of economic activity within Sweden and
in the other Scandinavian countries. The unemployment rate, even during the worst months of both
recessions was low by American standards. Most of
the unemployment that existed was either seasonal or
structural in nature, and was limited primarily to
the rural areas. One might legitimately question
the effectiveness of the investment reserve, given
an unemployment rate of 5 or 6 percent, or given a
sharp decline in exports. Would business firms be
as willing to invest if faced with a decline in export markets or a serious increase in unemployment?

It is also evident that the investment-reserve
program has a definite capital bias, and its effectiveness is uncertain, particularly with respect to less
industrialized rural areas characterized by a surplus
of labor resources. The capital-oriented industries
benefit more from the release of the investment reserve than labor-oriented industries. Industries
using skilled labor--the type that is least likely to
be unemployed--are more likely to use the reserve,
than industries using semiskilled and unskilled labor.

It has been argued that larger firms are more
likely to benefit from the investment-reserve system
than smaller firms. The larger firms usually have
ample liquid assets and, during a boom, can continue
their investment activity and, at the same time, take
advantage of the investment-reserve facilities. There
is little evidence, however, to support the notion
that the investment reserves are the exclusive domain
of the larger Swedish firms.

The effectiveness of the investment-reserve system depends on the extent to which it can stimulate a
volume of investment that is in excess of that which
would have been made in any case. Unquestionably, a
considerable volume of investment would have taken
place with or without the release of the reserves.
Certain investments are impossible to postpone.*

---

*In interviews with several managers of Swedish
business firms, the author gained the impression that

Nevertheless, business firms which make allocations to investment reserves are naturally aware of
the option that this gives them on future tax gains.
In order to realize these gains they must be prepared
to invest during periods when the reserves may be
used. The system thus stimulates preparatory planning
for investment expenditure and leads to a more rapid
reaction when the reserves are released. An attrac-
tive aspect of the investment-reserve system is that
reliance is placed on a voluntary and cooperative
relationship between government and business. Business firms are not required by law to set aside funds
in investment reserves; they do so voluntarily with
the knowledge that the government in granting certain
tax inducements expects in return the use of reserve
funds during a recession.

No economic stabilization measure is free from
defects. Government public works programs, for example, have serious flaws. They are started slowly,
are often chosen by political criteria instead of the
market place mechanism, and cannot be stopped once a
recession has been ended. The use of the tax credit
and accelerated depreciation as countercyclical fiscal
instruments also has many drawbacks.

The investment reserve is a useful addition to
the kit of stabilizing devices. Since many factors
contribute to recessions, a variety of stabilization
techniques is more useful than a limited number.

It is doubtful that the investment-reserve system could be used in the United States. The institutional differences between the United States and Sweden
are too great to permit a transplanting of this device.
There is much greater cooperation in Sweden between
labor, management, and the government. There is the

---

more lucrative investments were undertaken regardless
of the time period, while more marginal investments
were delayed in anticipation of an eventual release
of the investment-reserve funds. The investment
reserve, however, was regarded as an important factor
with respect to decisions to invest in certain projects during a recession. The author is of the opinion that a certain amount of investment, over and
above that which would have occurred anyway, would
have been undertaken.

knowledge among the three groups that cooperation is
necessary for survival in the world markets. Sweden
is also much smaller than the United States in terms
of both geography and population. Industrial concentration is largely limited to Stockholm and the
southern part of Sweden. A much greater diversity
in terms of industrial development and population
growth exists in the United States. More industry
and population is concentrated in New York than in
all of Sweden. Nevertheless, devices similar to the
investment reserve might be a helpful addition to
the list of techniques which the United States has
used to moderate the amplitude of industrial fluctuations.[5]

THE INVESTMENT TAX

The investment tax is a direct tax on investment.
It has been used on several occasions as a device to
reduce the level of investment when inflationary pressures were prevalent in the Swedish economy. The tax
was used in 1951 and 1952, but was withdrawn for 1953
and 1954. It was applied again on an annual basis in
1955, 1956, and 1957, but was not renewed in 1958.
After a hiatus of almost a decade, it was imposed on
certain types of investment in 1967.

This type of tax is a temporary levy on certain
capital expenditures; in particular, expenditures for
machinery and equipment, new or old, with an anticipated life of more than three years, and expenditures
for new buildings, or for the remodeling, rebuilding,
or expansion of existing buildings. The tax has also
been applied to the repair and maintenance of existing
buildings; however, a deduction of 2 percent of the
assessed value of the property was allowed for ordinary upkeep and maintenance. The tax has not been
applied to the purchase of used buildings. Expenditures for the development of mineral resources were
subject to the tax, unless deductible as current
operating expenses.

The investment tax is a flat tax levied on the
sum total of the taxpayer's taxable investments for
a given year less an exemption which has varied from
year to year. In 1956, for example, the exemption
amounted to 20,000 kronor, and for 1957, 30,000 kronor.
The rate of the tax has been usually 10 or 12 percent

of investment. However, the tax was reimposed on
certain low-priority investments in 1967 at a flat
rate of 25 percent. These low-priority investments
included all building activity with the exception of
residential construction, central government projects,
industrial plants, and school facilities. The tax,
designed to increase residential construction and
industrial investment and limit the growth of other
types of fixed investment, was applied to projects
started between March, 1967 and September, 1968.

An Evaluation of the Investment Tax

The investment tax is designed as an anti-infla-
tion rather than a revenue measure. It is levied
directly on the value of new investments in an effort
to keep capital investment within the limits of available resources. It attempts to cause a leveling out
in the business cycle by penalizing investment expenditures in periods of high economic activity, thus
causing a postponement of at least some investment to
periods when slack economic conditions would make such
expenditures desirable from the standpoint of employment.

The investment tax is an extra burden on the
investments of business firms, and may be placed in
the category of taxation on expenditures. The imposition of the tax on a business firm entails a worsening
of its liquidity and its profit-earning capacity. The
worsening of liquidity, however, is offset to a degree
when the tax is deductible as an operating cost for
the purpose of assessment of the national income tax.

Investment expenditures are one of four major
components of aggregate demand.* However, from the

---

*As a result of theoretical developments stemming
from the work of Keynes and of advances in the field
of national income accounting, it is possible to
identify the four major components of an economy's
aggregate-demand structure: consumption, investment,
government purchases of goods and services, and the
export-import balance. The components fit into the
familiar and fundamental identity equation.
$Y=C+I+G+X-M$, where Y=national income, C=consump-
tion, I=investment, G=government expenditures, X=ex-
ports, and M=imports.

standpoint of economic stabilization, investment expenditures create several problems: Firstly, investment expenditures have an impact on an economy's
productive capacity in that they are made for the
acquisition of capital goods, whose sole purpose is
to produce other goods and services. The productive
capacity and the rate of growth of an economy is
largely determined by the rate of investment. Secondly, investment expenditures, especially on inventories, are considered to be the most volatile of
the aggregate-demand components. There are greater
fluctuations in expenditures on capital goods than
on consumer goods. Therefore, the aggregate position
of the economy is largely the result of variations
in investment, which must be regarded as having a
dynamic impact on income, employment, and the business cycle. It is this volatility that the investment tax--and for that matter, the investment reserve
also--attempts to diminish.

It is possible to be certain of the direction in
which the investment tax will work. The imposition
of the tax is tantamount to an increase in costs.
Marginal, or less profitable investment, will not be
carried out. Dividend pay-out policies would be
affected to the extent that a firm would have to
secure a higher yield from its investment to maintain
its same dividends, or else reduce its dividends. The
imposition of the tax will cause some investment to
be postponed to a more desirable time.

If, however, the investment tax is to have full
effect, it must be a temporary one and not made permanent. An effect designed to postpone investment must
always be stronger than one that definitely aims at
putting a brake on investment. If firms have reason
to believe that the investment tax will be imposed
for a long time ahead, they will soon adapt their
estimates of earning capacity, and their financing
plans accordingly. Perhaps only the least profitable
investments will be abandoned. If, on the other hand,
firms know that the tax is only temporary, it is
likely that even more essential and profitable investments can be postponed for a year or so.

Erik Lundberg wrote the following in 1955 with
regard to the investment taxes of 1953 and 1955:

> The investment tax as a method of cur-
> tailing investments has been considered
> in Sweden to be preferable in many cases

to a raising of the rate of interest.
The tax can discriminate between different kinds of investments, and the
increased cost of investment does not
involve any increase in private incomes as an increase of investment
rates may. But a great deal of uncertainty surrounds the actual effects
on prices and demands of these investment taxes. The effects will be
influenced, e.g., by speculation in
the duration of the tax. Swedish
experiences do not allow any definite
conclusions to be made. So many
other factors were at work during
these years that statistical analysis
of the effects of the investment
tax is impossible.[6]

How far the investment tax is effective as an
anti-inflationary device is not clear. However, three
different viewpoints may be presented:

1. It has been argued that the investment tax
contributed to inflation by reducing investment that
might have led to increased production and hence to
a lessening of inflation. The proper objective should
be to increase the productive capacity of the economy,
not decrease it. An increase in the supply of capital
goods, or any measure that would result in plant
modernization or improved productive capacity, would
increase the outflow of goods and services to offset
increases in aggregate demand.* This idea can be
presented as in Figure 4-1.

----

*With full-employment of all resources a logical
concomitant of inflation, the question arises--How
can the supply of capital goods increase when all
available resources are being utilized? Increased
investment will place further strains on existing
resources. However, plant modernization and improved
technology brought about by investment could very well
result in increased output with fixed resources. Capital may be substituted for labor, and industries, as
they become more capital intensive, are capable of
greater output.
However, this argument is more applicable in the
long run. In the short run, with resources fixed, an

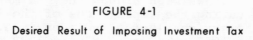

FIGURE 4-1

Desired Result of Imposing Investment Tax

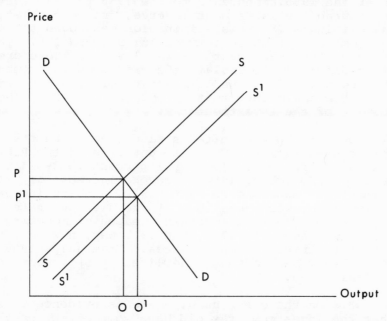

In the diagram, the price level is represented on the vertical axis, and output is represented on the horizontal axis. The original price level is represented by the symbol P and original output by the symbol O. Inflation is assumed to exist. Increasing investment, rather than decreasing it would increase the supply of capital goods, which, in turn, would increase the supply of goods and services. The supply curve, S, shifts to the right, S^1, with the results that output increases and the price level falls.

---

investment results in increased competition with the consumer and public sectors of the economy for scarce resources. The result is usually a rise in prices.

The investment tax would be more effective if demand-pull inflation exists. The appropriate remedy is to decrease one of the components of aggregate demand. If cost-push inflation exists, the investment tax probably would be ineffective.

2.   It has been argued that so many factors were
at work during the impositions of the investment tax
that an exact conclusion is impossible. For example,
under the 1955 amendments to the 1938 tax law that
introduced the investment reserve, free depreciation
was eliminated.* This elimination was bound to have
had some effect on investment in 1956 and 1957, years
in which the investment tax was levied. Therefore,
it is difficult to isolate the effect on investment
that resulted from the elimination of free depreciation from the effect that was brought about by the
levying of the investment tax.

Monetary policy effects also have to be taken
into consideration. The discount rate of the Riksbank
was raised in April, 1955 by 1 percent to 3-3/4 percent. In November, 1956, a second increase of 1/4
percent was made and in July, 1957, a third increase
of 1 percent was made, so that the discount rate was
5 percent. The most important weapon of monetary
policy during 1955, 1956, and 1957 was, however, the
direct restrictions on advances. From July, 1955 to
July, 1957, bank advances declined by 5 percent in
nominal value.

3.   On the other hand, there is evidence to show
that the investment tax did have some effect on the
Swedish economy. The combined effects of the credit
squeeze imposed by the central bank and the investment
tax (levied from the beginning of 1955 and expiring
at the end of 1957) have been estimated in two separate

---

*Free depreciation refers to the right of busi-
ness firms to write off machinery and equipment as
they see fit. Regardless of the anticipated life of
a machine, its entire cost could be written off in the
year of acquisition. Between 1938 and 1955, Swedish
corporations and economic associations were allowed
free depreciation of machinery and equipment--the
right to write off the cost of any piece of machinery
or equipment completely in the year of acquisition,
or on any other basis deemed appropriate.
It was argued that free depreciation contributed
to postwar inflation in Sweden, particularly in the
early 1950s, for the reason that business firms were
induced to make investments to acquire depreciable
objects at the very time that investment required
restriction rather than stimulation.

surveys of investment decisions to amount to a reduction of planned investment by 14 percent in 1955 and
1956. The credit restrictions seem to have been the
most effective measure, while the deflationary effect
of the investment tax declined in 1956 compared to
1955.[7]

There is also an indication that the investment
tax was at least partly effective in postponing capital expenditures to a time when inflationary pressures had diminished. Industrial investment in
Sweden went up by about 10 percent in 1958 over the
amount of investment in 1957.[8]

The Joint Economic Committee of the U.S. Congress,
in its report, Economic Policy in Western Europe, con-
cludes that the elimination of the investment tax for
1958, in addition to other measures taken at the same
time, contributed to an expansion of private investment expenditures in 1958 approximately twice as great,
in money terms, as that in the public sector.[9]

Although the tax was used as an anti-inflationary
measure, the revenue produced was considerable. In
1957, the tax raised 201,699,600 kronor ($39 million)
based on total taxable expenditures of 1,681 million
kronor ($300 million). In 1956, the tax yielded 87
million kronor on taxable investment expenditures of
727 million kronor.

The investment tax was discontinued in 1958 and
was not used again until 1967. There was a feeling
among some Swedish fiscal experts that the investment
tax had an uneven effect on investments in that it
penalized the larger and more efficient firms while
leaving the inefficient firms untouched. The tax, it
was felt, adversely affected Sweden's balance of payments because of the effect on the export-oriented
automobile and steel industries. In 1960, a purchase
tax was levied on industrial purchases. This tax, to
a certain extent, had the same effect as the investment tax.

The investment reserve supplanted the investment
tax somewhat as an instrument of economic stabilization. It was used as a countercyclical fiscal instrument in the 1958-1959 recession, again in the boom
period of 1960-1961, and for a third time in the recession of 1962-1963. The investment reserve possesses
a greater degree of flexibility than the investment

tax in that it can be applied to specific industries
or industries in general. The investment reserve can
also be used as an instrument of industrial location
policy.

OTHER STABILIZATION MEASURES

When a general decline in economic activity affects the labor markets of the whole country, a series
of employment measures may be used simultaneously.
These measures include emergency public works, extra
government orders from industry, and accelerated building construction.

Public Investment Reserves

Proposals for a public investment reserve of government, municipal, and government-supported projects
form the basis of an emergency national budget. It
is a stand-by budget for public works which is to be
used when unemployment reaches such proportions that
normal employment-creating measures are no longer
adequate. Appropriations for public-works projects
are voted for this budget. Financial powers are
delegated annually by the Riksdag to the Labor Market
Board, so that the budget may be drawn on it whenever
necessary.* However, on no occasion has it been
necessary to bring the emergency budget into operation.

The public investment reserve exists on paper.
It is a survey listing governmental work projects
which are scheduled for execution in the next few
years, but which could be undertaken ahead of schedule
in the event that unemployment occurred. The survey
includes projects of the government and the municipalities. Emphasis is placed on road building and
forestry projects, because these can be used during
periods of seasonal unemployment. The total of all

----

*Actually, the emergency budget can only be put
into force with the approval of the Riksdag. However,
to make it possible in an economic recession to start
relief works and to place government orders for industry without a loss of time, a special financial en-
titlement has been linked to the emergency budget.

projects in this investment reserve is many times
larger than the volume of construction that could be
undertaken in any one year, since the purpose is to
let the Labor Market Board choose among several possible projects in a given geographic area if and
when unemployment occurs there.

The public investment reserve is always updated
by annual revisions eliminating public-works projects
already executed either as emergency public works or
within the framework of normal public investment, as
well as projects which for various reasons have been
abandoned.

Government orders for commodities produced by
industry are also included in this investment reserve.
These orders are scheduled to be placed within a given
period of time, but can be placed ahead of schedule if
this proves necessary to create employment opportunities in industry.

Appropriations for emergency public works and
emergency orders for industry are voted in the general
emergency budget. However, funds for public relief
works which are used to combat seasonal unemployment
are obtained from the national budget. Each year a
certain amount is placed at the disposal of the Labor
Market Board.

To insure preparedness against unemployment, the
Labor Market Board makes grants to municipalities for
the advanced planning of municipal buildings and other
construction projects. The idea is to build up a
reserve of public works. The size of the grant is
determined for each municipality on the basis of its
local level of taxation. In recent years, the planning
grant has been approximately 50 percent of total cost.

Apart from the stand-by program for emergencies
which would be financed by funds out of the general
emergency budget, funds are regularly appropriated to
the Labor Market Board out of the national budget to
finance or subsidize public-works projects which are
necessary even in periods of full-employment to relieve
seasonal unemployment or local unemployment arising
for special reasons. The appropriations are made in
part from the budget of the Social Affairs Ministry
and in part from the budget of the Ministry of Communications. The latter appropriation is ear-marked
entirely for road building. If the total appropriation

proves inadequate because of an increase in unemployment above anticipated levels, the Labor Market Board
can request supplemental appropriations from the
Riksdag.

Public Relief Works

Public relief works are important as a means of
reducing seasonal unemployment, especially in the
northern part of Sweden where this type of unemployment is high among forestry and agricultural workers.
This device is also used to even out cyclical fluctuations in manpower demand. The relief works involve
the construction and maintenance of roads, the repair
of bridges, harbors, and channel facilities, the preparation of firebreaks, and other projects which can
be completed during a short period of time.

Investments in public relief works supplement
regular public-works programs which are planned on a
year-to-year basis. They are called emergency relief
works and are utilized whenever unemployment occurs.
The county labor boards are responsible for assessing
the need for relief works, but the decision to start
such works lies with the Labor Market Board.

Public relief works can be carried out either as
a state relief work or as a municipal relief work
subsidized by the Swedish government. A state relief
work is carried out either by the Labor Market Board
out of funds which are made available to it for employment stabilization purposes, from the orindary
budget, or by public institutions, such as the Royal
Board of Roads, when it comes to roadworks. A municipal relief work is carried out under the auspices
of the Labor Market Board by the commune or county
council. The costs of the relief work are divided
between the Labor Market Board and the commune.

Relief works are started when unemployment cannot
be alleviated by other measures, such as relocation
assistance or vocational training. The extent and
scope of the relief works is dependent upon the general
economic situation and the type of unemployment. Although the relief works have been used to combat seasonal unemployment, they are also used as a cyclical
employment measure.

The category of worker which has been employed on the relief works has come from the building and construction industry, agriculture, and forestry. For the most part, these persons lack the necessary training to fit into the type of jobs which are currently available in Sweden.

Public relief works are subject to a number of criteria which are as follows:

1.   They must be in inverse proportion to the level of economic activity--increasing when the level of economic activity is falling and decreasing when it is rising.

2.   They must be increased during the winter and contracted to a minimum during the summer to work effectively against seasonal unemployment.

3.   They must employ manpower which is difficult to place in other areas.

4.   The projects should be of such a type that they can be started quickly and discontinued quickly.

5.   Regard must be paid to the locale of these relief works from the standpoint of cost and from the standpoint of the absorption of the unemployed who cannot be moved to other areas.

The cost of executing public relief works varies from year to year. It amounted to 260 million kronor ($50 million) for the fiscal year 1961-1962 and 380 million kronor ($73 million) for 1962-1963. In the fiscal year 1966-1967, expenditures amounted to 391 million kronor, and 425 million kronor for 1967-1968.*

Placement of Government
Orders to Industry

Another employment-creating device used in Sweden is an increase in national and local governmental

---

*A rough estimate of the cost of a similar program in the United States would be $2 billion for 1967-1968. The estimate is based on the ratio of the two labor forces to each other.

purchases from industry. Orders are placed and financed either by the Labor Market Board in behalf of
the governmental units for which the purchases are
intended, or by the units themselves after consultation with the Labor Market Board. Funds can come
from two sources: (1) an increase in the regular
state appropriations for this purpose, and (2) special
funds which are made available to the Labor Market
Board. Purchases from industry may be made at the
onset of a recession or when a given industry is affected by a lack of sufficient orders to maintain
the employment of its personnel. For example, in
January and February, of 1968, public orders for machinery were increased to forestall a decline in
employment caused by a reduction in exports. The
Labor Market Board also obtained the government's
permission to extend subsidies to counties and municipalities covering 20 percent of the orders for machinery and equipment placed by them over and above
their previously established purchasing programs.

Increased government orders from industry was
used as one of a number of employment-creating measures in the recession of 1958. Orders amounting to
9,900,000 kronor were placed with the navy shipyard
at Karlskrona when it was faced with a general cur-
tailment in the navy's shipbuilding program. Other
orders were given to textile and clothing companies
and to other shipyards.

It is estimated that 2,000 jobs were created
during the 1958 recession through the placement of
government orders to industry. The total expenditures
in 1958 on industrial orders amounted to approximately
30 million kronor.

Housing Construction

Housing construction is also used to counteract
seasonal and cyclical employment. More than 90 percent of total housing production in Sweden is financed
with government loans, and employment in the building
industry can easily be influenced by the easing or
tightening of housing credit. The Riksdag decides
on an annual minimum number of housing credits to be
issued; however, if the employment situation warrants
it, these credits may be increased. The county labor
boards are given the power to grant starting permits
for building construction with an overall objective

of keeping this construction at a pace consistent with
the employment situation. The housing and employment
authorities allocate housing credits regionally in
accordance with both employment and housing needs.

Housing construction was used as an employment-
creating device during the 1958-1959 and 1962-1963
recessions. Total construction increased by some
10,000 houses in each of the two recessions. The
employment-creating effects were as follows:

1. In the 1958-1959 recession, employment attributable to increased housing construction ranged
from fifty in the winter of 1957-1958 to 7,000 in the
winter of 1958-1959. This represented approximately
20 percent of the total number of jobs created by the
various employment-creating measures. From the standpoint of job creation, housing construction was exceeded only by emergency relief works. By the summer
of 1959, employment had decreased to 3,000 as building permits were reduced to compensate for the upturn
in business activity.

2. In the 1962-1963 recession, increased housing
construction, together with the release of private
industry's anticyclical reserve funds, created approximately 10,000 jobs in building construction out of a
total of some 50,000 jobs that were created by all of
the employment programs.

3. During the winter period of 1967-1968 housing
expenditures and other related measures provided employment for some 5,600 workers.

SUMMARY

Government policies in Sweden have been aimed at
influencing the overall state of economic activity,
and economic-policy issues have revolved around how
to design a policy mix that will secure a desirable
rate of economic growth, maintain reasonable price
stability, and, most important of all, achieve a high
level of employment. The Swedish government has dis-
played a rather unique willingness to use a full
range of economic tools to accomplish these objectives.
In particular, taxation has been used to affect the
business cycle. The investment reserve is a key
policy instrument which has been used. It involves

the use of tax credits and tax reductions to enable
firms to build up reserves of investment funds which
can be used for investment during recessions. By
allocating part of its profits to the investment reserve, a firm receives an immediate tax reduction.
When the funds are invested under the rules established, they are not restored to taxable income.

The Keynesian model upon which the concept of
modern stabilization policy is based is easy to
comprehend. Whenever aggregate demand grows faster
than an economy's capacity to produce, it should be
reduced by some combination of fiscal and monetary
restraints. Conversely, there are times when productive capacity outstrips total demand, and it
becomes necessary to stimulate the growth of demand
by easing fiscal and monetary restraints.

However, as a practical matter, keeping aggregate
demand continuously in step with total output in all
economic sectors and avoiding inflation at the same
time is extraordinarily complex. In a country like
Sweden there is a tendency, which is stronger than
is generally realized, for excess demand to be si-
phoned off into higher prices and wages, rather than
into expanded output, once the sanction of unemployment is removed. Prices and wages are subject to
extreme upward pressures within a full-employment
zone. At levels of full-employment, all factors of
production move into short supply. Because of the
excess purchasing power which, by definition, is
present in the economy at such times, consumers will
not be disposed to resist higher prices for articles
in short supply. Producers, aware of this, will, in
turn, be disposed to grant wage increases rather than
run the risk of a cessation of operations. In a
countless variety of ways, internal costs creep to
higher levels, pushing prices before them.

The pressure of strong domestic aggregate demand
on both Swedish exports and imports has contributed
significantly to a balance-of-payments deficit. Exports have been retarded to some degree by a combination of domestic absorption and price effects. Goods
which otherwise would have been available for export
go to meet rapidly expanding demand at home. In part,
this is a reflection of the tendency for desired
investment to exceed saving. High aggregate demand
generates domestic price increases that spill over
to export industries and make them less competitive

in world markets. Strong aggregate demand also raises
import demands. In part, this merely reflects the
requirement of imports as a fixed proportion of inputs
in the production process when industrial output is
growing.

NOTES

1. Erik Lundberg, Business Cycles and Economic
Policy (Cambridge, Mass.: Harvard University Press,
1957), p. 52.

2. Curt Canarp, "Investment Reserves and How
They Can Be Used to Combat Recession and Unemploy-
ment," Skandinaviska Banken Quarterly Review, (Second
Quarter, 1963), p. 36.

3. Canarp, op. cit., p. 37.

4. Report of the Labor Market Board, 1969-1970
(Stockholm, 1969), p. 27.

5. For two recent studies of the investment
reserve, see Martin Schnitzer, "The Swedish Investment
Reserve: A Device for Economic Stabilization" (Washington, D.C.: American Enterprise Institute for Public
Policy Research, 1967); and Gunnar Eliasson, "Investment Funds in Operation" (Stockholm: National Institute of Economic Research, 1965).

6. Erik Lundberg, op. cit., p. 217.

7. Konjunktur Läget Hosten 1957, Meddelanden
Frän Konjunkturinstutet (Stockholm, 1957), p. 68.

8. National Central Bureau of Statistics,
National Income Accounts, 1950-1965 (Stockholm,
1966).

9. U.S., Congress, Joint Economic Committee,
Economic Policy in Western Europe, 85th Cong. 2d
Sess., 1959, p. 37.

CHAPTER **5** INCOME
REDISTRIBUTION

INTRODUCTION

Income distribution in a market economy depends
primarily on forces which operate through the market
system. In this system, people are rewarded in accordance with their contribution to marketable output which, in turn, reflects consumer preferences
and incomes. The implication is that persons whose
productivity in value terms is low will earn little,
regardless of whether the low productivity is attributable to lack of effort, lack of skill, or low
demand for the skill.

Fundamentally, then, inequality in the distribution of income is derived from certain institutional
arrangements which are associated with the operations
of a market economy, such as the pricing process.
High prices are set on scarce agents of production
and low prices on plentiful agents--results that are
desirable in many respects. High prices for the
scarce agents tend to reserve them for the uses which
are deemed most important on a price basis, and keep
them from being wasted in relatively unimportant uses.
Low prices for the more plentiful agents tend to lead
to their use in large quantities and to prevent their
being wasted in unemployment as they would be if high
prices were set on them. Thus, it is apparent that
high and low prices for various grades of productive
agents not only result from the operation of the pricing system, but are necessary for the rational allocation of resources in a market economy and to the attainment of equilibrium on the basis of market forces.

But regardless of the forces contributing to the
distribution of income, there has been general dissatisfaction with that distribution in Sweden and in

other Western countries over the years, and attempts
have been made to alter it. This dissatisfaction has
turned around three basic points: (1) income inequality leads to inequality of opportunity, (2) income inequality leads to political inequality, and
(3) income inequality can cause inadequate aggregate
demand and unemployment. Income inequality refers
in general to extreme income differences between
various income groups that existed in many countries
during the early part of the twentieth century and
which continues to exist today in such disparite
countries as the United States and the Soviet Union.

It is obvious why income inequality can lead to
inequality of opportunity in education and employment.
The wealthy can afford to send their children to the
best schools and provide them with the right contacts
in employment. Inheritances also compound this inequality through generations. The poor, on the other
hand, cannot afford quality education for their children, and much talent may be lost to society as a
result. Equality of opportunity is denied to many
who may be qualified in terms of ability and talent.

Economic superiority in terms of income may make
political dominance quite possible. Those who are
wealthy can finance their own or others' political
campaigns for office and thus successfully attain
power. In no country is this any more pronounced
than in the United States. Those who are wealthy
can hire expensive and successful lawyers to widen
the scope of legitimate action for themselves and to
resolve in their favor any legal conflict between
themselves and the less wealthy. The wealthy can
buy up and control mass communications media so that
they may shape public opinion in their favor. They
are frequently employers, and their employees may
feel constrained to vote for or support them. They
can take the time from their work to devote their attention to the avenues of power. Many of those who
are wealthy came into this wealth through no effort
or choice of their own, but through inheritance. Yet
society, particularly in the United States, accords
these persons a privileged position.

Another criticism of income inequality has
hinged around the problem of unemployment which has
confronted market economies for two centuries. The
severity of the problem has varied with time. During
the Great Depression of the 1930s, it was the foremost

problem in the United States and in the Western
European countries. However, after the end of the
Second World War, Keynesian economies developed as
sort of a lodestar for public policy decisions.
Basically, Keynes developed the theory that unemployment was caused by too little spending. Accord-
int to Keynes, the level of employment in an economy
is determined by the volume of production of goods
and services by business. This volume depends upon
how much spending is being done by consumers, other
business firms, and the government. If spending is
large, employment will be large, but if spending is
small, there will be much unemployment.

Consumer spending is the largest component of
the three types of spending which determine aggregate
demand. In the Keynesian framework, consumption is a
function of income. Moreover, as income increases,
consumption also increases, but not in the same proportion. In other words, the marginal propensity to
consume, which shows the relationship between an increase in income and an increase in consumption, declines as incomes increase. Inequality in the distribution of income results in the concentration of
income in the hands of those groups with the lowest
marginal propensity to consume. Tying this in with
aggregate demand is simple. Unemployment can be explained by traditional supply and demand analysis.
An economy's potential output of productive resources
rises from year to year. At times, aggregate demand
for goods and services may not grow as rapidly as an
economy's output potential. Then, demand will not be
large enough to provide employment for all of the
available labor resources. A redistribution of income to those groups with a high marginal propensity
to consume should increase the volume of consumption
and the level of aggregate demand.

However, it is safe to say that progress will
come faster if some degree of income inequality is
tolerated. Resources must be allocated into their
right use and labor given the right incentives. It
is significant to note that the communist countries,
like the United States and other Western nations, rely
on income differentials to allocate labor and to provide the incentives necessary to stimulate productivity. In fact few countries rely as much on material incentives to motivate workers as does the
Soviet Union. In many types of work, wage payments
are on a piece-rate basis. The merit of the

piece-rate system is that it can be used to stimulate
worker productivity and to distinguish between good
and bad workers. Peicework pay, wage differentials,
and bonuses to outstanding workers have always been
a part and parcel of the Soviet reward structure.*

Few, if any, rational persons would argue for
complete income equality. The results in terms of
resource allocation, loss of productivity, and lack
of incentives would be disastrous to any modern
society. It is much more desirable to eliminate the
glaring inequities that can result from extreme disparities in the distribution of income. It is necessary to insure all citizens of a minimum standard of
living, to provide equality of opportunity in employment and education, and to bring about a more equitable distribution of income. Admittedly, the last
objective is extremely hard to define: What is the
right degree of income inequality? It is apparent,
however, that Western society has favored arrangements that are designed to achieve some redistribution of income. National governments are, generally,
the most effective of all governmental instruments to
undertake income redistribution because the opportunities to circumvent their actions are most limited.

Both taxation and government expenditures are the
cornerstone of the modern welfare state which Sweden
epitomizes. The reason for this is clear because
taxes and expenditures, particularly transfer payments, are the chief means by which a government can
provide not only for a minimum standard of material
well-being for all of its citizens, but for the
greater degree of equality in the distribution of
income that the welfare state doctrine implies. The
development of the welfare state has required governments to use their power to alter the distribution of
money income that has resulted from the play of market forces. However, the effectiveness of the welfare state as a means to cope with the problem of the
distribution of income is limited. In other words,
the welfare state may achieve desirable results with

---

*Reliance on material incentives was justified
by Lenin himself when he stated that socialism could
be established "with the help of enthusiasm born of
the great revolution, on personal profit, on self-
interest, on economic calculation."

respect to the distribution of income up to a point,
but thereafter the principle of diminishing returns
sets in.

It is also necessary to mention the fact that
policies designed to promote full-employment of the
labor force will also have an impact on the distribution of income. Unemployment of available resources
can detract from productivity and thus result in a
loss of real income for society. In Sweden and in
other Western European countries, full-employment
has been the most important economic goal. The
unemployment levels generally equated with full-employment in the United States would topple governments throughout most of Western Europe. However,
as a result of full-employment policies, labor shortages have been endemic and inflationary pressures
persistent. Nevertheless, in countries like Sweden
jobs have been available to those who want them, and
general labor shortages have driven wages upward.

In Sweden taxation and expenditure policies of
the national government have played a prominent role
in the redistribution of income. A very high level
of employment has been maintained through the use of
fiscal, monetary, and manpower policies. The success
of these policies is the subject of this chapter.

THE TAX SYSTEM AS AN INSTRUMENT
FOR INCOME REDISTRIBUTION

Since the Swedish national income tax is progressive, there is a redistribution of income in the
direction of greater equality because the proportionate share of the upper-income groups in the total
income is reduced and the proportionate share of the
lower-income groups is raised. The progressivity of
the income tax structure brings about this result because the effective rate of taxation--the ratio of
total taxes paid to income received--increases with
the size of the income. This means, in other words,
that the proportionate share of the total tax burden
is greater for the upper-income groups, hence there
is a redistribution in the direction of greater
income equality.

While the national income is produced by the
collaboration of the productive agents--land, labor,
and capital--and is received by the owners of these

agents, it is consumed in the last analysis by individuals and families, and the factor which is important in their standard of living and general
economic welfare is the amount of income received
per individual or per family from all sources. The
broadest possible distribution of the national income is a two-fold division with wages and salary
income on one side and the various forms of property
income on the other. Property income consists of
income derived from the ownership of economic resources in the form of capital equipment or natural
resources. In national income accounting, property
incomes take the form of rent, interest, and profit.

A significant development in the distribution
of national income in Sweden is that there has been
an increase in the percentage of wages and salaries
relative to property income since the end of the
Second World War. During the period 1957-1966, wages
and salaries increased from 30.2 billion kronor to
65.6 billion kronor, while income of unincorporated
enterprises increased from 4.5 billion kronor to 6.5
billion kronor. Interest increased from 919 million
kronor to 2.1 billion kronor, and rent increased from
897 million kronor to 1.4 billion kronor. Corporate
profits increased from 2.3 billion kronor to 2.9
billion kronor.[1] Transfer payments, which would be
a part of personal income, but not national income,
increased from 4.1 billion kronor in 1957 to 12 billion kronor in 1966.*

It is necessary to remember that in terms of per
capita income Sweden ranks second to the United
States. However, the extremes in income distribution
are less pronounced in Sweden. In 1966, for example,
only eighteen Swedes reported a taxable income of 1
million or more kronor, and only four Swedes reported
a taxable income in excess of 2 million kronor.[2]

The redistributional effects of direct taxation
and transfer payments are readily apparent when they
are compared to personal income. In 1969, personal
income was estimated at 116.3 billion kronor. Transfer payments were estimated at 16.6 billion kronor and

---

*Personal income, as distinguished from national
income, in national income accounting, is the current
income received by persons from all sources, including transfer income, from government and business.

direct taxes at 34.4 billion kronor.[3] Transfer payments accounted for 14.3 percent of personal income,
and direct taxes represented 29.9 percent.

    Table 5-1 presents the distribution of income
before and after income taxes for 1967. The data
do not include tax-free social benefits of any
type. The term net income refers to that part of
Swedish income which is subject to the Swedish income tax. Net income can be identified with the
concept of preredistributional income. It corresponds
to the concept of adjusted gross income for income
tax purposes. In 1967, net taxable income amounted
to 81.7 billion kronor.

    Inequality in the distribution of income can be
measured with respect to either the receipt of income
or the ownership of property. Income is a flow,
measurable only over a period of time, such as a
year; property, a stock, is measurable at any given
point in time. The former may be thought of as the
flow of claims on the value of goods and services
produced, accruing to individuals or institutions;
the latter, as the stock of claims or rights to the
value of wealth, whether it be natural resources,
man-made capital goods, or consumer durable goods.

    The distribution of income before taxes is one
measure of inequality in the distribution of income.
In Table 5-2, before-tax income distribution in Sweden
is presented. Income in the sense that it is used
here includes wages and salaries, income of unincorporated enterprises, rent, interest, dividends, and
income from agriculture. Excluded are tax-free social
benefits of all types. The income corresponds to net
income before certain general deductions have been
made.

    In 1966, the median income for all income earn-
ers was 14,973 kronor ($2,900), the lower quartile
income was 6,497 kronor and the upper quartile income was 17,091 kronor. Although these figures appear low by United States standards (the median income
in the United States for 1966 was $7,651), it is
necessary to point out that the income earners in the
table include many students and others who work for
part-time incomes, and older persons who are also
in the labor force. Swedish income taxes are applicable to almost every income earner in Sweden as
evidenced by the fact that more than three million
Swedes paid taxes in the tax year 1967.

TABLE 5-1

Before and After Tax Income Distribution in Sweden for 1967

Distribution of Income Before Taxes

Income Class	Single Taxpayers	Percent	Married Taxpayers	Percent
0-10,000 kr.	601,284	35.8	102,102	5.8
10,000-20,000	677,393	40.3	355,519	20.1
20,000-30,000	308,633	18.4	545,341	30.9
30,000-40,000	62,689	3.7	387,226	21.9
40,000-50,000	16,455	1.0	188,585	10.7
50,000-100,000	12,599	0.7	165,926	9.4
100,000 and Over	1,595	0.1	20,331	1.2
	1,680,648	100.0	1,765,030	100.0

Distribution of Income After Taxes

Income Class	Single Taxpayers	Percent	Married Taxpayers	Percent
0-10,000 kr.	886,432	52.7	166,176	9.4
10,000-20,000	713,053	42.4	735,838	41.7
20,000-30,000	65,262	3.9	604,834	34.3
30,000-40,000	10,224	0.6	171,214	9.7
40,000-50,000	3,005	0.2	48,570	2.7
50,000-100,000	2,376	0.1	35,322	2.0
100,000 and Over	296	0.0	3,076	0.2
	1,680,648	100.0	1,765,030	100.0

Source: Skattebetalarnas Förening, "Fakta för Skattebetalare" (Stockholm, 1969), pp. 4-5.

TABLE 5-2

Distribution of Income in Sweden
Before Taxes for 1966

Income Classes	Percentage of Income Earners	Total Income	Percentage of Total Income
0-10,000 kr.	37.9	9,397.4	12.7
10,000-20,000	31.4	21,781.3	29.3
20,000-30,000	21.1	23,254.1	31.4
30,000-40,000	5.8	9,011.9	12.2
40,000-50,000	2.0	4,044.1	5.5
50,000-75,000	1.3	3,479.5	4.7
75,000-100,000	0.3	1,307.2	1.8
100,000 and Over	0.2	1,801.8	2.4
	100.0	74,077.3	100.0

Source: Statistiska Centralbyran,
"Skattetaxeringarna Samt Fördelningen Av Inkomst
Och Förmögenhet Taxeringsaret, 1967" (Stockholm,
1968), p. 10.

Swedish income taxes redistribute income in
three ways. First, of course, they do so because
they are much higher on large incomes than on small
ones; this means that as the general level of income
rises there is a continuous redistributionary effect.
Second, the taxation system redistributes income
toward those with more dependents, so that, generally
speaking, a married man is taxed more lightly than a
bachelor. Finally, to some extent unearned income--
income from property of any kind--is taxed more
heavily than income from employment. For example,
there is no exemption from either the national or
local income tax on interest on government securities.
Income from property is subject to both the national
and local income tax, and the property itself is subject to the national tax on wealth.

The national income tax, although steeply progressive, is not progressive through its entire
range. All incomes above the level of the tax-free
deductions are first assessed at the lowest rate of
10 percent. This rate is also the basic element in

the higher tax rates and may, therefore, be said to
constitute a proportional tax on which the higher
rates are based. Above the basic 10 percent rate
the progressity starts. It has been estimated that
the basic rate of 10 percent brings in around 70
percent of the national income tax revenues.4 Although this estimate may be high, it is necessary to
remember that most of the tax revenue comes from the
lowest tax rates since they hit the majority of the
income tax payers. Deduction of the local income
tax, which is proportional, also has the effect of
reducing the tax base for the national income tax.*
It can be said that the Swedish income tax system
is proportional throughout most of the income range.

Nevertheless, it is apparent that inequality in
the distribution of income is reduced to some extent
through income taxation. The reduction in the number
of upper-income taxpayers is particularly significant. Referring to Table 5-1, approximately 21 percent of married taxpayers had net incomes of 40,000
or more before taxes in 1967, but only 4.9 percent
had after-tax incomes of 40,000 kronor or more. The
upper 1.2 percent of married taxpayers was reduced
to 0.2 percent after taxes. At the other end of the
income scale, 25.9 percent of married taxpayers had
incomes of 20,000 kronor or less before taxes compared
to 51.1 percent after taxes. Before- and after-tax
shifts for single taxpayers are even more pronounced.

The heavy rates of Swedish taxation is apparent
when taxes are compared to income. In Table 5-3,
income from wages and salaries and direct taxes are
compared over a five-year period. Direct taxes include the national and local income taxes and contributions for old-age pensions and health insurance.
The marginal tax rate, which can be defined as the
ratio of a change in total direct taxes to a change
in income is also presented.

The increase in total taxes relative to income
can be attributed to two factors--an increase in the
rates of the local income tax and an increase in the
contributory rates for old-age pensions and health
insurance. To some extent the increase in taxes was

─────────────

*In 1967, deductions for the local income tax
amounted to 12.6 billion kronor.

offset by increases in transfer payments to households. In 1968, income transfers to households increased by 8 percent over 1967, and the increase for
1969 over 1968 was 10 percent.

TABLE 5-3

A Comparison of Direct
Taxes to Income from
Wages and Salaries

Year	Income from Wages and Salaries	Total Taxes	Effec- tive Tax Rate	Marginal Tax Rate
	(Millions of Kronor)		(Percent)	
1965	60,129	17,093	28.4	44.7
1966	66,705	19,179	28.8	31.7
1967	71,662	21,929	30.6	55.5
1968	76,325	24,673	32.3	58.8
1969	81,263	27,356	33.7	54.3

Source: Sekretariat for Economic Planning of
the Ministry of Finance and the National Institute of
Economic Research, "Preliminary National Budget,
1969" (Stockholm, 1969), p. 94.

Swedish direct taxes are much more burdensome
than American taxes on income earners. In Sweden,
the maximum marginal income tax rate is reached at
an income of $29,000, and in the United States the
maximum rate is reached at an income of $100,000.
Moreover, Swedish direct taxes cut deeper at all income levels than American direct taxes. In Table
5-4, Swedish and American direct taxes are compared
for various monthly income levels. Swedish taxes
consist of the national and local income taxes and
contributions for old-age pensions. The contribution for health insurance is excluded, as there is not
not a counterpart levy in the United States. American
taxes consist of the national income tax, the income
tax for the state of Virginia, and Social Security contributions. For each country, the taxes were obtained
from tax schedules used by employers. The rates for
single persons and married couples, with one wage
earner and no children, were used.

TABLE 5-4

A Comparison of Direct
Taxes in the United
States and Sweden for
Various Income Levels

Income	Tax on Single Person[a]	Tax on Married Couple[a]
United States		
$ 200	25.11	14.01
300	54.27	39.57
400	85.61	65.94
600	148.48	120.98
900	244.92	203.95
1,200	376.12	303.75
1,650	551.17	443.80
Sweden		
200	52,10	31.92
300	94.42	68.84
400	144.00	109.30
600	256.92	207.10
900	418.83	361.72
1,200	600.60	540.90
1,650	878.80	817.50

[a]For both countries, the taxes are preliminary withholding taxes. The Swedish local income tax used is 20 percent.

Source: United States: tax tables used by Virginia Polytechnic Institute; Sweden: Ministry of Finance, Skattetabell för Beräkning av Preliminär A-Skatt för Ar 1969.

Indirect taxes, to a certain extent, counterbalance the progressivity of the income tax. Sumptuary taxes on liquor and tobacco are quite high and account for 10 percent of national tax revenues. An element of regression is introduced, for the reason that the amount which a person spends on liquor or tobacco is not really dependent upon his income. With the present rates, the absolute burden upon

the lowest income groups from the taxes is substantial. Of course, it may be argued that the use of
these commodities gives rise to certain real costs
to society which do not appear as costs to the producers, and therefore are not reflected in the prices
for which the articles are sold.

In 1969, the value-added tax replaced the
general sales tax, which had been used for a number
of years. However, the economic impact of the value-
added tax is essentially the same as the general retail sales tax, in that the consumer ultimately pays.
The value-added tax accounts for around 19 percent
of national tax revenues. An element of regression
is introduced into the tax system for the reason that
the tax is a consumption-based tax which amounts to
a larger part of the incomes of the lower income
groups than for higher income groups. However, the
extent of the regressiveness of the value-added tax
is difficult to measure.

Table 5-5 presents the impact of direct and indirect taxes on various income groups. The data are
based on a family with one wage earner, without children.

TABLE 5-5

Impact of Direct and Indirect
Taxes on Income Redistribution
(Kronor)

Income Before Taxes	Direct Taxes	Income After Direct Taxes	Indirect Taxes	Net Income
8,000	1,020	6,980	1,675	5,305
10,000	1,480	8,520	2,045	6,475
15,000	3,250	11,750	2,820	8,930
20,000	5,000	15,000	3,600	11,400
30,000	9,160	20,840	5,000	15,840
40,000	14,020	25,980	6,235	19,745
50,000	19,285	30,715	7,370	23,345
75,000	33,570	41,430	9,945	31,485
100,000	49,090	50,910	12,220	38,690
200,000	115,270	84,730	20,335	64,395

Source: Skattebetalarnas Forening, "Fakta för
Skattebetalare," (Stockholm, 1968), p. 6.

The table indicates in a general way the impact of direct and indirect taxes in Sweden. Indirect taxes appear more proportional than regressive, but the table does not take into consideration different family circumstances. The impact of taxation on the redistribution of income is apparent. Income inequality is narrowed considerably through income taxation. When the tax rates for the city of Stockholm are applied to all sets of circumstances and applied to the incomes in the table, the pretax inequality of twenty to one is reduced to after-tax inequality of eight to one. Indirect taxes are excluded.[5]

SOCIAL WELFARE EXPENDITURES

The burden of Swedish taxation, the heaviest in the world, may to a considerable degree be explained by Sweden's extensive social welfare system. The bulk of Swedish social welfare expenditures is financed out of general national revenues, and by special levies on employers and employees.* These levies are paid not to the national treasury, but to special social security funds from which the benefits are paid. Most social security receipts and expenditures are, therefore, not reflected in the current budget of the government, but in autonomous budgets.

The Swedish government has assumed increasing responsibility for maintaining the incomes of those persons who do not have the ability to earn an adequate income through their own efforts. People beyond the working age, the disabled, the involuntarily unemployed, dependent children and their families, and other people with little or no incomes have received increasing amounts of social insurance and public assistance. Increases in social welfare expenditures have been at a much more rapid rate than an increase in national income. In 1960, health

---

*In France, which also has a very comprehensive social security system, 97 percent of the funds used for social welfare purposes is provided by taxes on employers and employees. Less than 1 percent is provided from the general tax revenues of the French government.

insurance benefits and medical services amounted to
2.9 billion kronor. In 1969, the cost has increased
to an estimated 11.4 billion kronor. Total expenditures on social welfare more than tripled during the
period 1960-1969.

Extremely large sums of money are distributed
through the medium of transfer payments. A transfer
payment is distinguished from other government expenditures in that no equivalent value in either
product or productive service is received in exchange.
Transfer payments are of several types. First of all,
there are those which directly benefit certain sectors
of society, such as family allowances, old-age pensions, sickness and accident benefits, and housing
allowances. Secondly, there are grants to certain
sectors of the economy, such as agricultural subsidies, which result in lower prices for certain goods
and services. With respect to transfer payments,
it should be noted that some of the services provided
by the government are, in effect, nonmonetary transfers. This would be true of such services as free
education, free medical care, and free school meals.
The recipients of these services benefit through ob-
taining them at a price below their real cost as
measured by the government expenditures for the resources necessary to provide the services. However,
these services absorb resources and must be distinguished from expenditures that result solely in a
transfer of income from one group to another group.

In the fiscal year 1968-1969, direct transfer
payments to households amounted to 15.6 billion
kronor. The comprehensive social welfare system in
effect in Sweden includes health insurance, old-age
and disability pensions, employee's supplemental
pensions, unemployment insurance, housing allowances,
and family allowances. The system is financed by
general revenues from the national budget, fees which
are carried in autonomous budgets, and grants to
local governments.

Several salient points need to be remembered
concerning the tax-transfer payment relationship in
Sweden.

1. The local income tax, which is proportional,
plays a very important role in the Swedish fiscal
structure. As the progressive rates for the national
income tax apply primarily to the upper-income brackets, the local income tax puts the heaviest burden on

single taxpayers up to an income of 36,000 kronor and
on married taxpayers up to an income of 55,000 kronor.

2.　The national income tax introduces an element
of progression into the tax system but only accounts
for a small percent of all income redistributed by taxation and transfers.　There is only a negligible shift
of the tax burden to upper-income groups.

3.　Indirect taxes accomplish a regressive coun-
terbalancing of the progressive income tax.　As a
source of national revenue to the national government,
indirect taxes accounted for 53 percent of tax revenues for the fiscal year 1969-1970, and direct taxes,
including the income tax, 47 percent.

Family Allowances

Family allowances are regular cash payments to
families with children, and are paid in all major
countries with the exception of the United States as
a social security benefit.　Payments usually cover
only gainfully employed persons and recipients of social insurance benefits.　Some countries start family
allowances with the first child; others start only
with the second child.　Family allowances are usually
financed by a tax on employers, or out of general governmental revenue.　The amount of the family allowances is either the same for all children, or it
increases progressively with the number of children
in the family.　The family allowance is usually paid
to the mother, and there are variations of the family
allowance which provide additional benefits for single
persons with children.　Also, youth allowances are
often provided for older children in families.[6]

The family allowance is a means of redistributing
income in such a way as to benefit the child-rearing
portion of a nation's population.　It is a fact that
children are more numerous in low than in high-income
families, thus reducing the margin of economic security
of these families, and often perpetuating poverty from
one generation to the next.　The family allowance, particularly in the industrial areas of France, to many
families is often the difference between poverty and
a minimum standard of living.*

---

*It is estimated by French authorities on the
family allowance that the ratio of the allowance to

As previously mentioned, Swedish family allowance
is paid at the rate of 900 kronor ($175) per child a
year. Unlike most countries with family allowances,
Sweden does not exclude the first child from receiving
assistance. The family allowance is not subject to a
means test--although this may change before long--nor
is it subject to personal income tax. It is the second largest expenditure item in the Swedish budget
after the basic old-age pension scheme. Like family
allowances in France and in other countries, the family
allowance includes more than just payments based on
the number of children in a family. There is also a
housing allowance which is subject to a means test,
and various allowances which are payable in special
circumstances, such as maternity grants.

The family allowance is financed from general
government revenues. There are no contributions from
employers and employees. In 1967, allowances were paid
for 1,770,000 children under sixteen at a cost of 1.6
billion kronor. This amounted to 1.3 percent of the
Swedish gross national product for 1967, 5 percent of
the national budget, and 14 percent of total social
welfare expenditures on the part of the national government. In addition to the regular family allowance,
special allowances are paid to single persons with
children, and to orphaned children living with rela-
tives. These allowances covered 169,000 children in
1967, and cost 167 million kronor. Added to these allowances are free holiday grants to children under
fourteen who come from families with taxable incomes
of less than 5,700 kronor ($1,100) a year. There is
an educational allowance for students over sixteen
which is based on a means test, with 75 kronor a month
being the maximum amount.

As a source of revenue to Swedish families, the
family allowance varies in importance. For example,
a family with five children would receive 4,500 kronor
in family allowances. In 1966, 11 percent of Swedish
families with five children made less than 12,000
kronor a year, while 63 percent of single persons
made less than 12,000 kronor. The family allowance
could conceivably amount to one-half or more of total
income to low-income Swedish families.

---

gross monthly earnings of the average production
worker is 28 percent in the Paris area.

The family allowance results in lateral income
redistribution between families in the same income
group. For example, a couple with no children and a
taxable yearly income of 12,000 kronor would have a
disposable income of 9,980 kronor. But a family with
two children would have a disposable income of 11,780
kronor after taxes. The 1,800 kronor differential is
accounted for by the allowance of 900 kronor per child.
A family with five children would have an income of
14,480 kronor. This means that two families with
identical taxable incomes of 12,000 kronor would have
different disposable incomes based on the number of
children each had. A family with no children would
have a disposable income of 9,980 kronor; a family with
five children would have a disposable income of 14,480
kronor, a difference of 45 percent. On the other hand,
a family with a taxable income of 48,000 kronor and no
children would have a disposable income of 30,139 kronor compared to a disposable income of 34,639 kronor
for a family with the same income but with five
children.[7]

Swedish social welfare critics feel that the current family allowance is inadequate as a means of
support of children, particularly for low-income families. They argue that cost-of-living increases over
the last twenty years have offset to a considerable
degree increases in the family allowance. Their point
is verified by a comparison of the cost-of-living
index to the allowance. In 1948, the consumer price
index was 100 percent; in 1966, it had increased to
215 percent. The family allowance amounted to 260
kronor per child in 1948 (the first year of the allowance) and 900 kronor in 1966. Using the consumer
price index to deflate the family allowance in terms
of real income results in an allowance of 559 kronor
per child in terms of 1947 prices.[8] This reduction
in terms of real income has led to recommendations
that the allowance be increased by a maximum of 420
kronor and based on a sliding scale relative to gross
income, with lower income families receiving a greater
allowance than middle-income families.[9]

It can be said in comparing the United States and
Swedish tax systems that a family allowance is built
into the United States system through the use of personal exemptions and deductions which amount to $700
per child. This means that families in the United
States receive a children's allowance which, when
based on current income tax rates ranging from 14 to

70 percent, varies from $98 to $490. This is a
savings to the taxpayer rather than a direct government outlay. The Swedish family allowance, on the
other hand, represents a direct outlay out of government revenues of 900 kronor ($180) a year per child
to rich and poor alike. The United States allowance,
however, is progressive and presumably benefits
upper-income families more than lower-income families.* The Swedish family allowance is a flat-rate
grant payable to all families with children, regardless of income status. Family needs are not involved,
and the allowance reflects partial compensation for
the imposition of excise taxes. It also reflects
compensation for the fact that there is no correla-
tion between wages and family responsibility in a
modern industrial society.

Housing Allowances

The provision of adequate housing for all persons is a paramount socioeconomic objective in
Sweden. Much emphasis has been placed on housing
construction and Swedish credit policies have been
subverted to this end as more than 90 percent of
total housing construction in Sweden has been financed
with government loans. Government housing credits
are designed to have priority on credit available in
the open market. Subsidies in the form of low-interest
loans, which are set at 4 percent and amortized over
a period of thirty years, are designed to stimulate
housing construction. The government pays the difference between this 4 percent and the current market
rate of interest, which averaged 7½ percent in 1967.

Rental allowances based on a means test are payable to Swedish families. Families with one child
and a joint taxable income of less than 7,000 kronor
($1,400), receive an allowance of 395 to 425 kronor
a year depending upon the part of Sweden in which
they are living. Families with more than one child
and with a joint taxable income of less than 12,000

------

*This assumes that an additional money income
has less utility or satisfaction to a family making
$25,000 a year than to a family making $4,000 a year.
On an a priori basis we can perhaps reason this way.
However, it may well be that the marginal utilities
of additional money would be similar to both families.

kronor ($2,400) receive an allowance ranging from
330 to 390 kronor a year depending upon the part of
Sweden in which they are living plus an additional
180 kronor a year for each child under sixteen.

However, for families with exceptionally low
incomes by Swedish standards, additional rental allowances are available. If joint taxable income is
between 6,000 and 8,000 kronor, and a family has
more than one child, a rental allowance ranging from
660 to 780 kronor a year, plus 230 kronor per child,
is paid. If joint taxable income is less than 6,000
kronor a year, the rental allowance is increased to
330 kronor for each child. Families with one child
and with a joint taxable income of less than 6,000
kronor receive an allowance ranging from 490 to 525
kronor a year.

The rental allowance was subject to revision by
the Swedish Parliament in 1968. It was proposed to
raise the allowance and the eligibility level. A
family with one child and joint gross income of less
than 20,000 kronor ($4,000) would receive 720 kronor
a year as an allowance. A family with two children
and a gross income of less than 25,000 kronor would
receive 1,680 kronor a year; a family with three
children and a gross income of less than 30,000
kronor would receive 2,680 kronor a year; and a
family with four or more children and a gross income
of less than 35,000 kronor would receive 2,880 kronor
a year.

Pensions

As family and housing allowances are designed
to improve the economic status of the family, pensions are designed to improve the economic position
of the aged and disabled. There is a basic, national
old-age pension as well as a supplementary old-age pension for everyone who reaches sixty-seven. The basic,
national old-age pension amounts to 420 kronor ($84)
a month for a single person and 630 kronor ($106) a
month for a married couple. However, at his discretion a Swedish citizen can apply for his old-age
pension at the age of sixty-three or defer it until
the age of seventy by accepting a reduction or premium
in the amount of the pension. The pension is financed
by a tax on the employee of 4 percent of income, with
a maximum payment of 1,200 kronor a year. The
employer contributes nothing and the government

finances 70 percent of the cost of the basic pension out of general revenues.

The benefits under the supplementary old-age pension program depend upon a person's earned income during the time he has been actively employed. The pension amounts to 3 percent of average annual covered earnings between 5,600 and 42,000 kronor times the years of coverage with the maximum set at 60 percent of earnings. The pension is tied to the cost of living, and is financed by a tax on the employer of 9 percent of the wages of each employee between 5,600 and 42,000 kronor.

The general level of total old-age pensions--basic national pensions plus supplementary pensions--amount to approximately two-thirds of the average annual earnings of the pensioner during his or her fifteen best years of income.

There are also basic and supplementary invalid pensions which provide the same amounts as the regular old-age pensions and are financed out of the same taxes. Both types of pensions provide for children's and housing supplements, as well as for a widow's pension which amounts to 90 percent of the basic pension and 40 percent of the supplementary pension.

Unemployment Compensation

Unemployment insurance, which is voluntary, covers the majority of persons who are exposed to the risk of unemployment. There are forty-seven unemployment insurance societies, each representing a particular union, but administered separately from the union to which the worker belongs. Benefits, which range between certain maximums and minimums, are paid on a daily basis and currently can amount to a maximum of 50 kronor ($10) a day, payable up to 200 days.* There is also a dependent's supplement of 2 kronor a day for the spouse and all children under sixteen. The compensation is financed by a levy on all insured persons, which ranges from 1 to 12 kronor a month according to the society, and

_____

*This is extended to 500 days for workers over sixty years of age.

government subsidies to the various funds which range
from 2 to 5 kronor per day of unemployment, the
actual amount varying with each society's incidence
of unemployment.

Approximately one-third of the cost of unemployment compensation is met by worker contributions,
and two-thirds by national government contributions.
The employer contributes nothing.

Disability Compensation

Disability benefits are financed entirely by
employer contributions which are based on payroll
and range up to a maximum of 1.2 percent. Benefits
are of two types; temporary and permanent. Temporary
benefits range from 6 to 52 kronor a day, based on
income classes and payable for ninety days. There
are supplements for children which range from 1 to
3 kronor a day based on the number of children.
Permanent disability benefits amount to eleven-
twelfths of earnings with a maximum benefit of
12,000 kronor a year. There is also a coterie of
ancillary benefits including a constant-attendant
supplement of 1,200 kronor a year and a funeral grant
of 600 kronor.

Sickness and Maternity Benefits

A compulsory health program covers all of the
population. It is financed by contributions from the
insured which are based on income. If a person makes
less than 2,400 kronor a year, he pays nothing. On
incomes above this amount, the insured pays an amount
for both cash and medical benefits which is based on
his income and the region in which he lives. The
employer contributes to the health program through
payment of a 2.6 percent tax on payrolls up to 43,500
kronor a year. The national government contributes
to the cost out of its general revenues.

There is a guarantee of income for loss of work
caused by illness. A standard sickness benefit of 6
kronor a day is payable to all insured persons. In
addition there is a supplement, which ranges from 6
to 52 kronor a day, and which varies directly with
income, payable to all persons earning more than 2,600

kronor a year. In addition, there are children's
supplements which range from 1 kronor a day for
one or two children, to 3 kronor a day for five or
more children under sixteen. A worker with two
children, hospitalized for two weeks, would normally
receive two-thirds of his income in sickness benefits.

Maternity allowances, which also range from 6
to 52 kronor a day, depending on income, are payable
for a period of 180 days; there is also a lump-sum
maternity grant of 1,080 kronor. In addition, there
is the provision of the free services of a trained
midwife before, during, and after childbirth and
free maternity care in a hospital.

The comprehensive health program covers all of
the population. It pays three-fourths of medical
fees and travel expenses, part of the cost of
medicines (vitally important medicines, such as
insulin, are free), and the total cost of hospital
treatment is free.

Swedish income-maintenance programs are designed
to provide an income floor in order to protect workers against risks that are not adequately met through
private means. An example is the provision of sickness benefits to workers. In the example below, a
worker with a wife and three children makes 2,000
kronor a month. His disposable income is computed
for a month, assuming a sickness of a month's duration, and compared with normal disposable income.

	From Normal Work	Sickness Income
Gross income	2,000	--
Sickness benefits	--	1,131
Taxes (income)	-530	--
Family allowance	225	225
Housing allowance	140	140
Disposable Income	1,835 kr.	1,496 kr.

The sickness benefit is computed at a rate of
39 kronor a day for twenty-nine days. The worker
himself would receive 37 kronor a day, which is the
sickness benefit payable on an annual income of 24,000
kronor a year. In addition, there is a supplement of
2 kronor a day for the three children. Sickness benefits are paid from the day after the worker fell ill,
hence the twenty-nine days.

Disposable income from sickness benefits and
the other transfer payments add up to 80 percent of
normal disposable income from employment. The sickness benefit is payable for as long as the illness
causes a reduction in working capacity of not less
than 50 percent. The family allowance is a continuous payment. For three children it is 2,700 kronor
a year, or 225 kronor a month. The housing allowance
is based on income, the number of children, and the
area of residence which is assumed to be Stockholm.

The Swedish system of income maintenance is far
superior to the American system, and also far more
costly. Its superiority is reflected in the provision
of free medical care for everyone, regardless of income, which has resulted in a lower infant mortality
rate and a longer life span. Old-age pensions in
Sweden afford the aged many more benefits and a
higher living standard than their counterparts in
the United States. In addition to the basic old-
age and supplementary pensions, housing and family
allowances are also available. There are pension
homes for persons who wish to do their own house-
keeping, and homes for those old people who need
permanent care. In each case, the charge is in
accordance with each person's means.

In 1967, social welfare expenditures in Sweden
amounted to 20.1 billion kronor, or 16 percent of the
gross national product. Included in this amount are
transfer payments to households under the social
security system, and expenditures on goods and services of a welfare nature. Included in the latter
category are expenditures on general health services,
old-age homes, public works, retraining of unemployed
workers, and free school meals. Table 5-6 presents
a breakdown of total welfare expenditures by major
categories, and the financing of these services by
the public and private sectors. Central administrative costs, which are minor, are not included in
the table.

It can be seen that most of social welfare expenditures in Sweden are financed by the national and
local governments out of general tax revenues. However, the apportionment of these expenditures varies
widely for the different types of social welfare
service. The cost of the family allowance is borne
entirely by the national government out of general
tax revenues. Health and hospital services are

TABLE 5-6

Total Social Welfare Expenditures in Sweden for 1967

Type of Expenditure	Amount of Expenditure	Expenditures Covered by Income from the Following Sources[a]			
		National Government	Local Governments	Employers	Insured Persons
		(T h o u s a n d s o f K r o n o r)			
Sickness	8,487,243	2,242,024	3,398,224	1,539,810	1,267,987
Industrial accidents	144,401	14,230	--	108,623	--
Unemployment measures	1,046,540	843,224	94,743	--	73,872
Old-age benefits	7,005,499	3,842,409	1,008,776	3,895,649	265,000
Families and children	3,120,575	2,279,833	840,742	--	--
General assistance	244,197	22,644	221,553	--	--
Military injuries	13,966	13,966	--	--	--
	20,062,421	9,258,330	5,564,038	5,544,082	3,170,395

[a]The contributions do not correspond with the amount of the expenditures for the reason that a surplus exists in various funds, but is not shown in the table.

Source: National Central Bureau of Statistics, "The Cost and Financing of the Social Services in Sweden in 1967" (Stockholm, 1967).

financed entirely by the national and local governments. Sickness insurance, on the other hand, is
financed almost entirely by employer and employee
contributions. Unemployment measures are financed
primarily by the national government.

About one-half of social security expenditures
are financed by the national government out of general
tax revenues. Transfer payments under the social
security system can be broken down by financing
sources. Approximately 12 billion kronor went
through the social security system as transfer payments. Of this amount 6 billion was contributed by
the central government, 3 billion by employee contributions, and 1.9 billion by employers. What this
means is that the Swedish taxpayer bears most of the
cost of social welfare directly.

Through government expenditure schemes, considerable sums of money are redistributed to taxpayers,
partly in the form of direct transfer payments, such
as family allowances and old-age pensions, and partly
through expenditures, such as free medical care and
schooling. The extent to which incomes are increased
through transfer payments and other welfare expenditures depends on a taxpayer's position on the income
ladder. Since public welfare measures are available
to all, irrespective of the level of income, and
since there is no means test for most of the direct
and indirect transfer payments, it is hard to estimate the effect of transfer payments as a supplement
to income at various income levels. However, a comparison of transfer payments and taxes for various
income groups is presented in Table 5-7.

Income inequality is reduced considerably through
government expenditures. The last column in the table
assumes that all redistributive measures are abolished,
and taxes to finance the redistribution are reduced
by the amount corresponding to the cost of redistribution. This tax reduction is assumed to be distributed
to each income group in proportion to what it paid in
taxes. An average income for each group is obtained.
The inequality between the average incomes for the
highest and lowest groups is about seventeen to one.
This inequality is reduced to seven to one after
transfer payments and other welfare expenditures.*

---

*Although the data in the table are ten years
old, it still possesses validity. Social welfare

TABLE 5-7

A Comparison of Tax Payments and Income Transfers in
Sweden by Classes for 1960

Income Group	Direct and Indirect Transfers of Income to the Group (Millions of Kronor)	Tax Payments by the Income Group	Average Income after Tax and Transfers (Kronor)	Average Income after Tax Reduction and Without Redistribution
- 4,000	2,867	425	---a	---a
4,000- 6,000	1,099	631	6,090	4,440
6,000- 8,000	761	787	6,910	6,170
8,000-10,000	774	1,083	8,100	7,890
10,000-12,000	830	1,379	9,410	9,600
12,000-15,000	1,225	2,381	11,050	11,740
15,000-20,000	1,469	3,301	13,720	15,110
20,000-30,000	1,193	3,431	17,800	20,660
30,000-50,000	453	2,044	24,060	30,890
50,000-Over	83	1,166	42,230	68,300
Total	10,754	16,628	---a	---a

aSince incomes of less than 1,200 need not usually be returned, the total income in this class is not known and the average income cannot be calculated.

Source: Swedish Taxpayers Association, "The Role of Taxation in the Redistribution of Income in Sweden" (Stockholm, 1962), p. 21.

Several other points can be made in connection
with income redistribution through government expenditures, which are as follows:

1.   Major gains in redistribution are confined
primarily to the lowest income groups. A break even
point, where taxes counterbalance gains from expenditures, is reached rather rapidly. The average gain
in the income group 8,000-10,000 kronor is 210 kronor.
More than half of the taxpayers were in the income
group 10,000-30,000 kronor. On balance, there is a
net loss to this group which was the middle-income
group. Taxes more than counterbalanced gains for
the majority of taxpayers who earned 80 percent of
total income. It is largely the average-income
groups who defray the cost of redistribution.

2.   Government expenditures tend to have an
equalizing effect on the standard of living. A
family with several children would gain through the
payment of family allowances, and depending on their
income, rental allowances. A single person would
lose through the payment of higher income taxes.

3.   Distribution of transfer payments between
income groups favors the nonactive segment of the
population over the active segment. This can be
attributed to the fact that old-age pensions constitute the largest part of the Swedish social
security system.

FULL-EMPLOYMENT POLICIES

It has been mentioned previously that there has
been a shift in favor of labor incomes and against
property incomes. This shift has been occasioned in
part by a tight labor market which has prevailed in
Sweden over the last two decades. There has also
been a movement out of agriculture in response to
the growth of better paying jobs in the urban industrial sector. This movement has been encouraged
through the provision of relocation allowances by the
Swedish government. The tight labor market has been

---

expenditures of all types have almost tripled in
Sweden since 1960. Therefore, the ratio has probably
narrowed.

responsible for not only an increase in labor's share
of national income, but a narrowing of occupational
differentials as well.

Sweden has had a very high level of employment
since the end of the Second World War. In fact, the
supply of labor has been so short that many workers
have been brought in from other countries. Unemployment has averaged less than 2 percent since the end
of the war. However, there has been a downturn in
employment during several postwar recessions which
also affected other Western European countries. It
must be pointed out that unemployment during these
recessions was moderate by prewar standards, reach-
ing a high of 4.3 percent in 1959.

It has been pointed out that the capital and
current budgets of the Swedish government exert a
major impact on the economy in terms of the level
of expenditures and the level of taxation. The
government's expenditures are a part of the economy's
total outlays on goods and services. They exert
their influence directly upon the economy by generating demand and, therefore, employment and income. If
the strength of demand for both consumption and investment in the private sector of the economy is not
great enough to generate operations at full-employment of resources, government expenditures are used
to add to the strength of total demand in the economy.
Special tax incentives are also used to stimulate
investment during a decline in economic activity.

However, the Swedish government has chosen not
only to use general measures of economic policy, but
also special measures to stimulate employment. Some
of these measures, such as expenditures on public
works projects, have been discussed in Chapter 3.
Manpower policies, which involve the upgrading of
the occupational and geographical mobility of the
labor force, also deserve mention. An aim of governmental manpower policy has been to transfer manpower
from regions and industries suffering from unemployment to those with a growing need for labor. Such
transfers can only be successful if the workers in
question have the skills necessary to secure new
employment. Consequently, job retraining courses
have become an integral part of what is called
Swedish labor market policy. The length of these
courses ranges from a few weeks up to two years.
Training is free, and tax-free allowances are made

to cover other expenses. To participate in job retraining, an applicant must be at least twenty-one
years old and be unemployed or in danger of losing
his job.

The number of participants in job retraining
courses during the fiscal year 1968-1969 was 100,000
which was around 3 percent of the labor force.
Government expenditures on job retraining amounted
to 200 million kronor. If the same program was used
in the United States, more than two million workers
would receive training at a cost of 1 billion dollars
--an amount which is more than the U. S. Department
of Labor spends on all of its manpower programs.
Training courses are offered in fourteen major occupational fields. For example, in the metal industry
field courses are offered in the following special-
ties: car electrician, car mechanics, tractor repair,
toolmakers, refrigeration mechanics, instrument repair, spray painting, welding, shipyard work, television repair, and a number of other specialized
occupations.

In Sweden, vocational training plays a paramount
role in labor market policies. Training courses are
scheduled by the Labor Market Board and administered
by the Central Board for Vocational Training. Some
courses are given by employers through agreements
with the local employment exchanges. There are
several types of training courses--beginning courses
for those entering the labor force for the first
time, advanced training for those who are already
employed, and job retraining for those who are unemployed and have no likelihood of being utilized in
their former occupation.

Sweden is the only country in the Western World
were relocation assistance is important as a device
to combat regional unemployment. Relocation assistance refers to the provision of financial assistance
to help a worker move to an area where employment is
available. It includes a payment of transportation
costs to the new area of employment, the cost of re-
moval of a worker's household goods, and a starting
allowance to support the worker until he gets his
first paycheck. In Sweden transportation costs to
seek employment are also paid for unemployed workers.
In addition, there is a special settlement allowance
which is designed to induce workers to relocate from
northern Sweden, where employment opportunities are

limited, into other areas of Sweden. In some cases,
homeowners who are induced to move are compensated
for any loss in the market value of their homes.

Swedish manpower policies are concerned with
the development and use of human labor as an economic
resource and as a source of individual and family income. It embraces the demand side of the economic
equation in the creation of jobs for specific individuals, groups, and locations. Examples are the
use of special public works projects to provide
seasonal employment, and employment programs for
the older and handicapped workers. Manpower policy
covers the supply side in the development of skills.
The emphasis placed on vocational training is an
example. Supply and demand are bridged in the
matching process through the use of relocation
assistance, and through the operation of a nation-
wide placement service. Information as to the existence of job vacancies in different parts of the
nation is broadcast daily over the radio. Advertise-
ments in the Swedish newspapers are also used to
inform the public on employment opportunities, and
bulletins are inserted periodically on television.

In Sweden, skill shortages rather than job
shortages have been a basic problem of the last two
decades. Fiscal and monetary policies have succeeded
in keeping aggregate demand at a high level during
most of this period. Manpower policies have been
aimed at increasing the mobility and skill of the
labor force. In this respect, they have inevitably
been a factor in the determination of income.

By far the largest part of the national income
takes the form of wages and salaries. Furthermore,
the percentage of wages and salaries has risen rapidly
since World War II. In 1967, wages and salaries
amounted to 73 percent of national income compared
to 66 percent in 1949. This increase can be attributable in part to a shift in employment from agriculture, forestry, and other low-paying industries,
into manufacturing and service industries. In agriculture, forestry, and fishing the number of workers
has been sharply reduced from 509,000 in 1960 to
345,000 in 1968. Shifts of workers into higher paying jobs requiring skills have been facilitated by
manpower policies, including job training and relocation allowances.

In the middle of the 1960s, the number of workers
in the Swedish labor force leveled off, and the size
of the labor force has hardly changed since then.
Only a slight increase in the labor force is forecast to 1980. This means that upward pressures on
wages will continue to exist in a tight labor market.

A COMPARISON OF INCOME
DISTRIBUTION IN SWEDEN AND
THE SOVIET UNION

It is difficult to compare income differentials
between countries for the reason that one has to take
into consideration the effects of both taxes and transfer payments. On a before-tax basis it can appear
that a considerable differential does exist between
various income groups, but income taxes can reduce
this differential considerably, and transfer payments
serve to redistribute income within groups. In comparing incomes in Sweden to incomes in the Soviet
Union, it is quite likely that after-tax differentials are considerably higher in the Soviet Union
because income taxes are far more progressive in
Sweden. After-tax comparisons ignore the fact that
transfer payments make up a considerable part of the
incomes of workers in both countries. In Sweden, an
income differential of ten to one between two families
before taxes can be reduced to six to one after taxes
(see Chapter 3 for tax rate comparisons).

A very rough comparison of income distribution
in Sweden and the Soviet Union can be obtained by
using income data in both countries for 1960. In
Sweden, based on income tax returns, assessed incomes for all practical purposes ranged from 4,000
kronor to 100,000 kronor--a differential before taxes
of 25 to 1. One-tenth of 1 percent of all taxpayers
received more than 100,000 kronor, and among those
with less than 4,000 kronor were pensioners, students,
and part-time workers. Those making above 100,000
kronor accounted for 1.6 percent of Swedish personal
income. In the Soviet Union, using a different set
of data, the range of monthly earnings in selected
occupations ranged from a high of $2,200 for persons
possessing special skills, such as opera stars, to
$30 for unskilled workers--an income differential of
seventy to one.[10] Not counted as a part of this

differential are special benefits which redound to
those who possess special skills or who occupy high
positions in the Soviet Union--estates, cars, and
apartments.

    The Soviet Union, like Sweden and the United
States, relies on income differentials to allocate
labor and to provide the incentives necessary to
stimulate productivity. These differentials, however, are limited primarily to wages, since practically all of the national income of the Soviet
Union is distributed directly or indirectly in this
form. Wages are determined by government action
rather than by the free play of market forces, and
constitute a device for distributing labor among
various occupations and industries in accordance
with planning objectives. Since property is owned
by the state, there is no income in the form of rent
which is paid to landowners. Interest does figure
in the national income to some extent, as a part of
income received by individual producers can be considered on the relatively small amounts of capital
which they own. Interest is also used as a device
to encourage personal savings, which is regarded as
necessary to put a brake on excess consumer demand,
and interest rate differentials exist in favor of
long-term savings deposits.

    From an economic point of view it is clear that
communism as it exists in the Soviet Union and other
countries, at no time has approached the theoretical
communist ideal of equality in the distribution of
income. Indeed, the Russians have found it necessary
to devise incentives not greatly dissimilar to those
used in the capitalistic countries--piece rates,
higher salaries for persons engaged in work regarded
as more useful by the government, and status symbols
such as automobiles and better housing for government
officials, factory directors, and other important
personnel. The main difference between communist
and capitalist incentives is that the government
rather than the market place decides in what areas
incentives shall be offered and higher wages granted.
The government decides which tasks are socially useful, and these vary from time to time. This system
is, in effect, one of state capitalism, for the state
is the only capitalist and uses capitalistic methods
to obtain its results.

    The Swedish and Russian social welfare systems
are similar in many respects. Medical care is free

in both systems. Higher education is free in both
countries; however, unlike the United States, the
emphasis is on quality rather than quantity, and
incompetents are kept out. Family allowances are
available in both countries, but the allowance starts
with the third child in the Soviet Union, compared
to the first child in Sweden. Sickness and maternity
benefits are paid in each country. However, unemployment compensation is not available in the Soviet
Union, although unemployment does exist.

     Basic social security in the Soviet Union is
financed from two sources--a payroll tax on employers,
which ranges from 4.4 to 9 percent of payrolls, and
by the Soviet government. The government pays the
whole cost of the family allowance. The payroll tax
is used to finance old-age pensions, sickness and
maternity benefits, and work-injury compensation.
However, the government actually covers at least 50
percent of the cost out of general tax revenues.
These revenues are obtained primarily from indirect
taxes, such as the turnover tax, which falls on the
Russian consumer.

     Not only are there wide disparities in income
in the Soviet Union, but there are also certain
privileges which redound to the advantage of various
groups--the Party elite, professional workers, such
as managers and engineers, and some highly skilled
workers. For example, special priorities are given
for housing, automobiles, and travel. These privileges extend into the field of education. It is
reported that children of upper-income families are
much more likely to receive a college education than
children of low-income families.[11] This may be attributed in part to family environment and in part
to political influence.

                   A COMPARISON OF INCOME
                REDISTRIBUTION IN SWEDEN AND
                   OTHER WESTERN COUNTRIES

     It appears that Sweden has a more egalitarian
society than other Western countries from the standpoint of income distribution. One measurement of
inequality is the distribution of personal income
before taxes. When Sweden is compared with other
Western countries, a smaller percentage of personal
income is concentrated in the hands of upper-income

earners. Erik Lundberg, in comparing before-tax dis-
tributions of personal income, found that Sweden had
a more even distribution of income than Holland,
West Germany, the United Kingdom, the United States,
and Japan.[12] The highest 2.5 percent of the income
earners received 11 percent of personal income in
Sweden compared to 27 percent in West Germany. His
explanation for the more even distribution of income
in Sweden is that wages and salaries constitute a
larger percentage of gross national product in
Sweden than in the other countries.

When taxes are taken into consideration, it is
possible to get a general idea of their effect on
income distribution in Sweden and other countries.
In 1966, total taxes, including social security contributions, accounted for 41 percent of the gross
national product in Sweden compared to 19.3 percent
in Japan. Sweden has the heaviest tax burden of all
Western countries, particularly from the standpoint
of the personal income tax. In 1966, the personal
income tax accounted for 18.3 percent of gross
national product in Sweden compared to 4.3 percent
in Japan, 4.6 percent in France, 9.7 percent in the
United States, and 10.1 percent in the United
Kingdom.[13] Denmark was second to Sweden with personal income taxes accounting for 13.7 percent of
the Danish gross national product. Generalizing
broadly, it may be said that lower tax levels reflect
a type of society that favors individual decision-
making. Higher tax levels are an expression of a
society in which the influence of the state is more
dominant.

In 1965, the top 5 percent of income earners in
Sweden received 16.7 percent of personal income before taxes. In the United Kingdom, the top 5 percent
received 19.8 percent of pretax personal income.[14]
After-tax income distribution widens the gap between
the top 5 percent in each country. In the United
Kingdom, the top 5 percent of income earners received
15.7 percent of after-tax income compared to 10.8
percent in Sweden. In each country, transfer payments are excluded. However, the redistributional
effect through transfer payments also favors the
Swedes in that they constitute a greater percentage
of household incomes in Sweden than in the United
Kingdom. In 1967, transfer payments accounted for
12.9 percent of household income in Sweden compared
to 10.1 percent in the United Kingdom.

SUMMARY

     The Swedish government has effected a redistri-
bution of income through taxation and expenditure
policies, and through the use of full-employment
measures, which include fiscal and manpower policies.
The result is the creation of an economy in which
the ratio of income inequality between the highest-
and lowest-income groups have been reduced to a
level which is certainly much lower than that which
exists in either the United States or the Soviet
Union.

     Poverty does not exist in Sweden, although
there are income earners who make well below the
median or average income. In 1965, 10 percent of
all Swedish families made less than 40 percent of
the average family income of 27,500 kronor.[15] However, this does not include transfer payments which
can and do make a substantial contribution to low-
income families. The family allowance, for example,
is free from the personal income tax, and to low-
income families with several children could add
several thousand additional kronor to family income.
There are also additional welfare benefits which also
put a floor under low-income families, and poverty in
terms of malnutrition and substandard health and
housing facilities has been eliminated through the
provision of medical care to all children.

     It is difficult to estimate the extent to which
full-employment, tax, and social welfare policies individually have affected the redistribution of income. Labor market policies, which have had as their
objective full-employment and the transfer of labor
to more productive branches of industry which offer
better pay, certainly have had some effect on income
redistribution. The enormous direct redistribution
of income through expenditure policy also has had an
income leveling effect. The gains to the majority
of the taxpayers may be more than counterbalanced by
the loss in taxation. The bulk of income taxes are
proportional, and the progressive income achieves its
redistributional effectiveness only at the high-income
levels.

     Political contributions to the process of income
redistribution by means of taxation and social welfare

measures have resulted in part in a tax burden that
is the highest of any major country in the world.
This burden may have caused a slower increase in the
rate of economic growth for the country, although it
would be difficult to prove. Highly progressive income taxation and the high tax pressure resulting
from expenditure policies are bound to have some sort
of restraining effect on the total investment of
labor and capital in the country. The inducement
to work longer hours or to invest money in venture-
some enterprises can be affected by income taxation.
However, it is impossible to measure this effect in
terms of lower production.

A positive factor with respect to the redistribution of income may well be the creation of a more
democratic society. Political power, based on vast
accumulations of income and wealth, would be difficult to attain in Sweden. The glaring inequality
in incomes and wealth and the special privileges
accorded the wealthy in the United States would be
socially unacceptable in Sweden.

The contrast in income redistribution in Sweden
and the Soviet Union is rather pronounced. In line
with Soviet antiequalitarian policy, personal income
taxes are among the lowest in the world. The Soviet
government derives most of its revenue from sales
taxes and other indirect levies that proportionately
hit the lowest-income groups hardest. In concentrat-
ing on sales taxes, the Russians have penalized consumption over the years to further production. The
Swedish national and local government derives the
bulk of its revenues from income taxation. Although
both countries have extensive social welfare programs,
transfer payments do not achieve as much effect on
income redistribution in the Soviet Union as is the
case in Sweden. Moreover, income inequality in the
Soviet Union is compounded by special prerogatives
which are accorded to the Party officials and the
scientific and technical personnel.

NOTES

1. Organization for Economic Cooperation and
Development, "National Accounts of OECD Countries,

1957-1966" (Brussels, 1967), p. 249; and Statistiska Centralbyran, "Statistisk Årsbok, 1968" (Stockholm, 1968), p. 360.

2.   Statistiska Centralbyran, "Skattetaxeringarna Samt Fördelningen Av Inkomst Och Förmögenhet Taxeringsaret, 1967" (Stockholm, 1968), p. 44.

3.   Sekretariat for Economic Planning of the Ministry of Finance and the National Institute of Economic Research, "Preliminary National Budget, 1969" (Stockholm, 1969), p. 101.

4.   Swedish Taxpayers Association, "The Role of Taxation in the Redistribution of Income in Sweden" (Stockholm, 1962), p. 6.

5.   Ministry of Finance, Skattetabell för Beräkning av Preliminär A-Skatt för Ar 1969, Tabell (Stockholm, 1969).

6.   For an analysis of the use of the family allowance in various countries, see Martin Schnitzer, "Guaranteed Minimum Income Programs Used by Governments of Selected Countries," Joint Economic Committee, 90th Cong., 2nd sess. (Washington, D.C.: Government Printing Office, 1968).

7.   Statens Offentliga Utretningar, "Barnbidrag Och Familjetillagg," Familjepolitiska Kommitten (Stockholm, 1967), p. 72.

8.   Ibid., p. 36.

9.   Ibid., p. 153.

10.   The Swedish income data derived from the 1960 Income Statistics of the Central Bureau of Statistics; the Russian income data from: Edmund Nash, "Purchasing Power of Workers in the U.S.S.R.," U.S. Department of Labor, Monthly Labor Review, Bureau of Labor Statistics (April, 1960), p. 362.

11.   Jeremy Azrael, "Bringing up the Soviet Man: Dilemmas and Progress," Problems of Communism (May-June, 1968), pp. 23-29.

12.   Erik Lundberg, "Sweden's Economy in an International Perspective," Skandinaviska Banken Quarterly Review (First Quarter, 1968), p. 4.

13.   First National City Bank of New York, "Monthly Economic Letter," (April, 1968), p. 43.

14.   The information for the United Kingdom was obtained from Central Statistical Office, "National Income and Expenditure, 1967," p. 33; and for Sweden from Statistiska Centralbyran, "Skattetaxeringarna Samt Fördelningen Av Inkomst Och Förmögenhet Taxeringsaret, 1966," (Stockholm, 1967), p. 11.

15.   Schnitzer, op. cit., p. 59.

CHAPTER **6** MONEY AND
CREDIT

INTRODUCTION

In a capitalistic market system, a great part
of the credit in use is extended by commercial banks,
although some is put out by other institutions or
directly between business enterprises. The commercial banks are usually privately owned and operate
for profit, though they are often subject to a large
amount of governmental interference and control.
Although the government does not usually own and
operate commercial banks, it is likely to operate
institutions for the purposes of central banking, of
which purposes one is the supervision and control of
the privately owned and operated commercial banks.
The government also may own and operate certain
types of credit institutions which private interests
either do not furnish at all or provide in insuffi-
cient quantities.

From a social point of view, the proper role of
credit in a market economy is a neutral one. Commercial credit is a useful instrument for facilitating
making and carrying out economic decisions which
would be in the interest of society. But commercial
credit should not be allowed to affect the content
and volume of these decisions. That is, commercial
credit should not be issued in such amounts or in
such ways as will cause prices to rise, profits to
increase, production to expand, and the overextension
of productive facilities to take place, so that a
boom period leading possibly to a recession is created.
In a similar fashion, contracting commercial credit
should not be a leading factor for contracting business.

While the total volume of credit is at least
partly under government control, even in the United
States, the distribution of commercial credit among
the business and industrial enterprises usually is
independent of such control. The commercial bankers
perform the function of distributing credit among
enterprises and industries on the basis of prospective profit and not according to some plan that is
supposed to take national needs into account. Under
ideal conditions, of course, the firms which could
bid most effectively for commercial credit would be
those whose products were most needed from a social
point of view. In actual practice, however, many
firms may be good credit risks because of the ready
sales of their products, even though the products are
far from being indispensable to social welfare.

Interest serves to allocate resources in a
capitalistic economy. The rate of interest selects
the most efficient processes and rejects the less
efficient. When quantities of capital funds are
available for investment, the question as to whether
they should be used to provide capital goods for
automobile production, or facilities for the production of shoes usually will be decided on the basis
of the amounts of interest that firms in these various fields of production are willing and able to pay
for the use of the funds. No producer in a free-
enterprise system will rationally and knowingly invest in capitalistic methods of production that do
not offer marginal rates of return greater than or
equal to the interest rate. Under state socialism,
there may be no explicit interest rate, but it is
just as important, albeit perhaps more difficult,
that the most efficient equipment and methods be
adopted first.

In countries with mixed economic systems, government control over the institutions of money and credit
is considerable. In pursuit of specific economic
policy objectives, governments have deliberately
intervened in economic affairs to further their aims.
Money and credit are particularly important areas,
for they provide the nexus through which transactions
are carried on. The instruments of money and credit
provide, in a number of ways, a contrast to those of
public finance. The budget, in most countries, is a
single once-a-year operation, and measures governments take are clear. However, the picture of money
and credit policy is much more confused. The

institutional arrangements vary from country to
country, and so do the monetary systems. Control
is normally divided between central banks and central
governments. The latter can divert the flow of
credit from areas which it would normally seek on
the basis of prospective areas, into areas which
they consider to be socially necessary or useful.
This is often done through the creation of special
purpose lending institutions which are supported by
funds from the state budget or from social security
contributions. Governments have also attempted to
sublimate monetary policy to national economic and
social objectives.

Monetary policy refers to central bank actions
to lessen fluctuations in consumer and investment
spending through the regulation and use of the supply
of money. It produces its effect upon the performance of an economy indirectly, by influencing the
level and composition of effective demand for goods
and services and the interest rate charged in the
financial markets. Its influence on aggregate demand
and the interest rate is indirect, being primarily
upon the stock of money held by households, business
firms, and nonfinancial institutions. Changes in
the degree of restraint or ease in monetary policy
have an effect on the total flow of expenditures,
and, in turn, on output, employment, and prices.
Monetary restraint reduces the availability of credit
and increases its interest cost, thus retarding the
flow of expenditures, output, employment, and income.
Monetary ease makes credit more available and reduces
its cost, and thus encourages an expansion in these
flows.

Although monetary policy instruments differ in
some degree from country to country, in general they
are of three basic types--open-market operations,
changes in reserve requirements, and rediscounting.
Open-market operations involve central bank purchases
and sales of primarily government securities from
commercial banks and other financial institutions.
Reserve requirements refer to the percentage of
deposits which banks must have on reserve in the
central bank. Rediscounting refers to the rate
which a central bank charges commercial banks for
borrowing on various types of credit instruments.
In addition, central banks also rely upon moral
suasion to encourage commercial banks to be more or
less lenient in the granting of loans. Its

effectiveness depends upon the extent to which
central banks can follow up their policy recommendations with threats of punitive action for noncom-
pliance.

Control over conditions governing the quantity
of money is inevitable in a modern industrial society.
This control has been vested in central banks. In
the United States, the Federal Reserve is responsible
for the implementation of monetary policy. In the
European countries--France, Sweden, and others--as
well as Japan, the central banks are responsible.
The central banks, however, are government-operated
and controlled, whereas the Federal Reserve Banks
are owned by member banks of the Federal Reserve
System. However, government ownership does not
necessarily mean government control. There are a
number of instances where the central bank, once
created and given its frame of reference, is left
to go its own way. This is also true of other
government financial institutions. In France, for
example, the public authorities exercise a tighter
control over the private credit banks than over the
state-owned institutions engaged in medium and long-
term credit.

In countries with mixed economic systems, credit
institutions such as commercial banks can be both
privately and publically owned. Commercial banks are
privately owned in Japan, West Germany, and Sweden.
In France, the largest commercial banks, such as the
Credit Lyonnais, are owned by the government. The
French government also owns all, or a controlling
part, of institutions operating in the field of
medium and long-term credit. It has used this ownership to direct their borrowing and lending policies
toward the attainment of economic and social objectives.

Governments in France, Sweden, and other
countries with mixed systems are a large accumulator
and investor of funds, and they exercise a great deal
of control over both external and internal capital
transactions. Thus, the impact of market forces on
the allocation of funds is affected by governmental
intervention in the field of credit. In Sweden,
capital markets have been to some extent segmented
by preferential treatment given to certain sectors
of the economy, particularly housing. The Swedish
government has consistently encouraged investment in

housing, and has channeled capital into this area. The government also controls all but certain specified new capital issues in an attempt to maintain low, long-term interest rates for priority borrowers. The provision of low-cost funds for residential construction is a major determinant of central bank monetary policy, and access to long-term funds is determined by control over capital issues rather than by free movements of interest rates in the market.

There are a number of types of financial institutions in European countries. In Germany, savings banks are owned by the German municipalities and are used to provide a source of capital for local needs. In Sweden, savings banks are privately owned. Specific purpose banks are quite important in the field of intermediate and long-term credit. In Germany, they serve to channel funds from the social security system and budgetary surpluses into areas of the economy that are in need of development. In France, there are a number of public and semipublic institutions, such as the Credit Foncier, which are supposed to grant long-term loans on mortgage to property owners, agricultural credit societies, and local authorities.

The point has been made that in the all-important field of credit governments participate in the market economies of such countries as France and Sweden to a considerable degree. This means that they can divert funds into areas which they wish to promote. Normal market forces are not allowed to operate freely. Funds are diverted from the national budgets, or from social security funds, into the capital market to be used for special purposes, such as to promote industrial development in depressed areas. In Sweden, the National Pension Fund, with its resources provided from the supplementary old-age pension fund, has grown to the point where it provides almost one-fifth of all the funds in the Swedish capital market. In fact, its resources are growing at such a rapid rate that it already is the largest supplier of capital in the capital market, although it has only been in existence since 1959. There is also the Investment Bank, which is supported by revenues from the budget. In each case, taxes divert resources from the private sector into the capital market.

STRUCTURE OF THE
SWEDISH CREDIT SYSTEM

The Swedish credit system is rather complex and diverse. At its apex is the National Bank of Sweden (Sveriges Riksbank). Essentially a bankers' bank, the National Bank is able to make use, in performing its function of regulating the supply and cost of money, of all the instruments of central bank policy; that is, changes in the rediscount rate, open-market operations, and changes in liquidity ratios. It also makes recommendations to the banks, especially with regard to qualitative credit control and the observance of credit ceilings.

There are sixteen commercial banks, the two largest, Svenska Handelsbanken and Skandinaviska Banken, accounting for over one-half of the total assets of the whole group. The commercial banks are subject to government control and regulations regarding the size of savings deposits, liquidity ratios, and the kind of assets in which their resources can or cannot be invested. In principle, they grant only short-term loans, secured by some kind of collateral. A typical feature is the predominance of savings and time deposits over demand deposits. The main forms of lending are: discounting bills, granting advances on current account and in the form of overdrafts, and granting fixed loans.

The national government is a large accumulator and investor of funds and it exercises a good deal of control over both internal and external capital transactions. Thus the impact of market forces on the allocation of funds is limited to a certain degree. The capital market has to some extent been segmented by the preferential treatment accorded to the housing sector. The government has consistently encouraged investment in housing and has channeled capital into this area both through mortgage institutions and banks. In recent years, about one-fifth of total housing construction has been financed out of the budget, and undoubtedly these housing preferences and subsidies have limited the availability of funds to other sectors of the economy and affected the terms on which funds could be obtained. The provision of low-cost funds for residential construction has had an influence on central bank policies.

Housing credits are favored in the open market since
the central bank gives priority to the floating of
bonds for this purpose.

Apart from the role played in the credit market
by the Swedish government through the central bank,
there are certain credit institutions which are
owned or controlled by the public authorities. A
government-owned commercial bank accounts for 12
percent of the total assets of commercial banks.
The National Pension Fund utilizes social security
funds to provide long-term capital. It has authority to invest in bonds and other debt securities.
In 1967, a new public credit institution, The Investment Bank of Sweden (Sveriges Investeringsbank AB),
was created for the purpose of financing investment
projects within industry and trade that will promote
employment and regional development.

Sweden also has a great many specialized credit
institutions, which are mainly concerned with mortgage lending. There are, for example, the city
mortgage societies, the residential credit societies,
and the general mortgage societies, all of which have
their own central institutions for the raising of
funds. The agricultural credit associations, which
grant long-term credit to agriculture, also obtain
their funds from a central organization, the Agricultural Credit Bank. Medium- and long-term credit
on ships is supplied by the Ship Mortgage Association
and the Svensk Fartygskredit. Private insurance companies also are a source of mortgage funds.

Savings banks are also a part of the Swedish
credit system. They were authorized to accept only
savings deposits, but since the beginning of 1956
they have also been legally authorized to open current
accounts, subject to certain regulations. Their investments consist mainly of mortgage loans, ordinary
advances, and bonds. Savings are also collected by
the Post Office Savings Bank and by various cooperative credit institutions.

Private insurance companies are another source
of funds in the Swedish capital market. They are of
particular importance in providing a market for housing bonds. Insurance companies also serve as a market
for municipal bonds.

The Central Bank

The Bank of Sweden (Sveriges Riksbank) is the
oldest central bank in the world. It was organized
in 1668 as a state-owned bank responsible to the
Swedish Parliament, after the failure in that year
of a predecessor institution, the Bank of Stockholm,
chartered as early as 1656 and considered to be the
first bank to issue ordinary bank notes. It is noteworthy that the Bank of Stockholm, although a private
institution, was for many practical purposes regarded
as a state institution; and from its beginnings, important questions pertaining to the bank were referred to the Swedish Parliament. The tradition
that the central banking institution is responsible
to the national legislature--a tradition which has
been embodied in a formal provision of the Swedish
constitution--is thus of very long standing.

The Bank of Sweden acquired the attributes of
a modern central bank only very gradually in the
nineteenth century. It was for a long period of
time a state commercial bank and the leading credit
institution in the country. In 1897, the Bank of
Sweden was given the note issue monopoly, and the
right of private commercial banks to issue notes
expired at the end of 1903. Operations of the Bank
of Sweden were restricted almost entirely to those
of a central banking character by the 1897 legislation, so that its transformation into a central bank
in the modern sense was completed by the end of the
century.

Legally responsible to the Swedish Parliament,
the Bank of Sweden operates under legislation which
expressly prohibits its directors from receiving in-
structions from anyone except the Parliament and its
banking committee. It is administered by a board of
directors consisting of seven members, of whom the
chairman is an appointee named by the king-in-council;
the other six directors are chosen by a joint group
of electors from both houses of the Swedish Parliament.
The chief executive officers of the bank--the governor
and deputy governor--are elected by the board of directors from among its members.

The operational independence of the Bank of
Sweden was seriously impaired during the 1930s, when
the ruling Social Democrats subordinated monetary
policy, then in disrepute, to the general economic

policy of the government. The subordination of
monetary policy continued into much of the postwar
period--as it did in many European countries, although
this phase was perhaps somewhat more prolonged in
Sweden than elsewhere. For a fairly extended period
the Bank of Sweden played an essentially passive role.
Until 1955, the bank pegged the government bond
market in order to permit flotation of the large
volume of bond issues necessary to finance budget
deficits and the housing program as the government
pursued a cheap money policy as an integral part of
its full-employment and social welfare programs.
However, monetary policy began to play a more active
role when the Bank of Sweden obtained authority to
impose effective minimum liquidity ratios on the
commercial banks.

The functions of the Bank of Sweden are as
follows:

1. It regulates the supply of money and the
level of interest rates on the credit market, for
which purposes it exercises the regular powers of
monetary policy.

2. It holds the country's main gold and foreign exchange reserves and is responsible for the
fixing of official exchange rates.

3. It conducts lending operations on a limited
scale--such lending being concerned primarily with
loans to state-owned corporations and certain small
loans out of special funds appropriated for social
purposes.

Monetary Policy

Monetary policy works primarily through controls exercised over the supply of money. In an
advanced economy this basically means control over
the volume of bank lending. In Sweden, the Bank of
Sweden is the chief agency through which such control
is exercised. The objective in controlling the money
supply, including bank lending, is to indirectly control spending. More specifically, control over the
money supply will be reflected in interest rate
changes, which, in turn, will have an impact on
spending. The brunt of this impact will be borne
by investment expenditures, as neither the consumption nor the government expenditures component of

aggregate demand is readily linked to the rate of
interest. Thus, the effectiveness of monetary policy
as an instrument of economic stabilization depends to
a major degree on the reaction of investment decisions to changes in the interest rate.

Monetary policy is exercised by the Bank of
Sweden in several ways which are as follows:

1. Through the use of liquidity ratios, which
are established for commercial banks and other lending institutions. Liquidity ratios are in some respects similar to legal reserve requirements of
United States commercial banks. Swedish commercial
banks' holdings of liquid assets, that is, mainly
cash and short-term government securities, are fixed
at a certain percentage of total deposits, excluding
savings accounts. These liquidity ratios are differentiated according to the size of the banks. For
example, for the largest banks they have been set
at 33 percent of deposits, and for the smallest banks,
15 percent. These ratios, of course, are varied from
time to time in accordance with monetary policy objectives. A decrease in a bank's liquidity ratio
reduces its capacity to lend, and an increase in
its liquidity ratio increases its capacity to lend.

2. Through discount rate adjustments, which
either increase or decrease the cost of borrowing on
the part of commercial banks from the Bank of Sweden.
In February, 1969, the official discount rate in Sweden was increased from 5 to 6 percent, and in July to
7 percent. Consequently, all of the rates in the Swedish credit market went up. The main reason for raising the discount rate was to reduce the outflow of
foreign exchange. During the first three quarters of
1969, Sweden's total gold and foreign exchange holdings
declined by 2 billion kronor.

3. Through open-market operations, which have an
impact on liquidity ratios of commercial banks. Open-
market operations involve the purchase or sale of
government securities in the money market.

Monetary policy was subverted during the period
following the Second World War to the general economic
policy of the Swedish government, which was the attainment of a high level of employment. Unitl the
latter part of the 1950s, monetary policy was passive.
The Bank of Sweden had to pursue a cheap money policy

in accordance with the full-employment and social
welfare policies of the government. Until 1955, the
bank pegged the government bond market in order to
permit the flotation of the large number of bond
issues necessary to finance budget deficits and the
housing program. The bank also exercised control
over capital issues, under which applications to
float long-term securities were screened to assure
that loans for priority sectors, such as the national
government and the housing market, received preferential treatment.

However, monetary policy in recent years has
been given freer reign by the Swedish government.
Sweden has an export-oriented economy, and rising
domestic prices have affected the international com-
petitiveness of Swedish industry. During the 1960s,
the discount rate was varied on a number of occasions. The Bank of Sweden has used penalty
rates to discourage borrowing on the part of commercial banks. In 1964, the bank introduced a penalty
rate of 9 percent on loans from it to any commercial
bank that exceeded 25 percent of the bank's own capital and reserves. In 1966, the penalty rate was
raised to 12 percent. In August, 1969, the bank, in
adopting a restrictive leading policy, stipulated
that commercial banks must deposit with it in a non-
interest-bearing account funds which correspond to
1 percent of their total credit obligations.

Commercial Banks

As previously mentioned, there are sixteen commercial banks in Sweden, of which fifteen are privately owned, and one, Sveriges Kreditbank, is
government owned. The four largest privately owned
commercial banks--the Svenska Handelsbanken, the
Skandinaviska Banken, the Stockholm Enskilda Bank,
and the Göteborgs Bank--account for 70 percent of
all commercial banking in Sweden. The largest bank,
the Svenska Handelsbanken, accounts for approximately
one-third of all commercial banking. These banks
operate throughout Sweden as well as internationally.
The Sveriges Kreditbank, which was created as a result of a bank reorganization in 1951, accounts for
about 6 percent of the commercial banking business.

Table 6-1 presents the assets of the sixteen
commercial banks as of April, 1969.

TABLE 6-1

Assets of the Sixteen
Commercial Banks in Sweden

Bank	Assets (Billions of Kronor)
Wermlands Enskilda Bank	1,308,276
Östergötlands Enskilda Bank	988,231
Smalands Bank	769,232
Göteborgs Bank	4,652,238
Stockholms Enskilda Bank	4,777,466
Skandinaviska Banken	13,970,686
Sundsvallsbanken	1,633,732
Skaraborgs Enskilda Bank	890,774
Uplandsbanken	1,118,832
Svenska Handelsbanken	16,519,376
Jämtlands Folkbank	189,731
Skanska Banken	1,487,693
Sveriges Kreditbank	6,709,932
Aktiebolaget Bohusbanken	107,553
Sparbankernas Bank	1,648,593
Jordbrukets Bank	433,135

Source: "Bankerna 1969," Kungl Bankinspektionen
(Stockholm, 1969), pp. 6-9.

The functions of the Swedish commercial banks
are as follows:

1.   They engage in the long-term financing of
industry.

2.   They act as underwriters for bond issues and
hold large portfolios of bonds and housing mortgages.

3.   They maintain stock exchange departments,
which act as brokers on the Stockholm Stock Exchange.*

4.   They receive savings and time deposits.**

---

*Around 90 percent of all transactions on the
Stockholm Stock Exchange are handled by the stock
exchange departments of commercial banks.

**A preponderence of time and savings deposits
characterizes the structure of Swedish commercial
banks.   Sight and demand deposits account for approximately 85 percent of all deposits.

5. They are responsible for foreign trade trans-
actions--a very important responsibility since foreign trade is a vital factor in Sweden's economy,
and fluctuations in it are quickly reflected in the
country's general level of prosperity.

All of the commercial banks in Sweden are joint-
stock companies operating under a government charter,
which has to be renewed every ten years. Amalgama-
tions with other banks and the opening of branch
offices in localities where banks do not operate are
subject to government approval. Regulations prescribe, among other things, certain standards in
regard to liquidity and minimum capital requirements,
and also state what kind of assets banks may hold.
Bank regulations generally require that loans must
be covered by specific security, either in the form
of collateral, such as mortgages or stock, or a
guarantee by a person other than the borrower. However, security provisions have been liberalized in
recent years.

The Swedish commercial banks may be described
as deposit banks in the sense that their activities
are principally based on deposits received from the
public. Deposits are received by the Swedish banks
on five different accounts--checking accounts, short-
term deposit accounts, long-term deposit accounts,
capital accumulation accounts, and savings accounts.
The difference between time and savings deposits is
that on time deposit accounts unlimited amounts are
accepted, whereas holdings in savings accounts are
restricted by law to a maximum of 15,000 kronor per
account. A preponderence of time and savings deposits is typical of the structure of deposits of
Swedish commercial banks. In April, 1969, these
accounts together amounted to around 75 percent of
the total deposits of commercial banks.

Traditionally, Swedish commercial banks are
concerned mainly with satisfying the needs of commerce and industry for short-term credit, and the
largest part of the banks' outstanding credits do go
to commerce and industry. The predominant form of
lending is the loan against a promissory note,
mainly on security in real estate. Other forms of
lending are discounting of bills, check accounts
with credit, and building credits. Discounting of
bills plays an important role in certain commercial
areas. It is important in the seasonal financing

of agriculture, and in the financing of automobile
sales from retailers to customers. As a rule the
commercial banks are not allowed by law to grant
loans without some form of guarantee in the form of
tangible or personal security. However, the banks
are able in certain circumstances to grant loans
without security. Such credit may be granted to
small employers and to private individuals. However, this credit is limited to specific amounts
depending on the type of borrower. A bank may not
extend unsecured credit to a greater total amount
than the equivalent of one-tenth of its own funds.

Savings Banks

Private savings banks also play a significant
role in Swedish banking. They are usually small in
size and differ from the commercial banks in that
they are nonprofit institutions with no shareholders.
Although the savings banks are private in ownership,
they are subject to government control since at least
half of their governing bodies must be appointed by
local government authorities.

Savings banks collect small or medium-sized
savings. They are limited by law to the restriction
of these savings to an amount not to exceed 100,000
kronor. This factor has limited the competition with
commercial banks over business funds, though competition is keen between both types of banks over personal
savings. The funds of savings banks are invested in
mortgage loans, loans to small business firms, loans
to local governments, personal consumer loans, and
government bonds. Swedish savings banks are of particular importance in the urban real estate market.
Most funds are invested either in mortgage loans or
bond holdings.

The basic principle governing the granting of
credit by the savings banks is that their funds should
be invested as securely as possible. Behind this
principle lies the fact that the savings banks possess
no share capital which could bear the brunt in the
event of a loss. This is the reason that much of
their funds consist of mortgage loans on urban and
agricultural properties. Although, in principle,
loans are supposed to be short term in character,
this rule is not strictly enforced. To a certain extent, the savings banks are allowed to grant fixed-
term mortgage loans up to a period of ten years.

Cooperation among the savings banks is highly
developed. A result of this cooperation was the
creation in 1942 of the Sparbankernas Bank, which
acts as a central bank for the savings banking system.
Legally, it is a commercial bank subject to the provisions of the Bank Act, and is included in the commercial banking sector. Funds which the savings
banks are at least temporarily unable to invest in
loans or securities, or which they wish to keep
readily accessible, are deposited with Sparbankernas.
This bank had assets in April, 1969, of 1.6 billion
kronor, which made it the sixth largest commercial
bank in Sweden. Most of its assets take the form
of loans and building credit accounts. The bank
also assists savings banks in the buying and selling
of bonds.

Savings banks play a rather important role in
the credit structure of the Swedish economy. In
1968, total deposits of the savings banks amounted
to 28.3 billion kronor compared to total deposits
of 41.2 billion kronor for commercial banks.[1] Advances to the public amounted to 26 billion kronor
for savings banks compared to 34 billion kronor for
the commercial banks. Deposits in savings banks
have increased from 7.4 billion kronor in 1950 to
28.3 billion kronor in 1968.[2]

The Post Office Savings Bank (Postsparbanken),
which together with the Postgiro (postal check
service) constitutes the Post Office Bank, is
a publicly owned institution which also provides an
outlet for savings. The Post Office Savings Bank
was formed in 1884. Its primary advantage from the
standpoint of savings lies in the fact that through
the very widespread network of post offices, it af-
fords facilities for depositing and withdrawing
money over a much wider area of the country than
either the commercial banks or the private savings
banks. Another point of some importance is that
the post offices generally have more extended business hours than the commercial and savings banks.
Interest rates on deposits are competitive with
those paid by the private banks, and there is a
maximum amount accepted for deposits of 100,000
kronor per account.

The Post Office Savings Bank is particularly
important in the field of housing loans. Early
emphasis in the investment of the bank's funds was

on the purchase of bonds from local governments.
However, during recent years, it has been very active in the market for housing loans and has granted
building credits of considerable amounts. Housing
loans in 1968 accounted for more than half of the
investments of the bank. Its deposits, however,
relative to those of commercial and savings banks
are small, accounting for around 10 percent of
total deposits in Swedish financial institutions.

The Postgiro is not a credit institution in the
strict sense of the word. It performs a checking
service to its members. No interest is payable on
holdings in the Postgiro, which amount to a considerable sum. For the last few years, however, it
has been possible to transfer balances of 50,000
kronor or more to an interest-bearing account, the
interest being calculated on the same rising scale
as for the deposit-transfer accounts of the commercial banks.

Savings deposits are accepted by the consumer
cooperative, Kooperativa Förbundet, though only from
its members. These funds are used entirely in the
financing of the cooperative's business operations.
Agricultural credit associations also accept savings
deposits. These associations are of a cooperative
nature and attempt to satisfy the needs of their
members for agricultural credit. There are twelve
central associations which are affiliated with a
national organization. To these associations are
attached 513 local branches to which farmers as
well as other organizations belong. The deposit
business is run by the central associations, while
lending is undertaken by the local branches.

Table 6-2 presents the deposits of commercial
and savings banks as of January, 1969. Included is
the Postgiro, which technically is not a savings
institution.

Specialized Credit Institutions

Apart from the commercial and the savings banks,
both of which conduct a number of activities, there
are a number of credit institutions in Sweden of a
more specialized type which engage in some particular
kind of lending or serve some particular segment of
the economy. These institutions are mainly concerned

with mortgage lending. Some are privately owned,
others are publically owned. There are special mortgage banks for agriculture, home building, and shipbuilding. An example of a mortgage bank is the Ship
Mortgage Bank. Its purpose is to grant long-term
loans on the security of ship mortgages. It is a
semiofficial institution in that its chairman is
appointed by the Swedish government, and its funds
for loans are obtained from the sale of bonds in
the open market.

TABLE 6-2

Deposits of Commercial and
Savings Banks in Sweden

Institutions	Deposits (Millions of Kronor)
Commercial banks	41,235
Savings banks	28,258
The Post Office Savings Bank	7,873
The Postgiro	4,405
Agricultural credit associations	3,733
Total Deposits	85,504

Source: Stockholms Enskilda Bank, Annual
Report for 1969 (Stockholm, 1969), p. 2.

Although a considerable proportion of the total
mortgage loans in Sweden are supplied by commercial
banks and savings banks, mortgage associations also
play a prominent role. These are of three kinds:
rural mortgage associations, urban mortgage associations, and housing credit associations. The rural
mortgage associations have the exclusive function of
granting fixed mortgage loans to agriculture, with
an upper limit placed at 60 percent of the assessed
value of agricultural property. The funds for these
lending activities are raised by a central institution, Sveriges Allmänna Hypoteksbank, through bond
issues on the open market. The urban mortgage associations give loans against first mortgages on urban
real estate. Their central institution is the
Konungariket Sveriges Stadshypotekskassa. The housing credit associations give loans against second
mortgages on urban real estate. These three systems

are organized on a similar plan in that they constitute sort of a cooperative undertaking. Borrowers are members of the associations. Each central
institution of the associations is supplied with
guarantee capital by the Swedish government. Moreover, the respective chairmen of the institutions
are appointed by the government.

    The Industrial Credit Bank (AB Industrikredit)
is an institution which was formed jointly by the
government and a few major commercial banks in 1934.
Its purpose is to provide medium- and long-term
loans to industrial firms, with priority given to
firms that are too small to have ready access to
the bond market. The loans of this institution have
never reached considerable proportions in the mortgage market. In 1967, loans of the Industrial Credit
Bank amounted to 773 million kronor out of total
mortgage loans of 31 billion kronor.[3]

    In addition to the various credit institutions
mentioned above, there are also state lending institutions, which have developed very strongly in
recent decades. Two of these institutions, the
National Pension Fund and the Investment Bank, are
important enough to merit separate treatment. Government credit institutions are of particular importance
in the agricultural and housing fields. Government
loans in support of agriculture take the form of
subsidies and guarantees to the various credit institutions which serve the normal credit needs of
agriculture. In the housing field a government
authority, the Svenska Bostadskreditkassen, supplies
credit as a part of a government program in support
of housing. This credit is provided beyond the limits
set by the regular credit institutions. For example,
regular credit institutions may provide credit up to
75 percent of the value of a house, and the Bostad-
kreditkassen, the remainder.

    Private insurance companies are a source of
capital funds in Sweden. Although their contribution
to the capital market has been passed by the public
insurance fund--the National Pension Fund--they are
still important. In 1967, the private insurance
companies administered assets with a combined value
of 24.8 billion kronor, an amount nearly corresponding to the value of deposits in the savings banks.[4]
The capital administered is invested mainly in gilt-
edged securities and in mortgages on real estate

up to two-thirds of the ratable value. Under existing legislation not more than one-tenth of that part
of the funds which relate to life insurance may be
invested in other than such assets. In 1967, mortgage loans constituted 30 percent of the investments
of the insurance companies, and investments in bonds
amounted to 43 percent.[5] Most bonds outstanding are
issued by the government and the housing sector.
The insurance companies provide a major market for
these bonds. Loans to local authorities constitute
around 8 percent of total insurance investments.

The National Pension Fund

In 1959, the Swedish Parliament established a
compulsory retirement system that was designed for
the purpose of supplementing the existing old-age
pension scheme. This system provides benefits that
are financed by the payment of pension contributions
by Swedish employers, which are calculated as a percentage of income for each employee. These contributions are paid by employers into a special fund,
which is the National Pension Fund. The fund is the
largest lender in the Swedish credit market. Its
assets at the end of 1968 amounted to 28 billion kronor. Although the fund is not administered directly
by the Swedish government, it is under its supervision. Since pension payments are still small relative
to the accumulation of funds, the assets of the fund
are expected to increase to 65 billion kronor by the
end of 1974. What this means is that there is a
diversion of income from the private to the public
sector. The Swedish government, through the National
Pension Fund, is in a position to divert the flow of
capital into areas which it wishes to promote.

The fund accounted for over one-third of the
supply of resources in the organized credit market
in 1968, and at times has subscribed to three-fourths
of the bonds issued in the bond market. The original
purpose for the creation of the fund was to counterbalance a decline in private savings. When the distribution of savings is examined for the private and
public sectors during the period 1960-1968, the National Pension Fund has increased its share of total
savings at the expense of the private sector. However, the savings of households and insurance companies
have also continued to increase during this period,
despite the fear of a decline as a result of the

creation of the fund. On the other hand, savings in
the corporate sector have declined.

Investments of the National Pension Fund are
allocated to four principal types of borrowers--the
business sector, the national government, local
authorities, and the housing sector. Loans to the
national government and to local authorities are
approximately equivalent to the contributions paid
by these sectors. However, the business sector,
which has paid in more than 70 percent of the total
contributions to the fund, has been granted loans
amounting to around 30 percent of the fund's assets.
Loans to the housing sector have accounted for around
40 percent of the total loans of the fund.

Table 6-3 presents the investments of the National
Pension Fund by types of borrowers for 1967.

TABLE 6-3

Investments of the
National Pension Fund
by Type of Borrower

Borrower	Account (Millions of Kronor)
National government	1,455.1
Housing credits	8,560.4
Communes	2,426.8
Industrial companies	4,915.7
Agriculture	582.4
Loans to premium payers	1,153.1
Foreign obligations	120.5
Deposits at banks	63.7
Total	19,277.7

Source: Statistiska Centralbyran, Statistisk
Årsbok, 1968 (Stockholm, 1969).

In 1968, the National Pension Fund accounted
for 19 percent of institutional savings in Sweden;
in 1960, the amount was 2 percent. This gain was
primarily at the expense of savings banks and life
insurance companies. In 1968, the breakdown of savings by institutions was as follows: commercial

banks, 31 percent; savings banks, 22 percent; National Pension Fund, 19 percent; life insurance companies, 14 percent; Post Office Bank, 7 percent;
agricultural credit associations, 3 percent; and
postal cheque accounts, 3 percent.[6]

At the end of 1968, 75 percent of the assets
of the National Pension Fund was invested in bonds,
4 percent in debentures, 8 percent in local authority
loans, and 13 percent in other types of credit.
Three-fifths of the fund's lending to business firms
has been through the purchase of industrial bonds
and debentures. The remainder has been in loans
through mortgage companies and premium payers. So
far the fund is not permitted to acquire shares in
Swedish corporations. This may be modified in the
future as the external financing requirements of
the business sector are expected to increase. There
is also the necessity on the part of the fund to
find new outlets for investment, as its resources
will continue to grow rapidly. This means that its
investment policies will continue to have a strong
impact on the credit market and on credit policy in
general.

The Swedish government does not have direct control over the National Pension Fund. Although the
fund is supposed to operate as an independent entity,
the government has appointive powers. The management
of the National Pension Fund is entrusted to three
boards of directors, each consisting of nine members
appointed by the national government. Some members
are nominated by union and employers' associations.
There are also representatives from the national government. The fund is limited in that it cannot buy
shares in industry--it is entitled to buy only national and local government bonds and local industrial
bonds. It can also buy unsecured debenture loans
publically tendered by a Swedish bank, and so-called
refundment loans. The latter type of loan means that
employers may under certain conditions borrow back
from the fund up to 50 percent of the contributions
paid by them during the preceding year.

The Swedish Investment Bank

The Swedish Investment Bank (Sveriges Investeringsbank) was created in 1967 for the purpose of
promoting long-term employment. Its funds are

obtained through the sale of government bonds to
the National Pension Fund. These funds are utilized
for industrial development loans to be used to promote structural concentration in the older branches
of industry, such as pulp and steel, and to acceler-
ate the growth rate of newer industries, such as
chemicals and engineering. Projects for investment
are supposed to be selected according to profitability, and there is supposed to be no subsidizing
of interest rates. Opponents of the bank argue
that a clash between the objectives of full employment and profitability is inevitable. They fear
that the Swedish government will use the bank to
establish unprofitable industries in uneconomic
areas in order to maintain employment or to check
the exodus of population from the northern part of
the country. As the bank has only been in operation
for a short period of time, its effect on industrial
development is difficult to assess.

The Swedish Investment Bank is a completely
state-owned corporation. It has a board of nine
members which includes representatives of the national
government, wage earner organizations, industry and
commerce, and banking. Although the bank is supposed
to be an independent credit corporation, its policies
are to conform to the basic outlines of the Swedish
government's general industrial and economic policy.
When the bank was created, it had an initial share
capital of 450 million kronor and a capital reserve
fund of 50 million kronor. Borrowing rights are to
be maximized at five times the capital. A state
guarantee for the bank's commitments up to 450 million kronor was made available during its first year
of operation.

The bank's capital was provided by appropriations
from the budget of the national government. General
sales taxes were raised in 1967 in part to provide
funds for the Investment Bank. The budget continues
to provide funds, although the main part necessary
to finance banking activities is raised through the
sale of bonds in the capital market. Unquestionably,
the Investment Bank is an example of the mixing of
private and state contributions. In fact, the
introduction of the Investment Bank is one example
of an increasing participation of the government in
the Swedish economy.

However, in countries with mixed economic
systems, governments exert a powerful influence over
the direction of investment in a way which has important implications for the capital market. In
Germany, the nature of the capital market is conditioned by the allocation of government savings to
enterprises. Since savings by the government sector
usually exceed investment, the government sector is
a large net supplier of investment funds to other
sectors of the economy. Most of these funds are
channeled to business by the banking system or in
the form of direct credits, thus bypassing the
organized capital market. With half of all residential construction being given government assistance, and building demand otherwise actively
stimulated by all levels of government, the demand
for long-term finance is so great that savings become available to other borrowers only at relatively
high prices.

Similarly, the Swedish government has encouraged
investment in various projects considered to be in
the public interest through various techniques such
as channeling funds directly from the budget into
housing construction. However, government housing
loans and interest subsidies have been granted on
principles which have partly crippled competitive
forces and consequently have pushed up construction
costs. In their attempts to catch up with the vigorous rise in demand, public authorities have found it
necessary to intervene in the capital market and give
priority to the financing of housing construction.
This intervention has tended to disrupt the normal
function of the credit system, and also makes it un-
necessarily difficult to carry on a rational monetary
policy, in particular, prior to the introduction in
the mid-1950s of flexible interest rates.

HOUSING

The provision of adequate housing is a major
government concern in Sweden. In housing, national
and local government units play a large part, with
the national government's share represented by loans
and subsidies rather than by direct ownership. A
wide variety of housing aid is available. These
include third mortgage loans; loans without interest
and in some cases without amortization; subsidies of

various kinds, including subsidies for old-age
pensioners, rural workers, and fishermen; and rental
and fuel allowances for low-income families. The
demand for long-term housing credit has exceeded the
supply of housing credit during most of the postwar
period. The persistent inadequacy of long-term investment funds has brought up questions of investment priority among prospective users. Free interest
rates, determined by market forces would have, of
course, equated the supply of funds with investment
demand, but at a cost to the Swedish government's
social objectives. The government has acted in
this situation to give investment preference to the
housing sector at the expense of other sectors of
the economy.

Almost all of the credit institutions in Sweden
are to some extent engaged in the financing of the
housing sector. The savings banks, which occupy a
leading position in this respect, the insurance
companies, and the Post Office Savings Bank grant
mainly mortgage loans up to 60 percent of the property
value, while a considerable proportion of the housing
credits of the commercial banks are secondary loans.
Self-liquidating building credits are granted principally by the commercial banks, but the Post Office
Savings Bank and the savings banks have also begun
to grant such credit in recent years. Specialization
exists between the official mortgage institutions,
which have been established in order to ease the
supply of long-term credits to the housing sector.
Stadshypotekskassan, the Urban Mortgage Bank, thus
grants primary loans exclusively, the Bostadskredit-
kassan, the Housing Credit Bank, is responsible for
secondary loans. Funds for these loans are acquired
by bond issues which are placed for the most part
with insurance companies and banks.

Housing credits are short term and must be repaid when the house is built. These short-term
credits are then replaced by long-term, cheaper
credits, usually granted by a credit institution
specializing in mortgage loans. These are joint-
mortgage loans, which were introduced in 1965 to
take the place of first and second mortgage loans.
The joint-mortgage loan has an amortization period
of sixty years. The savings banks and the Post Office Savings Bank together account for almost half of
the long-term mortgage lending, apart from the government housing loans. Mortgage banks, housing credit

societies, and insurance companies account for the
balance of mortgage lending.

The mortgage banks, the housing credit societies,
and mortgage companies acquire their funds for the
most part by issuing bonds in the capital market.
These bonds are brought by other credit institutions
--the National Pension Fund, insurance companies,
and banks--which make an indirect contribution to
the long-term financing of housing. In 1967, the
insurance companies held about one-third and the
National Pension Fund about one-fourth of all outstanding housing bonds. However, the role of the
National Pension Fund in this area is increasing in
importance. One-fifth of the bonds was held in the
portfolios of commercial banks, while the remainder
was held by the savings banks and the Post Office
Savings Bank.

The financing of housing projects has always
been considered to be a comparatively hazardous activity, so that the granting of short-term credit has
been considered to belong in the realm of commercial
banking. Long-term mortgage loans, on the other hand,
carry a comparatively negligible risk and have, therefore, been regarded as quite suitable for institutions
that are entrusted with the long-term savings of the
general public. These institutions are the savings
banks, insurance companies, pension funds, and mortgage companies. The housing credits that carry the
heaviest risk, the supplementary mortgage loans, are
granted almost entirely by the Swedish government.

In the field of financing, residential construction has long been a priority sector. Besides government housing loans and interest subsidies, monetary
policy has also been used to improve the flow of
funds to the housing sector. Among other things,
liquidity and investment quotas have helped to
channel the resources of the commercial banks and
the insurance companies, in particular, into the
housing sector. The Riksbank's control of bond and
debenture loan issues has been an efficient means of
improving the supply of capital available for housing.
Using these powers the Riksbank has, from time to
time, given the housing credit institutions priority
when granting permission to issue bonds. This control
has become more rigid in recent years as permission
to issue bonds has been granted only on condition
that the commercial banks grant new building credits

equal to the credit transfers made possible by the
new issue of bonds.

The accumulation in a comparatively short period
of time of large amounts of capital funds within the
framework of the National Supplementary Pensions
Scheme has had a considerable impact on housing credit.
Pensions are paid by employers into the National Pension Fund. A comparison between the investments of
the fund and the sources of pension payments shows
that the operation of the fund has brought about a
redistribution of capital from the business sector
to the housing sector. During the period from its
inception in 1959 to 1967, the business sector paid
in more than 70 percent of total premiums received
by the fund, but have received only just over 30 percent of fund investments. On account of this redistribution, business firms have been compelled to
increase greatly their borrowing from other credit
institutions, particularly the commercial banks.

In 1968, total housing construction in Sweden
was set at 95,000 dwelling units, of which 89,000
were to be financed by loans from the Swedish government.[7] However, 900 units from this program were
started in 1967 to support employment during the
winter. In late 1968, a decision was made by the
government to increase the number of housing starts.
Several thousand housing units were carried forward
from the housing program which was tentatively
planned for 1969. The quota of housing units built
without loans from the government was also expended
in 1968 from 6,000 to 14,000 units. Total housing
starts actually amounted to around 105,000 units--
an increase of 10,000 over the 95,000 units which
were planned at the start of the year.

SUMMARY

In a mixed economic system, the role of the government in the provision of money and credit is more
important than in the United States. The central
bank is usually nationally owned and subject to
governmental control. In some countries, monetary
policies are subverted to the general economic policies of the government. A less direct, but perhaps
even more pervasive, influence arises from the policies of some governments to direct a large proportion

of the available financial resources to selected areas of the economy, sometimes by-passing the normal market mechanism entirely in the process, but in any event sharply reducing the volume of funds free for investment in other areas of the market.

Governmental influence upon the supply and demand side of the Swedish capital market is far more extensive than in the United States. The Swedish government plays a central decision-making function in allocating the scarce supply of domestic savings. In terms of the provision of loanable funds to the market, public and quasi-public financial intermediaries play an important role in Sweden by transforming the very liquid assets for which the public displays a strong preference into the long-term financing of investment needs. Also in Sweden, the public ownership of transportation, utilities, and various industries is larger than it is in the United States. Many of these undertakings require external financing, and government ownership frequently implies preemptive rights to a portion of the capital market funds.

Swedish monetary policy is carried out through the Bank of Sweden. The basic monetary policy instruments are discounting, open-market operations, and liquidity ratio requirements. The liquidity requirements, which are differentiated by bank size and which are varied from time to time, are embodied in voluntary agreements between the central bank and the commercial lending institutions. Penalty rates are also imposed on those banks that do not adhere to the prescribed liquidity ratios. Along with the agreements concluded with the commercial banks, the Bank of Sweden's controls are also extended to the savings banks and insurance companies, in the form of requirements that these institutions reserve specified portions of new money for priority borrowers.

For a period of about twenty years, monetary policies of the Bank of Sweden were subordinated to the social welfare policies of the Social Democratic Party. A general easy money policy was followed during most of the period, which contributed to inflationary pressures in the economy. Since the 1950s, the Bank of Sweden has managed to gain a degree of autonomy in its decisions. In part rising prices and balance-of-payments problems have caused

a renaissance of Swedish monetary policy. In 1969,
the outflow of foreign exchange led to credit restraints more severe than ever before applied in
Sweden. The official discount rate was raised in
February from 5 percent to 6 percent and then again
in July from 6 percent to 7 percent--the highest in
Sweden since 1931. Furthermore, individual ceilings
were fixed for commercial bank borrowing at the Bank
of Sweden, a measure never before used in Sweden.
The liquidity ratios of the commercial banks were
raised and cash reserve requirements imposed. Four
different penalty charges were applied to banks that
were unable to maintain liquidity ratios or keep
their borrowing below the prescribed ceiling.

In recent years the role of the Swedish government as a provider of credit has increased in importance. In 1967, the Swedish Investment Bank, a
state-owned corporation, was created for the purpose
of promoting the development of certain industries.
The National Pension Fund, a quasi-public institution, uses the supplementary old-age contributions
to provide capital, particularly to the housing
market. There is also some talk among certain members
of the Social Democratic Party of the need to nationalize commercial banking. So far this can be considered
as so much leftist rhetoric on the part of a minority
within the party. There is no indication that Prime
Minister Olof Palme and the leaders of the party have
any interest in outright nationalization, nor does
there appear to be a need to do so, particularly
since the government is already capable of diverting
financial resources to meet social needs.

NOTES

1. "Svenska Handelsbanken," Economic Review,
index no. 9 (1969), p. 7.

2. Ibid., p. 7.

3. Stockholms Enskilda Bank, The Swedish Credit
Market, (Stockholm, 1968), p. 10.

4. Skandinaviska Banken Quarterly Review (Third
Quarter, 1968), p. 145.

5. The Swedish Credit Market, op. cit., p. 10.

6. Svenska Handelsbanken, Economic Review, index no. 6 (1969).

7. Sekretariat for Economic Planning of the Ministry of Finance and the National Institute of Economic Research, "Preliminary National Budget, 1969" (Stockholm, 1969), p. 101.

CHAPTER **7** LABOR AND
MANAGEMENT

INTRODUCTION

Management and labor in Sweden are strongly
organized. Both have formed central organizations--
the Swedish Employer's Confederation for the employers, and the Confederation of Swedish Trade Unions
and the Central Organization of Salaried Employees
for the workers. In addition to these groups, there
are the Swedish Confederation of Professional Associations, which includes professional workers--doctors,
lawyers, engineers, and teachers--and an organization representing civil service personnel called the
Central Organization of State Employees. Nearly
every Swede in the labor force is affiliated with a
union.

Industry-wide collective bargaining is the most
usual form in Sweden. Most unions are organized on
an industry-wide basis. For example, there is one
union for metal workers. Both skilled and unskilled
workers belong to it. However, this may differ from
trade to trade. Nevertheless, there are certain
points which are characteristic of the Swedish system.
If neither the labor or management federation in a
given trade gives notice of termination of contract
by a specified time, normally three months, before
it expires, the contract is automatically renewed.
Otherwise, the union usually makes the first move.
It holds a contract conference to decide its requests.
Delegates to such conferences--elected by the locals
in proportion to their membership--vote on the new
demands to be presented to management and elect negotiators. The corresponding organization on the employers' side discusses the specific demands of the
union, determines the approach that should be followed,
and marshals its bargaining forces.

190

Agreements that prescribe an obligation to negotiate before economic sanctions can be used were concluded between management and labor in the Saltsjöbaden Agreement of 1938. It contains agreements for industrial peace which have been accepted by both employer and employee federations. First, this agreement makes negotiations of labor-management disputes obligatory and sets forth the procedure in detail. Second, it provides restrictions on coercive action. Economic sanctions, such as strikes and lockouts, can only be used after direct negotiations between labor and management at the local and national levels have failed. Third, there is the provision which limits action against third parties, that is, secondary action against someone who is not directly concerned in the dispute in order to influence one of the parties involved. Fourth, there are provisions relating to the dismissal and layoff of workers. The employer has the unquestioned right to hire and fire as he sees fit. However, the agreement specifies that an employer must notify the local union two weeks in advance when dismissing or laying off a worker who has been employed at least nine months, except in certain circumstances, such as misconduct on the part of the worker.

Labor-management relations have remained consistently stable during most of the postwar period. In terms of work days lost through strikes, Sweden ranks very low among major industrial countries. In 1967, the United States lost 42,100,000 work days to strikes compared to 400 work days in Sweden. One basic reason for this contrast is the social responsibility in Sweden on the part of labor and management. There is little class animus in Sweden. Moreover, when collective bargaining contracts have been concluded, direct action, such as strikes, cannot be carried on during the period of the contract. Disputes must be settled peacefully. If the terms of a contract have been violated, an employer can take the union into court and sue for damages, or vice versa. It is only after the contract has expired that unions and employers are free to take any direct action to influence the terms of the collective agreement.

THE SWEDISH EMPLOYERS'
CONFEDERATION

The Swedish Employers' Confederation (Svenska
Arbetsgivareföreningen), or SAF, is the largest
organization of employers in Sweden. Not only the
greatest part of Swedish industry, but groups of
enterprises engaged in handicrafts, transportation,
and other services have associated themselves with
this organization in order to present a common front
in employer-employee relations. Forty-three employer
associations belong to SAF. These associations involve some 25,000 Swedish enterprises with around
1,200,000 workers.* The largest association in SAF
is the Swedish Metal Trades Employer Association
with 1,689 members and 312,468 workers. The second
largest is the Federation of Swedish Building Employers with 1,799 members and 97,014 workers. Other
large employer associations are the Swedish Iron and
Steel Works Association and the Swedish Textile Employers Association.

There are also a number of associations outside
of SAF, in banking and insurance, commerce, shipping,
agriculture and forestry, and service trades. The
cooperative movement and the fields of national and
local government have employers' associations of their
own. But the policies laid down by the SAF usually
set the pattern for wage negotiations.

SAF began as a defensive body to take care of
the employers' interests in disputes with labor unions.
This has meant that the top organization must maintain a united employer front and that, in turn, has
called for a concentration of power. SAF's employer
associations must get its approval of their constitutions or any amendments to them. Moreover, employers
who wish to become affiliated with any of the SAF
associations must be recognized by the paramount organization. Every labor contract must have SAF's
approval, and members are liable to penalties if
they ignore this rule or break the employer front
in an open conflict by making a separate agreement

---

*These data, provided by SAF to the author, are
as of January 1, 1967.

contrary to the SAF line. In fulfilling its chief
function as an assistant in wage bargaining, SAF has
a representative at all key negotiations. Finally,
it gives financial assistance to its members during
an open conflict, provided that the conflict is legal
and in conformity with the constitution of SAF.[1]

The organization of SAF consists of a general
assembly of 364 delegates chosen by the member associations, which usually meets once a year; a general
council of eighty members chosen by the associations,
which also meets once a year; and a board of thirty
directors, some chosen by the general assembly and
the remainder by the member associations. The board
has formidable powers in its task of organizing,
supervising member associations, and making decisions
about direct action. For example, it decides on all
measures contemplated in connection with strikes and
lockouts, unless this decision is referred by it to
the general council. Lockouts ordered or approved
by the general council or by the board are binding
for all members of SAF. Failure of members to observe
the terms of such resolutions entails the assessment
of damages by SAF against the offending member.

Each enterprise affiliated with SAF pays dues
to SAF and to the employer association with which it
is affiliated. Dues are payable in proportion to
the wages and salaries paid by an employer during
the previous year. The annual dues paid to SAF and
the employer associations average less than three
öre per employee and man-hour, and constitute around
three-tenths of one percent of the total annual bill
of the SAF membership. The dues are used to finance
the current work of SAF and to provide a fund from
which support is given to companies involved in industrial disputes.

The work of SAF covers primarily two areas:
labor relations and negotiations with its union
counterparts in the labor market, and public relations
with society as a whole. Labor negotiations consist
primarily in preparing, coordinating, and directing
the collective bargaining process. The employers'
associations within SAF and the trade unions, which
are also affiliated with national federations, in
the different branches of industry are the negotiat-
ing parties for national agreements, and it is they
who are ultimately responsible for the practical application of the agreements. Every collective

agreement which is intended to be binding on an
enterprise affiliated with SAF must, however, be
approved by SAF. There are also meetings between
SAF and its direct union counterparts, which usually
set wage patterns for the labor market. The settlements reached take the form of recommendations to
all of the federations affiliated with each group
to enter into collective agreements of specified
contents; such as wage increases up to a certain
cost ceiling.

THE CONFEDERATION OF
SWEDISH TRADE UNIONS

The Confederation of Swedish Trade Unions
(Landsorganisationen Sverige), LO, represents about
94 percent of all production workers in the country
and has around 1,500,000 members. Thirty-nine
unions with more than 6,000 branches are included
in this organization. LO was established as the
top organization of Swedish labor in 1898 to form
the connecting link in the collaboration of the
national unions which had developed during the preceding two decades. Initially, LO was an organization for joint defense--mutual assistance in case
of labor conflicts--and a center for the exchange
of statistics and other information. It now has
the responsibility of giving central guidance to
member unions in collective bargaining.

Local organizations, which constitute the
fundamental units of LO, are of three different
types. In each place where a productive enterprise
is in operation, the workers join a local union which,
in turn, is associated with a national union. If
there are several enterprises in the same industrial
branch in one place, independently working organizations called factory sections are organized at each
plant and are part of the local union. In places
where there are several branches of production represented and there is more than one local union
involved, these unions are combined into local
trade councils. These have no duties with regard
to wage policies.

The Swedish union movement has been marked by
centralism. There have been worked out within LO so-
called model statutes which the affiliated unions

must accept. According to these rules, the locals
do not have the right to take any sort of coercive
action without receiving the national union's permission. In connection with negotiations for wage
agreements, the members involved elect delegates to
a wage conference which discusses and decides the
cancellation of existing agreements. The wage conference appoints a delegation whose purpose is to
negotiate for a new agreement. When the negotiations are over, the result is laid before the wage
conference and the national union's board for examination and approval or disapproval.

If a union has exhausted the possibilities of
negotiation without being able to reach an acceptable result and decides in favor of open conflict,
it must according to law announce the work stoppage
seven days before the strike is called. Union rules
in such cases require a union to obtain the approval
of the board of LO of the announcement of the strike
if as much as 3 percent of the union's membership is
involved. If the union should refuse to ask LO for
permission or announce a strike against the will of
the board, it loses the right to economic and moral
support from all the member unions in LO.

The Confederation of Swedish Trade Unions and
its member unions provide the major financial support and membership for the Social Democratic Party
and own the Stockholm evening paper, Aftonbladet,
which supports the party's viewpoint. In addition
to Aftonbladet, LO contributes 4 million kronor
annually to the support of what is called the A-Press,
the publishing chain of the Social Democratic Party.
The directing board of the A-Press consists of three
LO officials and four from the party. Despite the
close working relationship between the LO and the
party, they operate independently. Nevertheless,
three-fourths of the members of the party are also
affiliated with the LO's unions, and Arne Geiger,
President of the LO, is a Social Democratic member
of the Upper House of the Riksdag.

The LO congress, which is the highest policy-
making authority, meets every fifth year. It is
attended by 300 delegates whom the national unions
elect in proportion to their membership. Each affiliated national union is entitled to at least one
delegate. The affiliates elect their delegates to
the LO congress either at their local congresses or

by a general vote of their members. The congress
elects an executive board, which consists of thirteen
members. The board, which meets once a week, is in
direct charge of LO's activities. Its general task
is to promote the coordination by the union affiliates
of their basic policies. There is also a general
council of 140 members which meets twice a year.
Its members are also elected by the unions in proportion to their membership. Between congresses,
the general council is the highest policy-making
authority.

Below the LO level, power in the trade union
movement is centered in the national unions, of which
the locals are dependent subsidiaries. The organization of the national unions follows the LO tripartite structure of congress, union assembly, and
executive board. Congress usually meets once every
three to five years. Union rules usually specify
that representatives to a congress are to represent
different districts, types of activities, and size
of locals in order to secure a truly representative
body. The executive board usually consists of seven
to ten members--the chairman, the secretary, and the
treasurer being full-time officials.

There is also another side to LO's role in
wage negotiations. According to their constitutions,
union affiliates are under an obligation to seek
the LO executive board's permission before issuing
a strike warning, if the members who would be involved in the strike amount to 3 percent or more
of the union's membership. Furthermore, the constitutions contain clauses which make it incumbent
on a union affiliate to seek LO's authorization for
a strike warning, if it wishes to receive LO's economic support in the event of a strike.

LO has the right and the obligation to assist
its affiliates in their wage negotiations and may
even present proposals for a settlement. If an
affiliate fails to accept such a proposal and is
receiving financial support from LO, the LO executive board can discontinue payment, provided that
two-thirds of its members vote for a decision to
this effect. In other words, a sanction seeking to
enforce compliance with the Lo executive board's
decision concerning the national union's wage policy
is applied only in connection with labor conflicts.
Usually, wage agreements are concluded without

conflicts, and in this case, the unions are not
under a constitutional obligation to submit the
agreement to the LO executive board for approval.

THE CENTRAL ORGANIZATION
OF SALARIED EMPLOYEES

Apart from LO, white-collar workers in both
the public and private sector have their own organization, the Central Organization of Salaried Employees, TCO (Tjanstemannens Centralorganization).
TCO is comprised of 27 unions with 2,500 branches.
There are 529,000 members, of which 300,000 are employed in private enterprises and 229,000 in state
and municipal administration. About 75 percent of
Swedish workers who are not engaged in actual pro-
duction--foremen, office employees of all types,
sales personnel, and engineers--are affiliated with
this organization. Membership includes workers in
agriculture, banking, commerce, insurance, railways,
state and local governments, and the armed forces.

The organization of TCO is based on the three
levels of a congress, general council, and a board.
Congress, the supreme authority, meets every third
year and consists of 200 delegates from the member
unions. The general council, elected annually, consists of 100 representatives appointed by the affiliated unions, and usually meets twice a year.
The executive board consists of ten members elected
by the congress and meets once a week. The board
has the power to participate in the general wage
negotiations of TCO unions where the results of the
negotiations affect other affiliated organizations
directly or indirectly.

The major unions affiliated with TCO are: the
Union of Clerical and Technical Employees in Industry,
107,000 members; the Foremen's and Supervisors' Union,
43,000 members; the Union of Municipal Employees,
40,000 members; the Federation of Civil Servants,
35,000 members; and the Union of Nurses, 19,000
members.

Beginning in 1966, wages and other conditions
of employment for government white-collar workers
affiliated with TCO unions were determined by collective bargaining of the same type as has long been

used for employees in the private sector of the
economy. Direct action on the part of employees
and the national government is permissible. In
other words, government employees may strike and
the government may impose lockouts, both in observance of the rules which apply to the rest of the
labor market. For bargaining purposes, the Swedish
government is represented by a special authority.
Statens Avtalsverk (the Board for State Collective
Agreements). In order to be valid, agreements
reached by Statens Avtalsverk on behalf of the state
must be approved by a special pay delegation which
is appointed by the Swedish Parliament.

Unions belonging to TCO are similar to other
Swedish unions in organization. There are different unions for different branches of economic activity. Some unions cover all workers performing
a certain type of work. For example, there is a
union for nurses and a union for elementary school
teachers. The unions are national, with regional
and local branches. Other TCO unions organize all
white-collar workers, regardless of their skills,
from the lowest to the highest salary brackets, who
work for the same employer or employers represented
in negotiations by the same employer association.

Three advisory bodies within TCO deal with
specific professional problems: one for technicians,
one for foremen, and one for teachers. In cities
where several TCO affiliates have local organizations, contracts and cooperation among the locals
are maintained through TCO local committees engag-
ing in propaganda and information of common interest.
These committees do not take any action in regard
to wage negotiations, however.

Regarding the structure of white-collar unions
--TCO affiliates as well as unions outside of TCO--
the usual pattern is a union consisting of locals,
which comprise either all union members within a
certain geographic area or at a certain enterprise.
Some of the unions promote cooperation among locals
within the same region through county or regional
bodies. A few unions are national associations of
employees in certain professional categories.

Under its constitution, TCO has the function
of promoting the establishment and maintenance of
effective white-collar unions. To accomplish this

task, it must have sizable financial resources.
Ever since the present TCO was founded in 1944, it
has pursued a policy of providing a sound economic
foundation for its affiliates, in part because the
possibility of a strike must be a real enough threat
in wage negotiations, and in part because effective
administration and negotiation require economic
strength. In 1967, unions affiliated with TCO paid
9 kronor per member as dues. For certain groups,
the dues also include contributions to unemployment
insurance. Membership dues in TCO union affiliates
averaged 136 kronor a year for workers in private
employment and 109 kronor a year for workers in public employment.

THE SWEDISH CONFEDERATION
OF PROFESSIONAL ASSOCIATIONS

     The largest group of salaried employees out-
side of TCO belong to the Swedish Confederation of
Professional Associations (Sveriges Akademikers
Centralorganisation) or SACO. It was formed in 1947
as an association of organizations for professional
workers who have passed examinations at a university
or similar institutions, or have specialized training based on the matriculation examination. Engineers,
lawyers, doctors, and university professors belong
to SACO. It is essentially a craft union movement,
using the specific organizational principle of academic training. In 1967, it had thirty-one organizations with 98,720 members.[2] About half of the members
are employed by the central government, a quarter by
local authorities, and the remainder are in the private sector or self-employed.

     SACO is nonpolitical, and the most important
principle governing its activity is that it is organized on a horizontal or craft basis. The criterion
of eligibility is a university degree or a profes-
sion, and each craft (doctors, lawyers, dentists)
organizes as one association, irrespective of the
place and sector of employment. There are many reasons for using this principle of organization. In
part it was because professional groups were being
squeezed by wage developments that they adopted this
principle of organization, since SACO believes that
the craft principle gives bargaining strength. Small
professional groups might in its view be sacrificed

in large vertical unions in the interests of the
majority.

When SACO was established in 1947, TCO and
the organizations of college graduates affiliated
with it discussed the possibility of merger. These
negotiations failed, primarily because the TCO and
SACO groups held different views on the principles
of organization of white-collar workers. TCO af-
firmed that workers who were college graduates,
should, in principle, join the same unions as other
groups of white-collar workers, while SACO felt that
the graduates should form separate unions--differ-
ences which to some degree reflected differences of
opinion on goals and means, especially concerning
wage policy.

Member associations in SACO are very small.
The largest group is the Association of Secondary
School Teachers, which in 1967 had 14,000 members.
Member organizations must keep SACO informed on important bargaining matters. The most important
bargaining provision is that the organizations must
respect agreements entered into by SACO as their
representative. As a corollary, they are also required to participate in any direct action on which
the executive board of SACO may decide. It is be-
coming increasingly common for SACO to bargain on
behalf of its organizations in the public sector.
Centralization on the part of the employer has made
this inevitable to some extent, but SACO has attempted to ensure that its members' craft interests
are not submerged by the other salaried workers
unions affiliated with TCO.

THE NATIONAL FEDERATION
OF CIVIL SERVANTS

A small central organization for salaried
workers is the National Federation of Civil Servants
(Statstjänstemannens Riksförbund) or SR, which caters
exclusively to senior civil servants and officers of
the armed forces. Higher civil servants were first
organized in 1904, and the present SR was formed in
1946 through a reorganization of the Civil Servants
Board dating from 1917. SR is the central organization for thirty-six organizations of civil servants in
the middle and higher salary ranges, with 18,325 members.

Only two of its member organizations have more
than 1,000 members--the Association of Civil Servants in Postal, Railway, and Telegraphic Services,
and the Officers' Association--and together these
accounted for two-thirds of total membership.

SR claims as its main virtues compactness and
homogeneity. The organization follows the usual
tripartite structure of a congress, general council,
and a board. The member organizations can bargain
independently about matters affecting only their own
organization, but SR must be informed if the matter
affects others, and it can decide to take part in
the negotiations. There is provision for bargaining delegations to be appointed by the executive
board for central bargaining, which is conducted by
SR. The employer is the central government, and
salary grades provide the range of civil servants
with whom it is concerned at national and depart-
mental level. The main reason for forming central
organizations of civil servants was the deteriorating
salary position of senior civil servants, and SR is
concerned to safeguard the interests of this small
and compact group.

A feature of the economic life of Sweden is
the extent to which business and labor are organized
into economic groups which are of considerable practical importance in relation to each other and to the
government. Most Swedish workers belong to a union
of one type or another. This includes professional
workers and high-level civil servants, who would not
normally be organized in most countries. On the employer side, there are also important trade groups
representing particular industries.

While the communists never have had any influence on the leadership of LO or the other con-
federations of unions, they were fairly strong
among the rank and file of the Metal Workers' Union
immediately after the Second World War and fomented
a devastating six-month strike in the metal industries in 1945-1946. Since then their influence has
steadily declined as a result of efforts on the part
of the Social Democratic Party, without ousters of
locals or individual members and without any legislation curtailing the civic rights of the communists.
Fluctuations on the local level occur, but communist
control or influence is limited to a small fraction
estimated at not more than 3,000 out of the total

union membership in Sweden. They are mainly in the
mining and construction industries. There is no
communist on the executive board of a national
union.

COLLECTIVE BARGAINING
IN SWEDEN

A novel procedure involving a considerable
degree of coordination of wage negotiations evolved
in Sweden during the 1950s. It has become customary
for the Confederation of Swedish Trade Unions, LO,
and the Swedish Employers' Federation, SAF, to
establish a basic pattern for wage increases and
other terms of employment of blue-collar workers in
mining and manufacturing. This pattern is laid down
in what is commonly called a central wage agreement,
although it is actually a joint recommendation from
LO and SAF to their affiliates concerning the contents of the collective contracts they are about to
conclude. The central bargaining agreements between
LO and SAF sets the pattern for the whole labor market. The settlements thereby reached have taken the
form of recommendations to all of the federations
affiliated with each group to enter into collective
agreements of specified contents, such as wage increases up to a certain cost ceiling. Most of the
agreements are concluded between a trade union on
one side, and an employers' association on the other.
The agreement is valid for all companies belonging
to the employers' association.

The wage negotiation procedure is essentially
as follows: LO and SAF reach a central agreement on
a recommendation to their affiliates concerning the
average size of wage increases as well as improvements which specific groups should receive, such as
changes in work hours, fringe benefits, and the like.
Thereafter, the national unions and their opposites
in SAF negotiate legally binding collective agreements based on LO-SAF recommendations. However, the
effects of the central recommendation reach far beyond
the LO-SAF field of organization, because all other
categories of private and public employees base their
wage demand on this recommendation.

On the labor side, coordinated wage negotiations are conducted by LO, which also has the task

of laying down the directives for the wage policy of
organized labor. The main responsibility for this
work rests with the LO executive board, which begins
planning a round of negotiations several months before the first contact is established with the
negotiators of the opposite side. The wishes and
demands of organized labor on the eve of a round of
negotiations are usually formulated in a statement
adopted by the LO general council. A proposal of
such a statement is submitted by the LO executive
board as a result of preparatory deliberations at
different levels. The wage policy statement of the
general council is formally a recommendation to the
unions--they are independent in their wage policy--
but in practice it is morally binding.

With the guidance of the general council's
wage policy statement, the different unions prepare
their proposals for new wage agreements and each
union submits them for discussion to its collective
bargaining conference, that is, a gathering of representatives of the union's locals elected for a given
round of wage negotiations. Some unions have replaced the collective bargaining conference by a
more permanent body called a collective bargaining
council, whose members are elected for longer periods
comprising several rounds of negotiations. LO is
usually represented at these conferences or council
meetings.

In negotiations with SAF, LO is represented by
its executive board and elected representatives of
some national unions which are not represented on
the board. As mentioned above, a central agreement
between LO and SAF is in the nature of a recommendation to the union affiliates concerning the contents
of the collective agreements they should reach, and
is therefore followed by negotiations between each
national union and its counterpart on the employer's
side. In the end, when nation-wide contracts have
been concluded for the different industries, negotiations ensue on the local level concerning the application of the industry's national agreement to the
plant and its work process, a procedure rendered
necessary in most industries by the widespread use
of piece rates.

When they meet at the bargaining table, labor's
demands are discussed and countered by management's
offers, bolstered in each case by a review of what

is happening in the industry and the overall economy.
It is a characteristic of all negotiations in Sweden
that the mainspring of debate and agreement is a
knowledge of economic facts, used not only to justify
wage demands, but also to test these demands in
terms of what they mean to the industry and to the
economy as a whole.

Agreements may be reached after a few sessions.
However, when an accord on certain issues appears
impossible and open conflict is imminent, an official mediator is required by law to intervene.
However, it is more usual for the conflicting
parties themselves to ask for official help. Eight
district mediators appointed and paid by the Swedish
government are supposed to help resolve disputes in
their respective regions. Special mediators may
also be appointed by the government. After concessions on both sides, the mediator can present a
formal proposal which may or may not be accepted.

Collective bargaining is free from compulsory
arbitration. Legislation enters only at three points:
It makes existing collective contracts enforceable
and compels arbitration in case of disputes over
their interpretation of application; it makes the
intervention of a government mediator obligatory if
the parties cannot reach agreement in negotiations
for new contracts; and it requires one week's notice
of strikes or lockouts if mediation fails.

Since the early 1950s, Sweden has enjoyed a
period of industrial peace unparalleled among the
free countries of the world. In 1951, LO and SAF
became concerned over the difficult and protracted
wage negotiations and the resultant high wage increases by which workers sought to offset the effect
of the price inflation stimulated by the Korean War.
In 1952, they agreed on a joint recommendation for
wage increases, referred to as the central agreement,
which has been binding on their affiliates and which
has set the pattern for the rest of the labor market.

Cases of contract violation and disputes over
interpretation or application which cannot be settled
by the parties concerned are taken to the Labor Court
--a seven-man body with two representatives from the
SAF and two from LO. If a case involves salaried
workers, a TCO representative replaces an LO representative. The Labor Court is a judicial body,

concerned primarily with declaring what the rights
and obligations of parties to a collective contract
are when disputes about it arise. The competence of
the court includes cases relating to individual employment agreements that are covered by provisions
in a collective contract, though it is not empowered
to deal with disputes that arise over individual
contracts of service which are not based on collective contracts. The Labor Court is a final court
of judgment. No appeals can be made against its
decisions. A union can take an employer before
the Labor Court and demand benefits in accordance
with the contract. An employer hit by an official
strike can take the strikers before the Labor Court
and demand damages which are limited to a maximum
amount of 200 kronor per person.

In 1966, the customary two-year central agreement between LO and SAF was extended to three years
in the interest of wage stability which both sides
considered to be important in order to keep Sweden's
export industry competitive. As in past years, the
LO-SAF agreement was followed by negotiations between
TCO and its affiliates with the employers' federation.
These in turn were followed by a series of negotiations between the Swedish government and LO, TCO,
and SACO, all of whom have members in the government
service. These were the first such negotiations in
history and were based on a law which went into effect
on January 1, 1966, through which Swedish government
employees achieved the same rights as those enjoyed
by workers in private industry, including the right
to strike. During the negotiations with the government, SACO, perhaps the most militant of the Swedish
labor federations, arguing that its members had
lagged far behind production workers in salary increases in recent years, called out part of their
membership in the first strike of national consequence
in two decades and the first strike in Swedish history
of government employees.

Normally, collective bargaining agreements are
set for a period of one or two years. When the contract has been established, direct actions such as
strikes, cannot be carried on during the period of
the contract. The Collective Agreements Act of 1928
defines the contractual obligations between labor
and management. Once entered into, a contract is
binding all along the line from the national federations to the individual employers and union members.

Even resignation from the organization does not free
anyone from the terms of the contract. During the
term of the contract, peace prevails. This means
that an individual employer can make his plans with
a greater degree of assurance that labor disputes
will not happen. This is important for competition
in foreign markets where delivery can often be up-
set by labor disputes.

Wage Policies

     Under the terms of the collective agreements,
wages in industry are differentiated to allow for
the fact that costs of living vary in different
parts of Sweden. Such wage differentials, tied to
the cost of living, are accepted by the unions.
Rates of pay for industrial workers and pay schedules
for salaried employees are generally differentiated
according to the place of residence of the employee.
In those sectors of the economy where wages and
salaries exceed minimum rates or where no rates or
schedules are applied at all, considerable non-
systematic differentials have emerged.

     Postwar Swedish wage policies of unions and
management have been influenced by the rapid rate
of economic expansion and high rates of employment
which have been achieved as a result of an economic
policy of demand management on the part of the
Swedish government. The strong demand for labor
which has characterized the period throughout has
given market forces considerable influence over wage
determination. The tension between the market forces
and the goals of labor and management engaged in wage
determination has been a dominant factor in Sweden.
A considerable wage drift has caused difficulties in
the wage policies of unions. Wage drift is a result
partly of institutional conditions and partly of the
market situation--the strong demand for labor.* It

_____

     *Wage drift can be defined as the difference
between the actual earnings recorded in a sector
during a period and the earnings which were expected
to follow directly from the terms agreed under the
contract for the period. It comprises all types of
wage changes which can arise in addition to those
determined by the agreement.

has operated against both LO's attempt to raise the
relative wages of workers in low wage sectors and
the salaried workers unions' attempts to keep pace
with the wage developments of industrial workers.

Another problem is the effect of a strong demand for labor in causing the sum of negotiated wage
increases plus the wage drift to surpass the average
room for wage increases which is created by productivity developments in the economy as a whole. The
wage policy followed by labor and management has
therefore been regarded as having an inflationary
effect by many people. During the 1960s, many
Swedish economists and politicians raised demands
for a governmental incomes policy, with its implication that the central government should control
agreements affecting incomes in some way in order
to insure that they are held within the limits of
productivity gains.

One facet of the wage system in Sweden is the
reliance on piece rates as a method of compensation.
In this respect, Sweden is similar to the Soviet
Union in that both countries employ payments for
piecework as the most important type of compensation
in manufacturing industries. Piecework methods of
wage payments in Sweden almost always take the form
of linear piece rates, which are generally geared
solely to units of quantitative output. Of the
total number of piece rates paid in manufacturing,
about two-thirds are paid at individual piece rates
and one-third at group piece rates. Individual
piece rates are important in the manufacture of
metal products, machinery, and transportation equipment, as well as in the steel industry and many
other establishments. Group piece rates occur
chiefly in the processing industries and in certain
service trades. The building industry relies almost
exclusively on group piecework. Rates are mostly
set by a schedule which applies to the industry as
a whole. This schedule is rooted in time-honored
traditions and is not based on work studies. In
recent years, however, work studies have been initi-
ated extensively in order to effect a revision of
the whole piece rate schedule.

Table 7-1 presents the standard forms of compensation in the manufacturing industries. Bonuses
are tied into straight piece rates as a form of
compensation.

TABLE 7-1

Methods of Wage Compensation
in Swedish Manufacturing
Industries

Plant Size by Work Force	Hourly Rates	Straight Piece Rates	Bonus	Total
51-100	37%	49%	14%	100%
101-200	31	47	22	100
201-500	31	47	22	100
501-1,000	32	42	26	100
1001 and Over	25	43	32	100

Source: Data provided to the author in 1969
by the Swedish Employers Federation.

Paying salaried workers by unit of output is a
rare occurrence. The industry which employs most of
them, engineering, pays less than 5 percent of the
work performed by salaried employees on this basis.
The piece rate in these cases amounts to only a
small bonus.

Systems for payment by results vary among
Swedish employers, but all are based wholly or in
part on the quantity of work. Pure and direct
piecework is used where there is a close and uniform
relationship between inputs of effort and outputs of
work. The building industry uses a pure piecework
system. But more common than pure piecework are
mixed or premium piecework systems, which give scope
for a variety of individual and group incentive
methods, through a combination of a certain fixed
sum of money per hour and a certain price per unit
of quantity. The time taken to produce a unit then
becomes fundamental, and gives rise to a great deal
of time study. Conventional time studies cover about
70 percent of Swedish industrial workers. Such
studies are also gaining ground in new fields where
piece rates had formerly been applied only to a
small extent.

White-collar workers in Sweden are normally
paid an hourly or weekly wage. Several types of
wage systems are used. The most rigid form of

wage-setting is called a standard tariff system and
means that a specified salary is attached to each
position regardless of a person's capacity or job
performance. The most important example of such a
system is the Swedish government's salary schedules
for civil servants, on which the salary schedules
of local governments are modeled as well. Positions
are listed by description and grade within a salary
schedule. There are four salary schedules. The
bulk of the civil servants are covered in Salary
Schedule A, in which salaries for different types
of workers ranged from 23,900 kronor to 67,340
kronor a year for 1969. The remaining three grades
cover special categories of workers. The top salary
range is for workers in Salary Schedule C. Salaries
in this schedule ranged from 74,480 kronor to
127,490 kronor a year.* Included in this category
are top level state employees. Among those persons
in the high wage category are university professors,
bishops in the Lutheran Church, government department heads, and cabinet ministers.

More flexible than standard tariff systems are
minimum tariff systems, which specify minimum salaries payable to employees with specific tasks. These
systems are aimed at stimulating employers to pay
salaries exceeding the minimum in accordance with
the individual employee's efficiency. The system
applies for example to bank employees, journalists,
restaurant employees, routine jobs in commerce, and
some groups of foremen in industry. All of these
systems provide for length-of-service increments
during periods of employment. Office workers in
private insurance companies are covered by a salary
zone tariff, which allows for consideration of individual merit both in grading and in the setting
of individual salaries within the zones corresponding to the grades.

Free, or individual, salary setting applies to
white-collar workers in mining and manufacturing and
in large sectors of commerce, and to some specialized
jobs in otherwise tariff-regulated jurisdictions.
The salary of each employee is set individually according to job content, personal merit, and efficiency.

---

*Salary schedules were provided by TCO to the
author.

Job classification and comparison of salaries based
on wage statistics are used by the unions as two
arguments among many others without, however, being
systematically integrated into the wage setting
process. In fields with free wage setting, the
unions negotiate general salary increases as a
floor for individual improvements: No employee
will receive less, but some or many will receive
more.

In public employment, especially the central
government, the unions of public employees have
achieved considerable influence on the establishment of positions open for promotion and the principles governing promotion, thereby offsetting in
part the rigidity of the salary system. The unions
are regularly invited to discuss with the ministries
concerned any significant reorganization plans and
devote on these occasions attention to the establishment of new jobs for promotion. Similar efforts are
also made in the annual revisions of the government's
salary schedules, which serve the primary purpose of
upgrading categories of positions.

Wage policy goals of salaried employees' organizations are different and less complex than the
goals of the unions of manual workers affiliated
with LO. Their primary aim has been to retain or
restore traditional income differentials of salaried
workers over manual workers. LO, in general, has
pursued policies which attempt to reduce income differentials between the worst and best paid groups of
workers. In the 1968-1969 wage negotiations, LO
demanded increases for low income workers at the
expense of those workers who were better paid. The
other federations of unions did not accept this
principle. A breakdown of wage negotiations occurred
in early 1969, as a result of disagreements among the
unions. The government established a mediation commission which apparently has given LO's concept of
wage equality between groups of workers more consideration than the views of the other unions.

Wage Policies and International Competition

Swedish industry can be divided into two sectors.
The first sector, which can be called the competing
sector (C-sector) is comprised of industries that
compete in the export markets, or with imported
goods. Included in this group are the manufacturing,

mining, forestry, shipping, and fisheries. The
second sector, which can be called the protected
sector (P-sector) includes industries that are protected from international competition either through
natural conditions or state regulations. C-sector
accounts for about 30 percent of total employment
in Sweden; P-sector accounts for the remaining 70
percent. Prices of goods in the C-sector are determined by trends in world prices, and prices in
the P-sector are determined by the development of
costs.

     During the period 1960-1967, world market
prices of goods produced in the C-sector increased
at a rate of 1 to 1.5 percent a year. At the same
time, average productivity in the sector increased
at a rate of 7.5 percent a year. However, total
wage costs in the C-sector increased at a rate of
9.4 percent a year.[3] This means that industrial
profitability in the sector has fallen and solvency
has been weakened during the period. Although the
international competitive capacity of industry in
the C-sector was maintained, it was at the expense
of profitability, which declined, particularly in
industries producing raw materials and semimanufac-
tured goods.

     In the C-sector, the level of productivity de-
pends mainly on corporate propensity to invest, which
is influenced by the profitability outlook. This
can, of course, be affected by economic policy and
wage agreements. It is by no means certain that
productivity will increase at the same rate in the
future as it did during the period 1960-1967. Moreover, if profitability must be strengthened to
stimulate investment, the scope for wage increases
will have to be narrowed. There is no doubt that
the volume of investment that is necessary for the
maintenance of the international position of the C-
sector will never be reached if earning capacity is
too low in the industries depending on foreign trade.

THE ROLE OF THE
SWEDISH GOVERNMENT

     Labor legislation in Sweden is limited to the
barest minimum, with the government and Parliament
complying with the insistence of labor and management

that they should be free to regulate the terms of
employment and their mutual relations by negotiations.
There is no legislation on compulsory arbitration or
minimum wages. There is no closed shop or union
shop. Legislation on hours and vacations is flexible, enabling labor and management to adjust the application of the statutory provisions involved in
collective bargaining to conditions in different
industries. The participation of the government
involves the provision of a mediation service, strictly
limited to mediation and without power for the mediators to hand down awards. There is also the tripartite Labor Court, with judges who represent the
government, labor, and management. It is responsible for the interpretation and application of collective agreements.

There exists, however, an interaction between
governmental economic policy and the wage policies
of labor and management. In principle, LO and SAF
operate their wage policies in the light of the
government's overall economic policy, although it
is not always evident where each side thinks the
division of function between government policy and
the labor market begins and ends. The government
can, after an evaluation of what ought to be the
fiscal policy guidelines in the short run, base its
policy on the presumption that wage policies are a
given datum for the coming period. In January, the
national budget division of the Ministry of Finance
presents a report on economic trends, which may or
may not give estimates of the likely scope for increases in income. The finance minister presents
his fiscal budget to the Swedish Parliament, and
discusses the requirements for economic equilibrium
in light of the budget report. He may suggest what
level of nominal wage increases is reconciliable with
stability. On occasion he has issued a warning about
the limited scope for wage increases.

The interrelationship between labor, management,
and the government is apparent in the operations of
the Labor Market Board, which is the organization
responsible for the operation of the Swedish employment programs. The Labor Market Board is a tripartite
board consisting of representatives from labor,
management, and the government. There are two representatives from the Swedish Employers Confederation,
two representatives from the Central Organization of
Salaried Workers, one representative from the Central

Organization of Professional Associations, one representative for female workers, one representative
for agriculture, and three representatives from the
government. The Labor Market Board, as mentioned
previously, is responsible for putting into action
various employment-creating measures, such as the
mangement of investment-reserve funds, and for
stimulating occupational and geographical mobility.
Other responsibilities include the supervision of
the public employment service, planning of projects
suitable to be carried out as emergency public works,
licensing of starting permits for housing construction, and advice as to the location of new industrial
establishments. The board functions as an independent
agency under the Ministry of the Interior.

    Labor unions in Sweden have been mainly active
in setting wages. The trade union movement in Sweden
has traditionally placed little emphasis on fringe
benefits in wage contracts, and instead has used its
political influence to obtain statutory social insurance systems applicable to all citizens. The government has by legislation provided numerous benefits
both for the workers and for those who are not actively engaged in the working process, such as children and retired people. The unions feel that the
advantage to workers of government-supported welfare
programs is that the coverage for individual workers
is not affected by loss or change of employment.
Thus, old-age pensions, unemployment compensation,
and other social welfare measures have been settled
by the political process, that is, legislated by the
Swedish Parliament and usually financed out of the
state budget. Recently, however, there has been a
tendency for collective bargaining to include fringe
benefits, such as life insurance and a system of
severance pay.

    There is no question that labor unions pos-
sess a closer working relationship with the Swedish
government than management. There has been an
association of organized labor with the ruling Social
Democratic Party which goes back to the last century.
Union affiliates in LO were required to join the party,
and failure to comply resulted automatically in ex-
pulsion. Although these rules were changed, the
close link between LO and the Social Democratic
Party remains. The party is not only represented at
LO congresses but also at the conventions of its affiliates, and LO is always represented at the party's

congresses. LO and the party cooperate closely
whenever public opinion has to be mobilized over a
major political issue. In parliamentary and municipal elections, both LO and its affiliates support
the Social Democratic Party by appeals to the
electorate and considerable contributions to cam-
paign funds.

Although this does not necessarily mean that
the Social Democratic Party is completely beholden
to the unions, it does mean that at least it is
generally receptive to policies which the unions
advance. In particular, the LO federation has supported the full-employment and social welfare policies of the party. Full-employment has always been
an objective of the highest order for the trade
union movement. This is so because of the economic
security and the opportunities for consumption associated with a high level of employment. Measures
designed to lead to an increased need for labor are
supported by the unions.

However, not all unions are associated with the
Social Democratic Party. TCO and its union affiliates have, in general, pursued a course of political
neutrality in elections. Some of the most acrimonious
labor disputes, in a country which is remarkably free
from labor unrest, have occurred between the government and government employees affiliated with SACO.
Strikes against the government have taken place over
wage disputes involving white-collar workers.

SUMMARY

The percentage of Swedes belonging to unions is
very high. Among blue-collar workers it is around
80 percent, and in manufacturing and mining it is
almost 100 percent. About 70 percent of Swedish
white-collar workers are organized. Virtually all
organized blue-collar workers belong to the Confederation of Swedish Trade Unions, LO, which has
1.6 million members in industry, agriculture,
forestry, commerce, public employment, and other
fields. There is also a close association of LO
with the dominant Social Democratic Party. The most
important white-collar federation is the Central
Organization of Salaried Employees, TCO, which represents public and private employees. The Swedish

Confederation of Professional Associations, SACO,
represents college graduates and persons with equivalent professional training and status in public
and private employment. The National Federation of
Government Officers, SR, with a membership of 19,000
represents civil servants in the upper echelons of
government. In addition, there are several other
minor federations representing a specific type of
worker. Their influence in the labor movement is
negligible.

        The employers side is also organized in Sweden.
By far the largest and most important employers organization is the Swedish Employers' Confederation, SAF,
which originally was formed as a defense mechanism
against trade unionism. It is made up of forty-three
employer associations, which represent some 25,000
business firms. In addition to the major portion
of the Swedish manufacturing industry, SAF also represents large and important groups of firms in the
handicraft trades, transportation, and other services. It is exclusively concerned with the interests
of firms as a contracting party on the labor market,
with primary attention paid to questions of wage
setting, employment, and relations with employees
and their organizations. There are also other employers' associations in the private sector which are
not affiliated with SAF. Employers' organizations
exist in the public sector as well. At the national
level, the Government Employees Negotiation Board has
the right to negotiate and conclude agreements with
the unions representing government workers. At the
local level bargaining has also become centralized on
the part of employers.

        The organizational structure for centralized
collective bargaining is thoroughly developed in
Sweden. The bargaining process is largely determined by the outcome of negotiations between LO and
SAF. Central negotiations take place according to
agreed practice between LO and SAF. Framework agreements are reached between the two organizations,
which take the form of recommendations to the unions
and employers associations to be used in their negotiations for the renewal of agreements at the
industry-wide level. The agreement covers the general range of wage increases that should be covered
in the collective agreements between individual
unions and employers associations. However, an element of rigidity has been introduced into the col-

lective bargaining process. While the contracts are in force, wage payments will usually increase substantially above the negotiated rate. This is the wage drift.

The actions of LO and SAF are regarded as having great importance in the development of the national economy. In practice, a mutual adjustment of the wage policies of these organizations and the economic policy of the government has taken place, even though both the organizations and the national government have carefully avoided trespassing on the freedom of action of each other. The increasing coordination of wage negotiations can be attributable to this mutual dependence between different interest groups, and between economic policy and the wage policy of these organizations.

Maintaining full-employment in Sweden is the responsibility of the Labor Market Board which administers the public employment office, area relocation and job training programs, emergency public works, and the investment reserve program. Labor and management are represented in the leadership of the board, which is an organization of great power connected with the Ministry of the Interior. In this organization, as in many others, the Swedish government and labor and management are united in encouraging policies of full-employment. To a certain extent, prime emphasis placed on full-employment has worked to the detriment of economic growth.

NOTES

1. See the Constitution of the Swedish Employers' Confederation (Svenska Arbetsgivareföreninger), arts. 34 and 42, pp. 21 and 23.

2. Ibid., p. 241.

3. Svenska Handelsbanken, Economic Review, index no. 2 (1969), p. 1.

CHAPTER **8** THE STATE AND
ECONOMIC LIFE

INTRODUCTION

A considerable amount of intervention is an indispensable condition for the establishment of even
the freest type of economic system. The very atmos-
phere for the conduct of business depends upon the
intervention of government to establish and maintain
the institutions of private property, freedom of
contract, money and credit, and a system of civil
laws for adjudicating the private disputes of individuals. Such institutions make possible an elabor-
ate system of private planning, in which individuals,
rather than government, organize and direct the production of goods and services in response to the
desires of consumers.

In Sweden, as well as in other Western European
countries, the government provides certain economic
functions which are as follows: First, it directs
the coordination of economic policy, and its various
administrative decisions determine some of the
boundaries or rules to which business firms must pay
attention in their own planning and decision-making;
second, it participates directly in the life of the
economy through its various agencies and enterprises,
and more indirectly through the regulation of business activities; third, it not only takes action to
provide for the distribution of the social income
of the country, but also for its redistribution by
means of taxation and transfer payments. Within
this framework provided by the government, the various operating agents, consumers, and producers, have
freedom to determine their actions as they see fit.

Since the war, the public sector has developed
much more rapidly than the private sector, and it

217

accounts for around a third of all domestic economic
activity. Within the public sector, the activity of
local governments has shown the most rapid rate of
growth, and since 1955 its share of public activity
has been larger than that of the central government.
However, the rapid expansion in local government activity is largely a direct consequence of, or governed
by, central government decisions, particularly with
regard to education and other public services.
Through the use of grants and national policy decisions the central government can influence the activities of local government units so that they conform with efforts to create a more efficient economy.

     Although the Swedish economy is predominantly
operated by private enterprise under free-market
conditions, the government is the ultimate coordinator
of economic activity. In addition to outright ownership or control of business, it also exerts an influence on the economy in other ways. It has been
pointed out in preceding chapters that the taxation
and expenditure policies of the government have been
used to effect an equitable distribution of income.
The budget has been used as a flywheel to raise or
lower the level of aggregate demand when needed, and
labor market policies are used to provide a balance
between the supply of and the demand for labor. However, the influence of the government is rather pervasive, and it is also necessary to look at other
aspects of its relationship to the national economy.
In particular, government ownership and regulation
of industry, the role of the national budget, economic planning, and industrial location policy will
be covered.

GOVERNMENT OWNERSHIP AND
REGULATION OF INDUSTRY

     The point was made in Chapter 2 that the Swedish
government, as well as local authorities, carries on
a number of commercial activities. Telephonic and
postal communications and most railway transportation
are supplied by government enterprises, and the
government is the most important entrepreneur in the
supply of electric power. Government-owned companies
also exist in mining, iron and steel, the forest industries, banking, and a number of other areas. Their
activities are fundamentally commercial in nature.

In addition, government ownership of industry has
expanded in recent years to include the creation of
a pharmaceutical company. In some cases, there is
mixed government and private ownership of industry.
As in the private sector, the planning and action
of government enterprises are based on commercial
calculation.

Government business activity has presented a
very heterogeneous picture, both with regard to the
different departments to which the enterprises are
responsible and the conduct of their activities.
The group consists of enterprises in widely differ-
ing fields of activity, which have a variety of objectives, and which are conducted in various legal
forms. The absence of a responsible central management has hampered effective collaboration and uniform policy. Apart from the credit institutions,
turnover of public enterprises in Sweden amounted
to 15.7 billion kronor in 1967. Recommendations
have been made to improve the coordination of government enterprises so that a greater uniformity in
policy can be achieved.

One of the recommendations is that the Swedish
Crown Lands Administration, the National Defense
Factories, and the Kreditbank should be transferred
to the Ministry of Industry and Technology.[1] An
investment trust would be formed under this ministry
for most of the government joint stock companies.
In principle, the only exceptions would be some
government-owned credit institutions, which it is
proposed would remain under the jurisdiction of the
Ministry of Finance, and those companies which are
under the supervision of the Ministry of Transport
and Communication. Another recommendation is that
Parliament be kept better informed of developments
in the public enterprises, through giving it greater
powers in the choice of auditors in the companies.

The pattern of government regulation of business resembles that of other advanced industrial
countries in Western Europe and North America. In
times of peace and prosperity, the importance of
direct controls diminishes, although in times of
crisis they may be extensively used. Ordinarily,
however, the direct controls are less important than
the general influence of the government in promoting
goals which appear to be the same as those of other
Western societies: a high rate of economic growth,

stability of the economy, an equitable distribution
of income, and an efficient use of national resources. Like other governments, the Swedish
government uses general measures of a fiscal and
monetary nature to level out extreme fluctuations
in the economy--tightening credit in boom times, for
example, or seeking to stimulate employment in times
of recession. Central bank authority over credit is
a major weapon in the government's arsenal. To a
much greater extent than most Western countries,
Sweden uses her tax laws as a fiscal device to help
in leveling out the business cycle.

In the more routine aspects of government control, such matters as import licensing and currency
restrictions are of no great present importance. A
very large proportion of foreign trade has been
liberalized, and imports and exchange controls are
limited to certain agricultural imports and to capital transactions. The krona has been steady on the
international market for some years at about 5.19
to the United States dollar. While capital payments
are subject to restriction, and some restriction may
also be applied to dividend and royalty payments,
convertibility with respect to ordinary current payments exists for nonresidents and to a considerable
extent for residents as well.

In the field of antimonopoly legislation, since
the war Sweden has adopted legislation providing for
the registration of cartels, investigations into the
state of competition, and the like. The scope of
this legislation has gradually been expanding. In
1946, for example, registration of cartel agreements
on request from the government was required. In
1953, a Free Trade Board was set up with power to
inquire into the interests of the community against
the harmful effects of restraint of competition.
Two restraints on competition are specifically forbidden: the practice of submitting uniform bids by
prior agreement, and resale price maintenance. In
1956, a new Price and Cartel Board was established
by the Swedish Parliament.

Government regulations concerning the use of
private property apply to the individual in Sweden.
For example, there are certain regulations which
pertain to home ownership. A person may own a home
and live in it himself or rent it out. He cannot,
however, charge any rent he so desires, as rent is

partially controlled by the state. The owner of a
house cannot tear it down and rebuild it as he sees
fit. He can only do this with a permit, and this
is acquired only under special conditions. The new
house must fit into patterns laid down by the city
plan. An owner also cannot evict a law-abiding
tenant when the contract has elapsed. Although he
can sell his house in the market at any time, an
owner cannot send income from the sale out of the
country without permission from a government agency.
Moreover, he must pay a tax to the state on profits
made from the sale of a house.

There are also other special regulations limit-
ing the powers of private owners. An agricultural
tenant, for example, has the legal right to have his
contract prolonged if he does not damage the property, and if the owner of the land does not need it
for himself. After a number of years, the tenant
has the legal right to assume ownership of the land
himself. Owners of forests have a legal obligation
to provide for continuous reforestation. Moreover,
an owner cannot prohibit people from walking in the
forests. If he puts up fences, he legally can be
forced to take them down again. The owner of a
beach may not prevent people from swimming and sun-
bathing there. He may not even build a house close
to the water on his own property, as that would soon
make all beaches private and leave no room for less
fortunate people.[2]

THE NATIONAL BUDGET

Basic information for the exercise of the
government's authority in the economic field comes
in part from the national budget, which is submitted
to Parliament early in January. This budget must be
distinguished from both the current operating budget,
which deals with the government's revenues and expenditures, and the capital budget, which deals with
the government's major capital expenditures. The
contents of the national budget can be described as
a discussion of the general economic developments
for the coming calendar year. It would cover what
may be expected to happen to gross national product,
the rate of economic expansion, private and public
investment, the trend of savings and consumption,
prices, external trade, and the like. Quantitatively,

the national budget takes the form of a balance of
resources for the coming year; that is, a table
showing the expected total supply of goods and services within the country, and the use of these for
different purposes. On the supply side, total
domestic production and imports are listed, and on
the demand (or use) side, private and public domestic
consumption and investments and exports are listed.

The idea of developing a national budget in
Sweden was inspired by work in other countries. A
scheme of this type was started in Norway. The
method which was to distinguish the work on national
budgets in Sweden is based on the inflationary gap
calculations--calculations of the strain ex ante
between demand and supply--developed by the National
Institute of Economic Research. These calculations
are used to establish a closer link between economic
forecasting and the shaping of general economic
policy.

The most important use of the national budget
is to provide an aid to economic policy. In the
national budget work an attempt is made to set forth
tendencies in economic development against a background of the economic policy being pursued. In
principle, the budget is given the task of prognostic-
ating developments with a given economic policy, and
suggesting what various combinations of political
means can be used to reach a given desired economic
position. The greater the amount of direct regulation in an economy, the greater can be the additional
task for the national budget work of acting as an
instrument coordinating economic policy. In such
cases, the budget has much the same duties as the
budget within a firm.

The national budget is drawn up by the Economic
Planning Division of the Ministry of Finance and the
National Institute of Economic Research on the basis
of materials received from the ministries and from
various administrative agencies and institutions.
Its procedure, basically, is to calculate total
supply, that is, production plus imports, at fixed
prices and then to subtract exports. The remaining
resources are divided between private and public investment and public consumption. For investments
and public consumption, statistics on plans for the
coming calendar year are available. Then, after a

correction has been made for expected changes in
inventories, the remainder is left for private consumption. Thus, the calculation shows how much is
left for private consumption after the other sectors
have received their shares--on the assumption that
development takes place in accordance with the existing plans in the various sectors.

The forecast of the national budget for the
Swedish economy in 1969 offers an example of its
operations. The prospects for exports and private
investment for the year were not particularly favorable. Forecasts of exports were based on an assessment of economic developments in Western Europe.
Since Sweden has an export-oriented economy, what
happens in other countries is bound to have an impact on foreign trade. The forecast was that the
rate of economic expansion in Western Europe would
be maintained in 1969 at around 4 percent, but that
the growth of foreign trade would decrease from 10
percent to 8 percent.[3] There would be a favorable
shift for Sweden in the distribution of trade by
countries. Investments in fixed assets by private
business firms were expected to increase at a rate
of 4 percent for the year. The investment data by
sectors indicated that engineering firms and steel-
works would increase their investments during 1969,
while an opposite development would occur in the
pulp and paper industry.

Inevitably there is some divergence between the
national budget and actual outcome in the economy.
Unpredictable events are bound to occur. It may be
a change in economic policy in other countries that
affects export prospects, or abnormal weather conditions with consequent effects on agriculture and
foreign trade. Errors in the primary statistical
material represent another cause of divergences.
This has been improved through the division of
statistical estimates into the different sectors
of the economy.

The national budget has some effect on the
planning of economic policy in Sweden. It enables
policy-makers to look at real economic problems as
a whole, from the standpoint of economic resources.
Since it is in the nature of a forecast, it gives
the government some indication of where trouble
spots might develop. As a result, remedial measures

can be developed. Business firms also have something
of a guideline to follow in making decisions concerning investment. However, actual governmental
economic policy is carried out in the regular state
budget, which consists of the current operating
budget and the capital budget. The state budget
exerts its influence on the economy in terms of the
level of expenditures, the level of taxes, and
whether or not it is balanced. In particular, the
balance in the budget is a reflection of the net
stimulus to demand and to employment and output
that is provided by the actions of the Swedish
government.

The balance in the state budget is a reflection
of the net stimulus to demand and to employment and
output that is provided by the actions of the Swedish
government. If the strength of demand for both consumption and investment in the private economy is not
great enough to generate operations at full-employment of resources, a budgetary deficit is used to
add to the strength of total demand in the economy.
It can act to reduce unemployment and move the economy
closer to its full-employment level. If, however,
the level of private and government demands without
deficit results in the economy operating at or above
its potential capacity, a budgetary surplus can be
used to dampen down the level of total demand.

NATIONAL PLANNING

The purpose of a national economic plan is to
harmonize the economic activities of different sections of society in the interest of optimal economic
growth and structural balance. A good plan provides
information on two matters: First, it provides a
forecast of how an economy should perform in the
future, and secondly, it provides a set or targets
which can be obtained through the implementation of
necessary measures.

Virtually all countries have government planning
policies of one sort or another to accomplish economic growth through proper resource allocation. In
developing a plan, two questions are involved--the
choice of the objectives and targets, and the extent
to which the government is committed to the implementation of the plan.

Economic planning can be classified as imperative or indicative.* The former would apply to a
centralized macroeconomic plan in an economy dominated by the public sector. The government would
assume direction by direct control and regulation
of output, prices, and wages. The latter would
apply to an economy in which the government indicates a series of goals, and indirectly stimulates
certain economic activities through the budget, taxation, and interest rates, to accomplish planning by
inducements. The free market, however, is recognized
as the normal mechanism of economic adjustment.

The Russian economic plan is an example of imperative planning. The planners, as would be true in any
country, have limited resources to start with, and
must allocate these resources to each economic sector
to maintain some kind of balance for the normal production of goods and services needed for the country.
Russian plans consist of selected physical targets
for output, employment, and consumption objectives by
sectors and regions. A plan is built around output
goals and the expansion in capacity needed for leading
industries and their supportive branches, and for
other sectors of secondary importance. A system of
input-output balances are used to derive the various
output and employment targets. Plans are drawn up on
the basis of directives from the leadership of the
Communist Party, which also controls the government.
Consumer sovereignty is pretty much disregarded, and
failure to fulfill defined goals redounds to the serious disadvantage of those who are responsible.

French economic planning is an example of
indicative planning.** It is much less extreme or
coercive than Russian planning, and it is essentially

---

*Actually, these two concepts can be too circum-
scribed. There are several degrees of economic planning, ranging from the authoritarian, command, type
of plan as used in Russia and China, to the very broad,
and not defined as such, monetary and fiscal plans of
the American Council of Economic Advisors. Most plans
are somewhere in between these two extremes, including
the French and Japanese plans.
**The term indicative may be a misnomer. Although
French planning is not imperative or mandatory, it does
attempt to direct the economy in a certain direction

viewed as a set of directives or guidelines which
help to guide the planning of private industry, as
well as the public sector of the economy. Nevertheless, there is a certain amount of intervention
on the part of the French government in the implementation of planning, which has taken the form of
indirect control over credit and taxation to encourage desirable economic and social objectives.
There exists in France a whole range of measures
which enable industries that conform to the plan
to be rewarded. There is access to credit. There
are tax concessions, and within the French policy
for regional development, subsidies for factories
and equipment. There are favorable interest rates
to encourage investment in certain areas.

Economic planning of the French type in which
a set of goals or targets are provided as objectives
to be achieved over a period of time, and an actual
planning mechanism provided to guide resources in the
desired direction, does not exist in Sweden. However,
planning which takes the form of economic forecasting
is used in Sweden as a source of information for the
government and private enterprise in the planning of
public policy.*

Swedish economic planning takes the form of a
long-term forecast which usually spans a five-year
period.[4] For example, the current long-term forecast covers the period 1966-1970. It covers such
subjects as capital input and economic growth,
regional trends and development, exports and imports, labor supply, labor demand in the manufacturing, retailing, and wholesaling areas, and the
need for government investment in certain areas.

---

and it does have the machinery to make its preferences effective. Although it does not fix an exact,
detailed, and rigid program for each industry, the
French plan does attempt to fit economic activity
into a general framework which it has outlined.
   *In France, planning is an integral part of eco-
nomic policy, and has assumed the character of offi-
cially authorized plans, which cover a four- or five-
year period. In Sweden, planning has no such official
recognition. There is no Swedish five-year plan, or
plan which is comparable to the French Fifth Plan.

The rationale of the survey is to provide information about the various sectors of the Swedish
economy, so that relevant economic decisions can
be made by government and private enterprise.

Previously Swedish long-term planning was entrusted to independent committees appointed by the
government. The latest plan, however, was carried
out within the Ministry of Finance, where a special
Economic Planning Secretariat was established.
Within the secretariat, a Planning Council was
created. This council is composed of representatives
of industry, labor, and public corporations, along
with the economic experts of the government. It
meets under the chairmanship of the Minster of
Finance and is responsible for the development of
alternative economic policies to be followed within
the framework of the plan or forecast.

The current economic forecast reflects a viewpoint that the individual's choice of consumption
of goods and services produced by both the public
and private sectors should be expressed by his preferences in the market place through prices that
correspond to the cost of production to the economy.
This arrangement ensures an optimum allocation of
natural resources in relation to consumer preferences. The view is expressed that fees and taxes
should be fixed at such a level that prices paid by
consumers reflect social costs, and that subsidies,
which keep prices lower than actual costs, should be
removed.[5]

A basic problem of resource allocation--the
distribution of labor, which is in unusually short
supply, between competing public and private uses--
confronts the Swedish economy. This problem of
balancing the labor requirements of the public and
private sectors of the economy with a labor shortage is brought out in the long-term forecast. The
supply of labor forecast is based on the following
elements: forecasts of the population broken down
on the basis of sex, age, and marital status; forecasts of the labor participation rate in various
groups of the population; and forecasts of the number
of working hours per year.

The forecast indicates that the supply of labor
will remain virtually unchanged not only during the

period 1966-1970, but during the decade of the 1970s
as well. The Swedish government is now in a position to undertake policy measures which are
aimed at increasing the quality and quantity of
labor. These measures include a heavy emphasis on
job training and retraining, the importation of
workers from Finland, Italy, and other countries,
and the movement of surplus labor from the farms
and forests into areas of labor shortage.

The government is also able to plan in detail
the development of those sectors of the economy in
which production and distribution are directly its
responsibility. It can also act similarly for
sectors in which it plays a more indirect, but
nevertheless important, role through the use of subsidies, construction permits, and other devices, in
influencing production and distribution. Important
sectors are agriculture and housing. For example,
agricultural policy is based on the forecast of a
decline in agricultural employment from 265,000 persons in 1965 to 195,000 in 1970.[6] This decline called
for a policy which aims at the consolidation of farm
land into larger and more viable economic units, and
at a greater mechanization of agriculture to sustain
an increase in production at a necessary rate of 5
percent a year to support the population.

Government planning, as applied to the private
sector of the economy, involves the provision of
information through the use of the long-term forecast, to firms to follow in making policy decisions.
No direct controls or coercion is used to see that
firms make the right decisions, and in the application of general economic instruments, such as credit
and finance policies, there is no discrimination
between firms.

Parliament has nothing to do with the long-
term forecasting or with any sector plans which
might develop. The plans are never submitted to
Parliament for approval, and the government has on
the whole no special or selective means at its
disposal to make the economy develop in accordance
with a plan. The main function of the long-term
forecast is to serve as background for public policy
and for private discussions and decisions.

Economic planning in Sweden would also involve
a business cycle policy. The main target of this

policy has been full-employment. Forecasting is
made by the Labor Market Board, and policy is based
on the forecast. The instruments used in business
cycle policy are: the investment-reserve fund
scheme, which is intended to stimulate corporations
to make investments in plants and machinery in order
to level out business fluctuations; and labor market
policy, which is designed to create employment and
stimulate job mobility.* The major problem connected
with business cycle planning is the difficulty of
anticipating business cycles. Even when appropriate forecasts have been made, time lag problems
have often appeared.7 These time lags have been
difficult to circumvent, even though in a parliamentary system such as Sweden's fiscal policy
measures can be effected within a shorter period
than is possible in the United States.

INDUSTRIAL LOCATION POLICY

     Another way in which governments intervene in
economic life is through the use of policies designed
to influence the location of industry. Normally in
a laissez-faire economy, industries would locate in
those areas in which they could make the greatest
return on their investment. Market factors, rather
than the conscious efforts of governments, would
determine the location of industry. Moreover, governmental intervention to influence industrial location would be opposed on the grounds that efficient
allocation of resources would be hindered.

     Sweden has had an industrial location policy
as far back as the middle of the 1940s. For a long
time activities were of an advisory nature but during
recent years have come to include direct supportive
measures. In 1963, the investment-reserve funds were
released for the purpose of encouraging the location
of industry in the northern most part of the country.
This area has had the highest percentage of unemployment in Sweden, not only in periods when unemployment
is high in the rest of Sweden, but also when it is
low. Continued structural unemployment, especially

_____

     *See Chapter 3 for the analysis of investment
reserve and labor market policies.

in forestry, has underscored the need to create job
opportunities in this area. Investment-reserve funds
for industry as well as forestry were made available
for projects started in northern Sweden. For example,
the funds were used to erect or enlarge plants, procure machinery and equipment, or for other eligible
purposes.

Also in 1963, the Labor Market Board began to
grant local authorities permission to use funds
allocated to public-works expenditures for the construction of industrial buildings. State subsidies
were issued for one-third of the building cost. The
condition upon which the subsidies were granted was
that the buildings had to be constructed in an area
designated as the Northern Development Area. In
1965, this form of aid was replaced by direct state
industrial location subsidies which went directly
to companies rather than to local authorities.

Financial support to influence the location of
industry now takes two forms: investment subsidies
and loans. Subsidies do not have to be repaid, but
loans have to be paid off in installments within a
period of twenty years. Interest on the loans are
set at the current market rate, which in 1969 was
7½ percent. In some cases, loans may be free of
interest for a period of up to three years. Loans
and subsidies cannot exceed two-thirds of total investments in a given project, and subsidies by themselves cannot exceed 35 percent of total investment
costs.

The overall gain in terms of employment, resulting from industrial location incentives is rather
modest. During the period from 1963 to 1967, some
17,500 jobs were created in northern Sweden as a
result of industrial location aid.[8] However, these
figures do not provide a reliable gauge of the effectiveness of location policy. An element of uncertainty is that no one knows what proportion of the
investments made with the help of industrial location
aid would have been made, had it not been available.
Furthermore, data on the effect on employment are
also unreliable, as they are based on estimates
provided by the companies themselves when applying
for aid, and this could mean an overstatement of
the number of vacancies that would be created by
the new projects.

TAX POLICIES

It is generally recognized that economic growth
in democratic, largely free-enterprise societies can
stem from a number of sources and that the importance
of any single source--whether it be a larger labor
force, more capital, more education, or a general
advance in technology--may vary considerably from
country to country. To stimulate economic growth,
tax devices have been used as an instrument of economic policy in the Western countries. All sorts of
liberalized depreciation schemes, investment allowances, and tax exemptions have been tried. The
basic reason for the use of these devices is to
stimulate growth through the stimulation of investment. Investment is required, not only to increase
the total stock of equipment and buildings, but also
to allow labor to be employed on increasingly more
productive jobs as old plants and machinery are replaced by new. Tax incentives can be used as a
macroeconomic device, available to all industries,
or as a microeconomic device, available to some industries, but not to others.

Few countries can exceed Sweden in terms of the
use of sophisticated tax policies to accomplish given
economic goals. Sweden has pioneered the use of
income tax devices designed at least in part to making the economy more resistant to depression and to
influence the propensity to invest. In the period
between the two world wars, for example, Sweden introduced very liberal rules for inventory valuation
and liberal depreciation schedules on machinery and
equipment. She has also been a pioneer in the use
of countercyclical tax policy, with the employment
of the investment reserve.

The investment-reserve system has been described
in its role as a device to iron out economic fluctuations by encouraging private corporate savings
in years of high profits, and private capital
expenditures in years when the government wishes to
stimulate investment. The promotion of economic
growth was not one of its stated aims, perhaps because the sponsors of this legislation were more
interested in improving the timing of capital expenditures than they were in raising the amount of

it. But there is reason to believe that the investment-reserve system has contributed to the growth
as well as the stability of the Swedish economy,
and since similar schemes have been introduced in
other countries with the avowed objective of promoting economic growth, certain possibilities are apparent.

It is possible that in stimulating investment
activity during an economic downswing, the investment reserve has contributed to economic growth.
Clearly, an efficient anticyclical policy may contribute to economic growth even if it has no effect
on the aggregate amount of investment over the cycle.
By tempering the growth-hampering effects of under-
development and stagnation, such a policy may contribute more to economic growth than a policy which
aims exclusively at raising the level of investment
without regard to the cycle.

Ordinarily, the release periods are used for
accelerating investment programs already planned, or
for undertaking certain low priority investments,
such as research laboratories, the profitability of
which is not easily calculated. An understanding
of the profitability of such investment might be
balanced by comparatively cheap financing through
the use of the investment reserve. Last but not
least, the release of the investment reserve means
that firms which would have stopped or delayed their
investment programs because of bad times may be induced to proceed with them in accordance with the
original plans. The release of the investment reserve furnishes them with the cheap and easy money
necessary to offset the poorer economic prospects.

Accelerated Depreciation

A very common tax incentive device is accelerated depreciation. When a government increases depreciation allowances, it reduces the tax burden on
a firm, at least on a short-term basis. One advantage
of accelerated depreciation is that it is equivalent
to an interest-free loan. That is, since the firm
is not required to pay the tax during the immediate
period, it has the use of a greater supply of funds,
interest free, which it would not have had without
accelerated depreciation.

It is also true that accelerated depreciation
means that the firm will be able to pay off the investment project in a shorter period of time. This
means a significant reduction in risk and uncertainty
both of which increase with the life of the asset.
This factor serves to stimulate investment by raising cash flow, by raising present value, and by
lowering the discount for uncertainty.

In its depreciation rules and in the changes
that have been made in them from time to time,
Sweden has been motivated not only by tax considerations, but by a desire to influence the investment
decisions of business taxpayers and build up the
financial strength and liquidity of such taxpayers.
Indeed, the provisions governing the depreciation of
machinery and equipment, including ships, may be regarded as one of the major areas in which Swedish
tax policy has sought to influence the business
cycle. The rules currently in force for the depreciation of machinery and equipment are as liberal
as those of any of the advanced industrial countries
in the world; within broad limits they give corporations the right to write down the value of machinery
and equipment in the way which in their business
judgment is most appropriate to the needs of the
business.

Sweden has also experimented with various depreciation methods. In 1938, a policy of free depreciation was adopted.* Under this policy, a
corporation was allowed, for income tax purposes,
to write off machinery and equipment as it saw fit.
Thus, the entire cost, or any portion of it, which
a corporation considered appropriate, could be
written off as an expense in the year of acquisition

---

*The 1938 provision had as its basic policy
objective the creation of a more nearly depression-
resistant economy through the use of devices to
stimulate investment.
    The free-depreciation provision was limited to
corporations, economic associations, savings banks,
and mutual insurance companies. Individual proprietors and partnerships were restricted to the
use of annual depreciation rates based on the
estimated useful life of the item.

of the asset, subject to two restrictions: (1) Depreciation for tax purposes in any year had to coin-
cide with depreciation taken on the books for that
year, and (2) in no case could total depreciation
taken on the books and reported on the tax returns
exceed the original cost of the asset.

However, in 1955, free depreciation was replaced by a more restrictive depreciation policy,
for it was felt that the free-depreciation system
was contributing to inflation.   The combination of
high taxes and high profits induced some corporations
to acquire capital items in order to increase depreciation allowances rather than for ordinary business
reasons.   This led to increased corporate spending
and to more inflation at a time when the problem
was to keep capital expenditures within the limits
of available resources.*

The new system of depreciation, however, is
quite flexible as an instrument of public policy.
A brief summation of depreciation policy allowed in
Sweden with respect to machinery and equipment is
as follows:

1.   The taxpayer may use a 30 percent declining-
balance method which means that depreciation in any
one year cannot exceed 30 percent of the year-end
book value of the taxpayers' machinery and equipment.
Under this rule, 30 percent of the cost of the equipment can be written off the first year, 30 percent
of the remaining balance the second year, 30 percent
of the remaining balance the third year, and by the
end of the five years, the cost of the equipment has
been written off.   The 30 percent is the ceiling;
the taxpayer can take less if he chooses--5 percent
of book value one year, 30 percent the next year,
and so on.

2.   Instead of the 30 percent declining-balance
method, a company may at any time take a straight-line

*The present Swedish system of investment
reserves was introduced in 1955 as a partial compensation for the loss of free depreciation.   The
investment-reserve scheme was introduced with the
hope that it would be an effective instrument for
stimulating business investment when needed, not
otherwise.

deduction of 20 percent of the book value of its
machinery and equipment. Under this rule, it can
write off the cost of the machinery and equipment
in five years.

In any particular year, the company can use
either the declining-balance or straight-line method.
However, whichever method is selected must be applied to all of the machinery and equipment. In
other words, the declining-balance method cannot be
applied to some items and the straight-line method
to others. These methods and percentages apply only
to machinery and equipment. Buildings are depreci-
ated at straight-line rates which are often as low
as 3 percent.

The use of both the declining-balance and
straight-line methods is shown in the following example. The cost of the machinery is assumed to be
100,000 kronor. The declining-balance method is
used and 30 percent of the cost (30,000 kronor) is
written off the first year. The balance is 70,000
kronor. For the second year, the declining-balance
method is used, and 30 percent of the balance or
21,000 kronor is written off. The balance is reduced to 49,000 kronor. For the third year, 30
percent of this balance or 14,700 kronor is written
off. The balance is now 34,300 kronor. For the
fourth year, the straight-line method is used (20
percent of the original cost of the machinery) and
20,000 kronor is written off. The balance for the
fifth year is now 14,300 kronor. The straight-line
method is used and this is written off. As a percentage of the total cost of the machinery, the
annual writeoffs are 30 percent, 21 percent, 14.7
percent, 20 percent, and 14.3 percent for the five-
year period.

If the employment situation requires it, the
Swedish government may decide that business firms
which procure within a stipulated period of time
machinery and equipment for permanent use in their
own enterprises--agriculture, business, and forestry
--by purchase or by producing it themselves, or sign
a contract for future delivery, will be entitled to
an extra depreciation allowance of 30 percent of the
cost, in addition to the regular declining-balance
or straight-line depreciation allowed under tax
legislation. In addition, the taxpayers may deduct
10 percent of the cost from taxable profits in their
income tax returns. When machinery is contracted

for future delivery, the 10 percent deduction will
be made for the fiscal year during which delivery
has been made. The extra depreciation allowance and
10 percent deduction from taxable profits apply to
both national and local income taxation.

The government has been given considerable dis-
cretionary powers. It may make the claim to tax
benefits contingent on fulfillment of stipulated
conditions, and it may extend the tax benefits to
business firms throughout Sweden or in specified
areas only. The government can also determine the
kind of machinery and equipment procurement which
can establish a claim to tax benefits. If the government wishes to promote the location of industry in
certain areas, this tax incentive can be limited to
taxpayers in these areas.

If the procurement of machinery has been
financed by the withdrawal of money from an investment-reserve fund, the tax benefits under the special
depreciation allowance cannot be claimed.

For machinery and equipment delivered immediately upon placement of the order, the extra first-
year allowance of 30 percent and the allowance
available under the regular tax legislation would
amount to a total of 51 percent of the price in the
fiscal year when the purchase was made. For example,
assume the machinery cost 100,000 kronor. Using the
regular declining-balance of 30 percent, the depreciation deduction would be 30,000 kronor. This would
leave a balance of 70,000 kronor. The extra first-
year allowance of 30 percent is applied to this
balance. The deduction would be 21,000 kronor.
The balance is now 49,000 kronor. Fifty-one percent of the cost of the machinery, or 51,000 kronor,
has been written off.

Inventory Valuation

Sweden's tax provisions governing the valuation
of inventories are designed to eliminate the taxation
of inflationary profits and to permit the strength-
ening of corporate resources against the possibility
of inventory price declines. Although provisions
exist in other countries to accomplish the same purposes, none takes the same form as Sweden's. Since
the depression of the 1930s, tax policy with respect

to inventory valuation has allowed business firms
discretion within certain limits, to take greater
or lesser deductions in any year for inventory
write-downs.

The basic rule in Sweden is that the valuation
of the inventory entered by the taxpayer in his
books of account shall govern for tax purposes.
This rule provides that a taxpayer, after first
writing off all obsolete or unsaleable items in
full, may write down the balance of the inventory
by 60 percent to a floor of 40 percent of cost or
market value, whichever is lower. Cost is determined on a first-in, first-out basis.

SUMMARY

Business is affected in many ways by the
activities of government. It is government that
provides the institutional foundation upon which
business rests, the legal framework within which
it functions, and many of the instruments through
which its activities are carried on. The economic
system within which business functions is shaped by
the government; the character of its performance
depends upon decisions that are made by government.
The demand for the products of business and the
nature of its costs are influenced by public regulations, by the character of public expenditures,
and by the types of taxes that are used in raising
public expenditures. Its expectations of profit or
loss depend to some extent on the policies adopted
by central banking authorities in controlling the
volume of credit and on those pursued by government
in balancing its budget, accumulating a surplus, or
running a deficit.

The Swedish government exercises a considerable
degree of influence over the activities of business
firms. Tax policies are designed to provide incentives to stabilize the rate of investment over the
business cycles and also to promote economic growth.
Industrial location incentives are provided to encourage firms to locate in depressed areas in the
northern part of the country. Economic planning
provides a forecast of potential developments in
the economy over a given period of time.

The main approach of economic planning in
Sweden involves the employment of fiscal, monetary,
and industrial location policies as means of promoting desired economic development. The large public
sector gives Swedish policy-makers leverage in the
implementation of these policies. This leverage is
particularly marked in the central government sector
where the use of subsidies gives it a strong influence
over agricultural production, housing construction,
and other areas of production. The Swedish government is also directly responsible for the production
of goods and services. Public agencies have to
produce regular estimates of the development of
demand and plan their production and investment
accordingly.

NOTES

1. Svenska Handelsbanken, Economic Review,
index no. 2 (1969).

2. Gunnar Adler-Karlsson, Functional Socialism:
A Swedish Theory for Democratic Socialization
(Stockholm: Bokförlaget Prisma, 1969), p. 37.

3. Sekretariat for Economic Planning of the
Ministry of Finance and the National Institute of
Economic Research, "Preliminary National Budget,
1969," (Stockholm, 1969), p. 10.

4. The forecast is published by the Ministry of
Finance, "The Swedish Economy, 1966-1970."

5. Ingvar Svennilson, "Swedish Long-Term
Planning--The Fifth Round," Skandinaviska Banken
Quarterly Review (Second Quarter, 1966), p. 38.

6. "The Swedish Economy, 1966-1970," op. cit.,
p. 116.

7. Martin Schnitzer, "The Swedish Investment
Reserve: A Device For Economic Stabilization"
(Washington, D.C.: American Enterprise Institute
for Public Policy Research, 1967), pp. 31-35.

8. Svenska Handelsbanken, Economic Review,
index no. 5 (1967), p. 2.

CHAPTER **9** SWEDEN: THE
MODEL SOCIETY

INTRODUCTION

The Swedish economy can be characterized as a
mixed economy. Although the public sector is large,
the economy is dominated by private enterprise where
production and investment decisions are determined
primarily by market forces. In the Swedish economy
around 90 percent of what can be called the agents of
production is owned by private industry and individuals. There has been a selective socialization of
some of the most important functions within the totality of functions which is called ownership. Other
functions are regulated under the Swedish system.
However, the main forms of governmental intervention
in the economy are fiscal and monetary measures,
which are designed to maintain a high level of economic activity. These measures have been the hallmark of economic policy, not only in Sweden, but in
other Western European countries as well since the
end of the Second World War.

Before the end of the Second World War, while
the Western countries were laying postwar economic
plans, a central problem bothering the policy-makers
was the maintenance of full-employment. Unemployment
had long been a major problem of capitalism, and was
responsible in main for the catacylsmic upheavals
that took place in the capitalistic countries during
the 1930s. It was thought by the policy-makers that
other problems would take care of themselves if this
problem could be solved. The central goal to be
pursued was then one of achieving full-employment
through the use of public policy.

One of the most important economic developments
of the twentieth century has been the attempt of

239

governments to modify inequalities in the distribution of income. Unquestionably, income inequality
has led to political and social inequalities in those
countries that pride themselves as having democratic
societies. Moreover, the institution of inheritance
undoubtedly has tended to perpetuate inequality, although the precise outcome is dependent on sociolog-
ical and demographic factors. Within the framework
of a capitalistic system, Western countries have
developed weapons for combatting income inequality--
progressive taxation of income and wealth, and the
provision of social services, such as medical care
and education, of particular benefit to the lower-
income groups.

A utopian society does not exist in any country
in the world. The perfect system has not yet been
developed. Certainly, the United States and the
Soviet Union, the two great powers of today, are far
removed from the ideal model of the just society
which has been desired by many persons throughout
the ages. This just society, however, is hard to
define. One example is the type of society which
was developed by Edward Bellamy, a Boston journalist,
in his book called Looking Backward, which was published in 1887. The hero of the story is put to
sleep by a hypnotist and remains in a state of suspended animation until he awakens 113 years later.
He learns that a gradual transition from his old
society to a new one has occurred.

In the year 2000, all industry is nationalized
and all citizens between the ages of twenty-one and
forty-five are required to serve in an industrial
army. This industrial army is divided into ten
departments covering all branches of industry, each
department being under the control of a lieutenant
general. Each lieutenant general is elected by a
vote of all of the retired members of the department
he heads, thus avoiding the undesirable effects of
having the workers select their own bosses. The
general-in-chief of the whole army is the President
of the United States, and he is elected by all the
men in the nation not connected with the industrial
army. No wages are paid, but all citizens, be they
active or retired, receive an equal share in the
national income. At the beginning of each year,
every American citizen is given a credit card marked
off in dollars and cents, and every time he makes a
purchase the amount is punched out of this card. If

any surplus is left over at the end of the year, it
may be used the following year, or returned to the
common fund. There is no need for an individual to
save any of his annual income, since incentives which
impel workers to do their best are patriotism prizes;
and if any man who is capable of working refuses to
do so, he may find himself in solitary confinement
until he sees the light.

It is unlikely that this type of society will
develop, at least in the near future. Moreover, it
is to be doubted that Bellamy's society is all that
desirable. One weakness in Looking Backward is the
problem of incentives. Patriotism and honor are not
beyond the realm of possibility for economic activity,
but it is doubtful that human nature could be changed
sufficiently to make such incentives practical.

THE MODEL SOCIETY

In general it can be said that the goals of a
model society should be as follows:

1. The provision of employment for all persons
who are able and willing to work.

2. An equitable distribution of money and real
income among all citizens so that economic and social
deprivation does not exist.

3. An increase in the level of real gross national product from year to year so that the standard
of living for all citizens continues to rise.

4. An emphasis on the quality as well as the
quantity of life.

Full-employment is in itself a desirable economic
goal. It is the prime function of an economy to enable everybody willing and able to work to earn a
living, and only a fully employed economy performs
this function. Maximum output is desirable given the
community's willingness to work, and here again full-
employment is a necessary condition.

A more equal distribution of income is one of
the major objectives of a model society. The major
uncertainties of an industrial society are those of

unemployment, premature death or disability of the
head of the household, prolonged illness, and old
age. These uncertainties can be taken care of
through social security programs. However, the use
of social security measures is contingent upon the
happening of a particular event, such as unemployment. Families with extremely low incomes are often
unaffected by most social security measures. It then
becomes necessary to provide some minimum standard
of well-being for these families through family allowances, housing subsidies, and free medical care.

What a nation can afford in the way of a redistribution of income is in a broad sense a function
of its real per capita income. What is important
from a welfare standpoint is the availability of
goods and services per person; it is reasonable to
talk of an improvement in the material well-being
of a people only if, over time, each person has a
growing volume of goods and services at his disposal.
Economic growth involves, in other words, an increase
over time in the actual output of goods and services
as well as an increase in an economy's capability to
produce goods and services.

The survival of mankind has emerged as one of
the major themes of the 1970s. In the United States,
the world's leading polluter, the concern expressed
for years by scientists and conservationists spread
to the general public in the late 1960s. In addition to each citizen's personal experience with foul
air, bad water, excessive noise, overcrowding, and
disappearing landscapes, the impetus behind the rising concern over the environment has also come from
the Malthusian warnings on population. There is the
question of whether or not man will complete the
destruction of his planet or learn to live in harmony
with it.

To a certain extent there is a contradiction
between economic growth and the quality of the environment. Economic growth results in part in smoke
and fumes from more cars, litter from more cans produced, and pollution of streams from the increased
output of factories. It now has become necessary to
start thinking about things which are tangential to
environment. However, it is possible to resolve the
conflict between growth and environment by using
rational measures to solve the problem of pollution.
But it is apparent, particularly in the United States,

that environmental problems far outweigh national
efforts to find solutions. Unfortunately, given
the present set of national priorities, solutions
will be long in coming.

It is possible to evaluate a country on how well
it provides for the economic and social well-being
of its citizens. Although there is no such thing as
a utopian society today, there are those countries
which appear to have done well in providing the
greatest good for the greatest number of their people.
Sweden is an excellent example of one such country.
It displays a willingness and ability to act in order
to correct problems that arise in society. The approaches that it has used to create employment, eliminate poverty, and create aesthetic beauty in its
cities are very resourceful and have been emulated
by other countries. In its general humanitarian approach and willingness to help lesser developed societies, Sweden must also be rated highly.

Although Sweden unquestionably deserves a high
rating on the attainment of the goals of a model society, it is necessary to point out that extenuating
circumstances have favored this development. First
of all, it has avoided participation in the two major
wars of this century--wars which dissipated the resources and talents of other European countries.
Secondly, Sweden is a very homogeneous country; unlike the United States and the Soviet Union with
extremely heterogeneous populations, there are no
minority or racial problems. Thirdly, the population
of Sweden is small relative to the land area and resource base. Problems of population pressures would
not affect Sweden nearly as much as a densely populated country like Belgium.

Also, there appears to be in Sweden a willingness to experiment with new ideas, and a capacity
to utilize measures to achieve various economic and
social goals. Poverty, as it is defined in the
United States, does not exist in Sweden. Although
there are low-income groups which are easy to identify
--single persons with children, unskilled workers,
pensioners, small farmers, and disabled persons--
transfer payments buttress incomes in these groups
and put an income floor beneath them. Labor market
policies exist to create employment opportunities
and job training for those persons who are capable
of working.

Progressive income taxation and transfer payments have been used to create a more even distribution of income among income groups than in other Western industrial countries. Although this policy of creating a more egalitarian society is not without its costs, it can be said that disparities in economic and social power between upper- and lower-income groups based on income and wealth ownership are narrowed considerably. Perhaps this policy is more consistent with democratic principles than policies in the United States which favor the rich over the poor. Tax policy is a prime example of how the rich are favored in the United States. Interest payments on state and local bonds are exempt from the Federal income tax. The wealthy investor receives a tax haven which reduces the effective rate of the tax. Moreover, treatment of capital gains is also designed to favor wealthy investors.

Employment

Most European countries, including Sweden, have maintained low rates of unemployment during the postwar period. In this respect, there has been a complete turnabout from the period of the 1930s, when unemployment rates were high in all countries. In Sweden, unemployment rates have been kept below an average annual rate of less than 3 percent. To accomplish this performance, fiscal, monetary, and labor market policies have been used. Heavy stress has been placed on finding jobs for all persons who are willing to work. Even sheltered employment is provided for handicapped and older workers. Moreover, priorities in terms of financial allocations have been given to measures designed to upgrade the quality and the mobility of the labor force.

However, full-employment has not necessarily provided an unmixed blessing. Although overall unemployment has been kept at a low level, the full- and overfull-employment has put pressure on the price level. Wage drift, a phenomenon referred to in Chapter 7, has helped exacerbate the problem of rising prices. The problem, at least over much of the last decade, has been to control inflation. During the period, 1964-1968, the consumer price index increased by 34 percent, and the wholesale price index increased by 14 percent. There was also a balance-of-payments deficit in each of the five

years.1 In 1969, however, the consumer and wholesale
price indexes rose by only 2 percent, but a number of
restrictive measures had to be taken during the year,
not only to offset a heavy outflow of foreign exchange, but also to neutralize overheating tendencies
in the Swedish economy.

Income Redistribution

Sweden has the second highest money per capita
income in the world. There are those who predict
that Sweden may well have the highest per capita income in the world by the end of the century.2 This
per capita income can be translated into a high
standard of living, but what is important is that
the disposition of this standard of living is much
more equal than in the United States, and probably
more equal than in any other developed country in
the world. There are no slums as exist in the
United States or, for that matter, in some other
European countries. Neither is there a large section
of the population which is unemployed or poor. This
is an achievement which is more important than the
maintenance of a very high standard of living. There
has developed in Sweden a high degree of equality
and a great freedom for every individual to develop
the best of the abilities nature has given him.

The personal income tax is highly progressive
and contributes to a greater equality in the distribution of income after taxes. Although there are
wealthy families who own or control a considerable
amount of industry in Sweden, their power and influence is limited to a greater degree than in the
United States. Taxes on income and profits are
devised so that it is profitable for private owners
to reinvest them in business activities. The tax
system is used to stimulate the owners of industry
to expand, and thus to provide more employment opportunities and a higher rate of productivity. Although it is possible to make a fortune in Sweden,
the conditions under which it can be made are rather
circumscribed. A condition is that the fortune
would be made only if it contributed to the creation
of employment and the production of socially useful
products. Also, in the process of production, some
thought has to be given to its effect on the quality
of the environment.

Social welfare measures are comprehensive. One
of the basic characteristics of the Swedish economy
is the provision of a number of welfare measures to
insure the average person against the vicissitudes of
life. There is security from the cradle to the grave
which does indeed provide protection for everyone.
This security is expensive and is paid for by the
taxpayers out of taxes which amount to more than 40
percent of the gross national product. But, given
the objectives of the welfare state which are a more
equal distribution of income and the provision of
social services to everyone, it is hardly surprising.
The basic lesson for the United States which can be
learned here is simply that to create a better society in which poverty, pollution, and other problems
are solved is going to cost money. Taxes will have
to be increased considerably and the American public
should be conditioned to this fact.

Economic Growth

During the period 1952-1965, real gross national
product in Sweden increased at a rate of 4.2 percent.[3]
This rate was higher than comparable rates for the
United States and the United Kingdom, but lower than
the growth rates for Japan and West Germany. However,
it is important to point out that Sweden has operated
from a highly developed economic base, while a part
of the rapid Japanese and West German growth rate can
be attributable to wartime recovery. In other words,
it is harder for Sweden to maintain above-average
rates, because its economy is functioning at an advanced level. It is also significant to note that
the Swedish economy has shown a high degree of stability in terms of economic growth. The standard
deviation for the growth rate is low compared to the
growth rate itself. For example, the standard deviation for Sweden is 1.5 percent over the period 1952-
1965, compared to 4.2 percent for Japan and 2.7
percent for the United States.[4] This means that the
rate of growth in Sweden has been relatively stable,
with few and rather small deviations from the average
of 4.2 percent.

Within the period 1960-1964, household incomes
in Sweden increased by 46 percent compared to 24 percent in the United States and 74 percent in Japan.[5]
Most of this increase in Sweden was absorbed by price
rises and direct taxes. Real household consumption

increased by 31 percent compared to 44 percent in
Japan and 59 percent in the United States. In terms
of the proportion of household income that was claimed
by direct taxes, Sweden was very high. Direct taxes
absorbed 34 percent of household income in Sweden
compared to 22 percent in West Germany, 15 percent
in the United States, and 14 percent in Japan. Rising prices absorbed 25 percent of household incomes
in Sweden compared to 39 percent in the United King-
dome, 35 percent in West Germany, 23 percent in
Japan, and 17 percent in the United States.

     However, a rising standard of living does not
necessarily dispel all economic and social ills.
Often full-employment and economic growth have been
accompanied by urban decay and pollution of the environment. Also, private goods of doubtful value
have been produced at the expense of public goods.
Yet economic growth is necessary to alleviate social
and environmental problems. Job training, better
housing, reliable transit systems, clean air and
water--all of these require financing that only a
rich and expanding economy can afford. There does
not have to be a contradiction between economic
growth and the quality of life, so that to have one,
the other has to be forsaken. Growth can be redi-
rected into areas which improve the quality rather
than the quantity of life.

     In Sweden, a considerable part of the resource
base is diverted by the government into areas which
do indeed improve the quality of life. An increasing
number of public goods are not subject to the private
market place: education, welfare, subsidized housing,
parks, clean air and water. This shift from private
to public goods can be considered in part as a tribute
to the private sector of the economy in that it has
met consumer demands for automobiles, household durable goods, and other goods and services. The problems
of consumer consumption have been pretty well solved.

     In its attention to the production of public
goods, Sweden can be rated highly. Resources are
channeled into the construction of schools and hospitals and the provision of medical care for everyone.
Education is free for those who are qualified to
benefit by it. The share of gross investment going
into the construction of housing is relatively high
compared to other Western countries. In 1965, the
number of completed dwellings per 1,000 inhabitants
was 12.5 compared to 7.8 for the United States.

Environmental Protection

New environmental protection legislation went
into effect in Sweden in July, 1969. The legislation provides comprehensive regulations concerning
various kinds of environmental pollutants and wastes
from industrial and municipal installations. These
regulations apply to a wide area of economic activity.
Covered are the discharge of waste water, solid matter, or gases from land, buildings, or installations
into lakes and other water areas, and the use of
land, buildings, or installations in a manner that
may disturb the environment through air pollution,
noise, vibrations, or light. A new government agency,
the Environmental Franchise Board, was established
by the new legislation. This board has court status
and is responsible for the issuance of licenses,
which must be obtained by any new industrial install-
ation that will have some sort of adverse effect on
the environment. Licenses are necessary for mines,
iron works, metal refineries, cement factories, nuclear power plants, detergent factories, and other
types of industrial activities.

The environmental protection law sets up the
following standards:

1. Pollution and the discharge of both oil and
other refuse at sea are forbidden in Swedish territorial waters.

2. In order to combat the discharge of sulphur
dioxide occasioned by the extensive use of heating
oil, the sulphur content is now limited to 2.5 percent by weight. In Stockholm and other major cities,
the limit has been set at 1 percent.

3. Rules have been imposed to reduce the discharge of motor exhaust. Starting with the vehicle
models of 1971, carbon monoxide and hydrocarbon discharge will have to be reduced to 45 grams per kilometer and 22 grams per kilometer respectively. The
lead content of gasoline is also to be reduced.

4. Noise is also regulated, particularly with
respect to the honking of horns, and noises created
by supersonic civil air traffic.

5. Special regulations also cover the use of
chemical preparations such as pesticides and biocides.

The use of mercury is banned in the preparation of
seed disinfectants.

The legislation includes rules regarding proce-
dures for dealing with private claims against environmental disturbances. A private individual may
sue the pollutor in a real estate court, demanding
prohibition against environmentally damaging activity
or a ruling establishing compulsory precautions.
For those who are found guilty of violating the rules
of the environmental protection law, fines or a maximum of a one-year prison sentence may be imposed.

Government subsidies are used to encourage the
development of methods designed to improve the quality of the environment. Industrial firms are to
calculate environmental protection expenses as part
of their production costs. But bearing in mind that
costs of this kind can constitute an intolerable
burden for firms which were set up before demands
for environmental protection were ever made, the
Swedish Parliament has allocated an annual sum of
50 million kronor for a period of five years to
defray up to 25 percent of the costs of environmental
protection investments by older firms. Government
subsidies covering up to 50 percent of the costs
involved are available to the communes in order to
hasten the development of sewage purification plants.
The higher the degree of purification, the higher the
subsidy. Communes are also responsible for the construction of recreational areas, and are supported
in this activity by subsidies from the national government.

There are several agencies in Sweden which are
responsible for environmental protection. The central
administrative organ is the National Nature Conservancy Office. The main tasks of the office are to
further the interests of nature conservancy in connection with social and industrial expansion and to
survey the pollution accompanying such developments
as well as to direct measures designed to control
and combat the same. There is also the Environmental
Franchise Board, which grants licenses under the
provision of the new law on environmental protection;
the Committee on Poisons, which administers laws relating to biocides and toxic preparations; and the
State Planning Office, which draws up directions
for building policy.

LESSONS FOR THE UNITED STATES

It is currently fashionable to catalogue the
faults of the United States, but all too often those
who criticize have no solutions to correct them. Instead, they point vaguely to some sort of communistic
state in which the faults will disappear through the
firing squad, osmosis, or some other process. However, there is absolutely nothing about the real
communist states, such as the Soviet Union, to indicate that they do a superior job in eliminating the
flaws which beset the United States. It is possible
to work within the framework of the capitalistic
system by using taxes, money policy, Federal spending,
and subsidies to correct such problems as poverty
and pollution. The problem is that sacrifices will
have to be made, and it is up to the government to
take the lead in providing a diversion of resources
from the private to the public sector.

First of all, poverty should be eliminated.
Admittedly, this is much easier to do in a country
like Sweden which has a small and homogeneous population. But it can be done in the United States
through family allowances or some form of a guaranteed
income. The coexistence of poverty and wealth cannot
be justified on economic or moral grounds. The Nixon
Family Assistance Plan is a step in the right direction. Coupled with the guaranteed income, there
should be emphasis on job training. A national program of public works should be supported by the
government in order to provide employment for mar-
ginally employed and unemployed workers. Low-cost
housing should be provided as a matter of public
policy to all low-income families. Grants to equal-
ize teachers' salaries between rich and poor areas
of the country are also necessary in order to equal-
ize educational opportunities.

A central theme which has been emphasized
throughout the book is that the welfare state is
expensive. The tax burden in Sweden is the highest
of all countries, but in other countries, such as
France and West Germany, taxes take more than a
third of the gross national product. Unquestionably
to support the desired changes in the United States,
taxes will have to be raised. As a start, loopholes
in the personal income tax structure which favor the

wealthy and special interest groups should be closed.
These loopholes encourage speculation in real estate
and the stockmarket--activities which do not benefit
the masses of people. Closing the loopholes should
result in increased tax revenues of at least several
billion dollars. It also appears desirable to utilize some form of a national sales tax, perhaps of
a value-added type. Although critics of a sales tax
say that it is regressive, the fact remains that
remedies to cure poverty and pollution cost money--
more money than can be raised through income taxation alone.

It also appears that more governmental regulation and protection of the public interest is necessary. A department of consumer affairs should be
created to protect consumers from false or misleading
advertising and defective products. Doctors' salaries and the cost of medical care should be under
government supervision. It is indeed unfortunate
that many doctors have used the Medicare program as
a bonanza to enhance their own personal financial
interests.

SUMMARY

A model society depends upon one's definition.
It has been defined in this chapter as an economic
and social system in which poverty and economic and
social deprivation have been eliminated, and the major
vicissitudes of life are covered through some sort
of social protection. Equality of opportunity is
also a fundamental desideratum, but this does not
mean that everyone is supposed to be equal. The
quality of life is also a factor which has become
increasingly important as many countries appear to
be destroying themselves through pollution of the
environment.

Sweden has gone as far as any country in creating a model society. In material terms the standard
of living is very high. More important there is an
equitable distribution of this standard of living
in that there are no radical extremes between rich
and poor. No one lives in deprivation. Basic protection against old age, sickness, and unemployment
is provided by the state. Taxation and government
expenditures have been used to redistribute income

downward in order to assure that everyone can have
some claim on the output of real goods and services.
Although accomplished at some cost, the rate of unemployment has been maintained at a low level for
several decades. In this connection, manpower policies have been particularly effective in training
Swedes for the labor market.

As far as the United States is concerned, the
point is simple. Much must be done in the area of
human welfare before it can qualify as a model society. The coexistence of too much poverty and too
much wealth is unfair, indecent, and what is more,
critical, and dangerous. It produces crime and vio-
lence which pervades every major city. To solve the
problem will require more imagination and resource-
fulness than the United States has shown to date.
However, a country which is capable of landing men
on the moon should also be capable of solving its
domestic problems if it is willing to put forth the
effort. The effort will be costly, but it is probable
that the American public is willing to share the burden provided that the wealthy and the special interest
groups also have to pay.

NOTES

1. Skandinaviska Banken Quarterly Review,
(Second Quarter, 1969).

2. Svenska Handelsbanken, Economic Review,
index no. 9, (1969).

3. Erik Lundberg, "Sweden's Economy in an
International Perspective," Skandinaviska Banken,
Quarterly Review (First Quarter, 1968), p. 2.

4. Ibid., p. 5.

5. Ibid.

ABOUT THE AUTHOR

Martin Schnitzer is Professor of Finance in the College of Business Administration at the Virginia Polytechnic Institute. He serves as a consultant to the Joint Economic Committee and the House Ways and Means Committee of the U.S. Congress. He also served as a member of President Nixon's task force on public welfare and was among those instrumental in developing the Family Assistance Plan. He is a specialist on Sweden for Congress and has published monographs on this country for the American Enterprise Institute and the Joint Economic Committee. He has also received research grants to support work in Sweden.

Professor Schnitzer was formerly the Editor of the Virginia Social Science Journal. He has published a number of articles and books in comparative economic systems, labor mobility, and public finance.

Dr. Schnitzer received a Ph.D. in Economics at the University of Florida and has done advanced work in summer institutes at the Harvard Business School and the University of Virginia.